Edited and designed
by David Dew

Contributors

Richard Birch
Scott Burton
Ian Greensill
Dylan Hill
David Jennings

Paul Kealy
Lawrie Kelsey
Craig Thake
Nick Watts
Robbie Wilders

Cover artwork by Duncan Olner
Inside artwork by Stefan Searle

Published in 2025 by Pitch Publishing on behalf of Racing Post, A2 Yeoman Gate, Yeoman Way, Worthing, Sussex, BN13 3QZ.

Copyright © Pitch Publishing and Racing Post, 2025. Every effort has been made to trace the copyright. Any oversight will be rectified in future editions at the earliest opportunity by the publisher.

All rights reserved. No part of this book may be reproduced, sold or utilised in any form or transmitted in any form or by any means, electronic or mechanical, including photocopying, recording or by any information storage and retrieval system, without prior permission in writing from the publisher.

Pitch Publishing specifies that post-press changes may occur to any information given in this publication. A catalogue record for this book is available from the British Library.

ISBN 978-1801509497

Printed by Short Run Press

RACING POST

THE TRAINERS

Ed Bethell	4-13	James Owen		40-47
Karl Burke	14-23	Hugo Palmer		48-57
Jack Channon	24-31	Kevin Ryan		58-65
Owen Burrows	32-39	George Scott		68-75

THE STATS

Last season's leading Flat performers by Racing Post Ratings   **76-83**
Last season's leading Flat performers by Topspeed ratings   **84-89**

GUIDE TO THE FLAT **2025**

THE EXPERTS

View from Ireland	**91-93**
Ante-post analysis	**94-95**
Ten to follow	**96-98**
Names to make it pay	**102-107**
View from France	**108-112**
On the up	**114-115**

THE KEY HORSES

A-Z of key horses who can make a mark this season	**116-188**
Key horses listed by trainer	**189**
Index of horses	**190-191**

William Knight's string walk down the side of Warren Hill at dawn in Newmarket as preparations get under way for the new season

RACING POST

ED BETHELL

Regional's Ascot aim

AFTER playing catch-up with star sprinter **Regional** last year, Ed Bethell begins this season in a happier frame of mind.

His seven-year-old gelding, who cost a mere 3,500gns at the Tattersalls horses-in-training sale four years ago, won the Betfair Sprint Cup at Haydock in 2023, but plans for a defence of his title last year went awry after running fourth in the Group 3 Hackwood Stakes at Newbury in July.

"He's wintered well and looks really good. I'm delighted with him," says Bethell *(right)*. "We've taken our time with him and hopefully we'll see him out in May either in the Duke of York Stakes, the Greenlands Stakes at the Curragh or the Temple Stakes at Haydock.

"Last year we struggled with him after a bad spring and we were playing catch-up all year. He scoped dirty before the Nunthorpe, so we pulled the plug and gave him a big holiday."

Regional had finished runner-up in the Greenlands Stakes before filling the same position in the Group 1 King Charles III Stakes (formerly the King's Stand) over five furlongs at Royal Ascot behind Australian flyer Asfoora, then fourth in the Hackwood.

GUIDE TO THE FLAT **2025**

WINNERS IN LAST FOUR YEARS 58, 43, 22, 22

"Perhaps the season was a touch disappointing but I was very happy with his performances," says Bethell. "He did finish second in the King's Stand, which was a pretty big run, and finished second in a Group 2. Frustrating is probably the best way to describe it.

"He'll be aimed at Royal Ascot again, either the Diamond Jubilee or the King's Stand. I would imagine it would be the King's Stand.

"Last year he was entered in the July Cup but he didn't run because I thought the ground was definitely softer than good to firm.

"I think we could enter him again for that or maybe the Maurice de Gheest. After that it could be the Nunthorpe, then the Betfair Sprint Cup at Haydock.

"It's all geared to trying to win the Sprint Cup he won two years ago. We might consider the Breeders' Cup at the end of the year, but we'll see what the lads think. There's a lot of water to go under the bridge first before we think about that."

Regional was one of three Bethell runners he had at the royal meeting. Mickley became his first Royal Ascot winner when landing the Britannia Stakes and was then sold to race in Hong Kong, where he has since won a £115,000 handicap, and Elim finished sixth in the Kensington Palace Stakes.

Although she didn't win in four subsequent outings, **Elim** ran consistently well in good races, including second in the Group 2 Sceptre Stakes at Doncaster, ending her season 18lb higher on a mark of 101.

"She's wintered well and is a big, strong girl now," says Bethell. "I think I might start her off in the Chartwell Fillies Stakes, the Group 3 over seven at Lingfield in May.

"After that we'll see where we are and try to win Listed or Group 3 races and get some black type for her pedigree."

Point Lynas began last season with victory in a mile handicap at York and ended it by winning a Listed mile race at Pontefract.

This year he began his season in a mile race on turf in Doha in mid-February when he finished second to earn £88,000 and now Bethell could start looking at European Group races for him.

"He's training really well," says Bethell, "but it's not easy for a horse rated 112 over here. So we'll be looking abroad to earn as much money as we can."

Bethell has three entered for the Lincoln Handicap at Doncaster – Naepoint, Old Cock and James McHenry.

"**Naepoint** probably won't get into the Lincoln, so I imagine he'll start off in the Spring Mile, the consolation race. He had a good season last year, winning three times for us and looked a real progressive type.

"**James McHenry** has wintered very well, but it depends how he's training whether I find an easier option for him.

"**Old Cock** also did very well last year, winning three of his six races. He was a big, raw horse who's improved for the winter. He won't run on anything other than good or good to firm, so it would have to be a good-ground Lincoln.

Point Lynas scores at York last May

RACING POST

ED BETHELL
MIDDLEHAM, NORTH YORKSHIRE

RECORD AROUND THE COURSES

	W-R	Per cent	Non-hcp 2yo	Non-hcp 3yo	Non-hcp 4yo+	Hcp 2yo	Hcp 3yo	Hcp 4yo+	£1 level stake
Newcastle (AW)	17-155	11.0	2-36	2-34	0-6	0-10	6-27	7-42	-56.37
Redcar	16-60	26.7	4-18	1-9	0-0	0-1	9-22	2-10	+26.77
Haydock	13-62	21.0	0-15	1-4	3-7	0-3	8-26	1-7	+15.27
Ripon	11-47	23.4	0-6	3-8	0-0	1-1	4-18	3-14	-1.23
Southwell (AW)	11-66	16.7	3-8	5-16	0-0	0-2	1-15	2-25	-17.21
Carlisle	9-34	26.5	2-12	2-4	0-0	0-1	3-10	2-7	-4.15
Pontefract	9-44	20.5	0-9	2-5	1-2	0-3	4-12	2-13	+7.33
Beverley	8-38	21.1	2-10	1-3	0-1	0-0	3-16	2-8	-10.36
Doncaster	8-55	14.5	1-6	1-13	0-1	0-2	4-22	2-11	-17.22
Nottingham	7-27	25.9	3-6	0-7	0-0	0-0	4-10	0-4	+5.20
Hamilton	7-31	22.6	0-3	1-3	0-0	0-1	5-16	1-8	-5.64
Thirsk	7-40	17.5	1-17	0-6	0-0	0-1	4-11	2-5	-1.38
Wolverhampton (AW)	7-40	17.5	0-6	3-8	0-0	0-4	2-14	2-8	-12.72
Catterick	4-18	22.2	1-1	0-2	0-0	0-1	2-3	1-11	-5.78
York	4-49	8.2	0-6	0-2	0-4	0-1	2-19	2-17	-18.00
Musselburgh	2-16	12.5	0-1	0-5	0-0	1-3	1-4	0-3	-7.63
Sandown	1-3	33.3	1-1	0-0	0-0	0-0	0-0	0-2	+4.50
Wetherby	1-6	16.7	1-2	0-1	0-1	0-0	0-1	0-1	-3.13
Ascot	1-12	8.3	0-0	0-2	0-2	0-0	1-5	0-3	-3.50
Leicester	1-13	7.7	0-2	1-4	0-0	0-2	0-3	0-2	-11.33
Ayr	1-17	5.9	0-4	1-2	0-0	0-0	0-4	0-7	-15.75
Newmarket	1-21	4.8	0-4	0-1	0-1	0-2	1-10	0-3	-17.75
Epsom	0-1	0.0	0-0	0-0	0-0	0-0	0-0	0-1	-1.00
Yarmouth	0-2	0.0	0-0	0-0	0-0	0-0	0-1	0-1	-2.00
Lingfield (AW)	0-3	0.0	0-0	0-0	0-0	0-1	0-0	0-1	-3.00
Chelmsford (AW)	0-4	0.0	0-1	0-1	0-1	0-0	0-2	0-0	-4.00
Kempton (AW)	0-4	0.0	0-0	0-0	0-1	0-1	0-1	0-1	-4.00
Newmarket (July)	0-5	0.0	0-0	0-0	0-1	0-0	0-4	0-1	-5.00
Goodwood	0-5	0.0	0-0	0-2	0-0	0-0	0-1	0-2	-5.00
Newbury	0-8	0.0	0-0	0-4	0-1	0-2	0-0	0-1	-8.00
Chester	0-8	0.0	0-0	0-2	0-0	0-1	0-4	0-1	-8.00

Number of horses racing for the stable **145**
Total winning prize-money **£1,378,539.96**

■ Watch out for Andrea Atzeni in the saddle for the stable — he has a strike-rate of 22% over the last five years

Callisto Dream: has a Classic entry but might be seen to better effect over further than a mile

"He'll be trained with that in mind. It would be an ideal race for him if it comes up as nice ground because it's a flat track that suits him down to the ground."

Callisto Dream has an entry in the Irish 1,000 Guineas after ending her two-year-old season with a well-backed debut victory at Carlisle over six furlongs in September.

"She won her debut well and it was no secret we liked her a lot," says Bethell. "She's done okay over the winter but we'll see how she does in the spring before deciding where we start her, whether it's another novice or in a Guineas trial. Her pedigree would suggest she might want a bit further than a mile.

"So it wouldn't surprise me if she didn't make the Guineas entry and we found her going over a bit further. I don't know yet. I want to see how she trains in the spring before making any plans. But I like her a lot and I think she's going to be a really nice filly this season."

Another possible Classic hope is **Danger Bay**, by French Derby winner New Bay, who ran impressively to finish a close runner-up on his only outing last season over a mile at Haydock against an odds-on favourite who had already had two runs and subsequently ran in the Group 2 Royal Lodge.

"He split two quite highly rated horses," says Bethell. "He looks the type to hopefully win his maiden over a mile and a quarter. Whether he's a Derby horse, a high-end handicapper or Listed horse remains to be seen.

"But he showed me all the right signs last year for a big, tall, angular horse. To be able to do what he did at the start of August was quite impressive and he's done exceedingly well over the winter.

"I'll start him off in that mile-and-a-quarter maiden at the Lincoln meeting, all being well. If he was to do well there, then you might look at another novice or you might look at a Derby trial.

"He's very, very smart. Even if he's not a Derby horse, I think he's going to be a very nice horse for the season. He could find himself in the King Edward VII or the King George V handicap at the royal meeting. He's in and around that kind of bracket."

Fluorescence is another who impressed on her only start last season when winning over six furlongs at Southwell in October.

"She won well. She's not the biggest and she's from a fast family, so whether she'll stay seven would be a question mark in my mind. She showed a very good turn of foot and had been working well up to the race.

"You can't draw too many comparisons with what she beat. So, do we start her off in the Fred Darling or go for another novice and see how we get on? We'll see how she comes on in the spring."

Kings Merchant was a model of consistency last year, winning four of his nine outings, finishing second twice and third once, earning the sobriquet "just a typical sprint handicapper" from Bethell.

"I'd imagine we'll be looking at Saturday races, fast ground, six furlongs and see how we get on. He was amazing last season because he doesn't do a lot for me at home. I thought he'd be on the transfer list coming into the season, but he seems to turn it on at the track, which is great. I prefer it that way."

Yorkshire is a "pretty good horse" who ran eight times last season, winning his opener over seven furlongs, his last over the same distance with a third victory sandwiched between them. He ended with a rating of 95.

"He'll start off in a handicap at Southwell and if he were to win there, he'll go for the Listed Lady Wulfruna Stakes at Wolverhampton in March over seven. Then we'll give him a short break before aiming him at stakes races over the summer."

Make a careful note of **Paborus**, described by Bethell as "the most exciting of the whole bunch" for whom he has high hopes.

After readily landing a couple of novice races over seven furlongs at Redcar and Carlisle, the four-year-old performed even more impressively over the same distance on the all-weather at Southwell in October. The handicapper was so impressed, he raised Paborus 13lb to a mark of 103.

"He won his handicap by five lengths on the bridle and I'd imagine he'll go for the Listed Spring Trophy at Haydock in May, then the Group 3 John Of Gaunt the month after that at Haydock again, both over seven.

"He won't go up in trip. If anything, he might come back in trip to six and, if he were to do well in either of those races, we might give him a special entry in the Diamond Jubilee [6f, Royal Ascot].

"Or we might bypass that and have a look at the Lennox Stakes [Group 2, 7f] at Glorious Goodwood, but ultimately his big target, or the race I'd love to try and get him high enough for, is the Prix de la Foret [Group 1, 7f] on soft ground at Longchamp on Arc weekend.

"He needs a bit of juice in the ground. If I have any horse that can bridge the gap between a stakes horse and a Group 1 horse, he's the one."

Paborus has Bethell excited for the months ahead

RACING POST

Azure Angel (right): has joined the stable from Roger Varian

"He's wintered incredibly well. He's grown, filled out, he looks a monster."

After spreadeagling a field of fillies at Southwell in October on her third start, **Rogue Sensation** tackled colts in a seven-furlong Listed race at Deauville the following month, finishing a highly promising half-length runner-up to earn a rating of 98.

"She's a nice filly, although possibly she hasn't grown as much as I'd have liked to see her do, but she's lengthened and put on weight. If the ground isn't too soft, I think we might start her off in the Fred Darling, see how she goes and take it from there."

Newbury's traditional Guineas trial is over seven furlongs but Bethell thinks his filly will probably come down in trip to six, with the Listed Chelmer Stakes for fillies over that distance as her early-season priority.

"I don't think she'll get a mile, so we won't think about the Guineas. She's quite fast. I know she's by Too Darn Hot and from quite a stout family, but she probably doesn't help herself in her work to allow her to settle enough to get the trip.

"She might get an entry in the French Guineas but the problem is she wants top of the ground."

Intrusively ran on strongly after a slow start to finish third in the Group 2 Richmond Stakes at Glorious Goodwood, cantered home in his maiden at Nottingham, before ending the season with a creditable fifth of 20 in the Weatherbys sales race at Doncaster to earn a rating of 97.

"He's done well over the winter," says Bethell. "I quite like the idea of starting him off in the Listed Prix Montenica at Chantilly in March, although I have a feeling I might get diverted to the Prix Djebel at Deauville in April. We'll see how he trains in the spring and go from there."

Azure Angel was bought out of the Roger

Varian yard in the winter after winning four all-weather starts, and Bethell has high hopes for his new purchase.

"She's rated 87 and has done exponentially well since coming to us," he says. "She's very nice and was rated in the 90s in her pomp. She'll be out in the spring and we'll be trying to get some black type for her."

Another to take careful note of is **Kirkdale**, who won comfortably at Catterick on his third outing to earn a rating of 78, which Bethell thinks could underrate the gelding.

"I think he could be a snip off that. So too could **Counting Cards**, who's rated 76 and has been campaigning over six. Both horses could run over seven to a mile and could improve through handicaps. There's definitely two nice horses in there."

Codiak is "a lovely" Make Believe gelding who is unraced after having a few niggly immature issues last year.

"He could develop into a nice horse if he strings it all together this year. He'll race over a mile and a quarter to a mile and a half and wants nice ground."

From his stock of two-year-olds, Bethell has no hesitation in singling out **Return Of The Gods**, who cost £350,000 and is a half-brother to 111-rated Gimcrack winner Cool Hoof Luke.

"He's a nice-moving colt who will be a bit of fun for his owner," says Bethell, whose Thorngill stable sent out 58 winners last year and earned $1.088 million.

"I'm hoping we can improve on that, but that all depends on whether the big horses turn up.

"I hope they do because I want to be consistently hitting £1 million prize-money each year," he says. "I have 78 horses and as long as they stay healthy and sound I'm really excited."

Reporting by LAWRIE KELSEY

RACING POST

KARL BURKE

Powerful squad can ensure good times continue

WINNERS IN LAST FIVE YEARS 121, 119, 117, 100, 60

KARL BURKE'S Spigot Lodge stable produced a phenomenal performance in 2024, confirming its place at Britain's top table – and his team is well worth following again this campaign.

His record-breaking year brought 121 winners and more than £4 million prize-money, leaving him fourth in the trainers' championship, his highest to date, and that figure was boosted to £5m with prize-money from overseas.

RACING POST

This season his Middleham Moor yard in North Yorkshire will house close to 200 horses, around 90 of which will be well-bred two-year-olds, making him hopeful of another season packed with winners.

"Last season was fantastic. I'd love to think we could replicate it, but you need a lot of luck and the horses have to stay sound," he says. "Having said that, on paper it looks the strongest bunch we've had."

So, what to watch out for? Probably top of the list is **Swingalong**, a five-year-old mare whose last seven runs have all been in Group 1 six-furlong sprints.

There was talk of owner Sheikh Juma sending her to the paddocks, but the team decided to try for an elusive Group 1 prize before definitely retiring her at the end of this season.

Last year she finished runner-up in the Queen Elizabeth II Jubilee Stakes at Royal Ascot, beaten half a length by Khaadem; second three weeks later in the July Cup a neck behind Mill Stream; then filling the same position in the Champions Sprint at Ascot, beaten a head by Kind Of Blue.

All those races will help form her programme again, but when and where she starts off will depend on how she's training in the spring.

"I would imagine it will be the Group 2 Duke of York in May, then on to Royal Ascot for a Group 1 and take it from there," says Burke. "She's wintered well and I'm very happy with her."

Also on the sprinting roster will be **Elite Status**, third in the 2023 Norfolk Stakes and winner of Listed and Group 3 races last year, before finishing unplaced in the Betfair Sprint Cup at Haydock and the British Champions Sprint at Ascot.

"He's come back looking in great shape and has really strengthened well," reports the trainer. "I'm looking forward to him and I'm hoping we can turn him into a top-class Group 1 sprinter with a bit of luck, but he's got a bit to find to do that. He wouldn't want it soft; he'd want decent ground."

Another highly rated inmate is **Poet Master**, who has a mark of 115 after landing the Group 2 Minstrel Stakes over seven furlongs at the Curragh, finishing fifth in Doncaster's Group 2 Park Stakes and ending the season with a creditable fifth in the Group 1 Prix de la Foret at Longchamp over seven. On ground that was officially very soft, he led over a furlong out but weakened in the last 100 yards.

"He's done really well for his break," says Burke. "He'll be aimed at all the Group 1, seven-furlong races and he might just prove he's quick enough on slow ground over six. He'll be out early and ready for the spring."

Marshman is another member of Burke's sprinting team, who was quick enough to finish second in the Gimcrack as a two-year-old and won a Group 3 in France the following season.

The five-year-old ran at all levels up to Group 1 without success until opening this year with victory in a Newcastle handicap over six.

He followed up by winning the Listed Kachy Stakes at Lingfield in early February against four higher-rated rivals before tackling the Listed Hever Sprint over five furlongs at Southwell later in the month, when he failed by half a length to haul back Clarendon House from an outside draw.

"Hopefully, we can get him up to Group company somewhere along the line. His optimum distance is six and he likes good ground," says Burke.

Another stable star sure to make headlines again is last season's Ayr Gold Cup winner **Lethal Levi**, who beat stablemates **Silky Wilkie** and **Korker** to give Burke an unprecedented 1-2-3, Scotland's richest Flat race. He'd saddled the 1-2 with Always Alight and Daring Destiny in 1998, while Daring Destiny won it four years earlier.

The handicapper raised Lethal Levi 7lb to a rating of 109 after his victory, which means

PREMIER EQUINE
ENGLAND

Turnout Rugs

Stable Rugs

Coolers

Sheets

Saddle Pads

Horse Boots

Therapy

PROUD SUPPLIERS TO THE RACING COMMUNITY

To apply for a trainer's trade account, please contact:
sales@premierequine.co.uk | Order Line 01469 532279
www.premierequine.co.uk

he will probably be running in Listed races and possibly Group 3s.

"I imagine he'll be taking in some Listed races along the line, and maybe a Group 3, but equally he could run in some of those top handicaps as well," says Burke. "We'll just see how it goes. He's done very well over the winter."

Night Raider ended the year with a smooth win over six furlongs in a Listed race at Newcastle, making it four out of four on the all-weather.

"We think he's a Group horse in the making," says Burke. "We're thinking he could go out to Dubai for Super Saturday [March 1] for a Group 3 over five and if he performed well there he could get an invite for the Group 1 Al Quoz on March 30 at Meydan.

"He wants good fast ground, so we'd have to wait for the summer time over here."

Burke is looking forward to running **Serving With Style** this season after she won a novice stakes race at Goodwood, then ran disappointingly in the Group 2 May Hill at Doncaster before ending the season runner-up in the Group 2 Rockfel Stakes at Newmarket.

"She should definitely progress but wants a bit of cut in the ground. She ran well in the Rockfel, we were delighted with her. She had a frame to fill and I'm sure she'll be a lot stronger this year."

Al Qareem has been a real money-spinner

for Burke, winning eight races and almost £470,000 prize-money in his four seasons at Spigot Lodge, including last season's Group 3 Cumberland Lodge Stakes at Ascot for the second year in succession.

"He's a fantastic, tough old horse and will be campaigned in Group 2s and Group 3s again. We tried stretching him out in the Prix Royal-Oak at Saint-Cloud [1m7½f] but I think his best distance is probably a mile and a half, maybe a mile-five on slow ground. He's a relentless galloper at that trip.

"He'll be ready to run early when the ground's right and he might have a trip to France."

Holloway Boy has performed well in Dubai this winter, finishing a short-head second in a Group 2 mile, then third in a Group 1 over nine furlongs.

"He has the chance of going to Qatar, dropping back to a mile, or staying in Dubai to run on Super Saturday. If he ran well there he could get an invite to the World Cup.

"But at the moment he's on the cusp. He's thrived out there and done really well; he's enjoyed the climate. Some of those older horses can find an extra gear when they go out there.

"He definitely stayed the nine furlongs, so I'm not sure what his optimum distance is. But I'd be loath to drop him back to a mile now and, who knows, he could even stay a mile and a quarter."

Andesite, who won over six furlongs on

Holloway Boy: could run at Dubai World Cup meeting

RACING POST

KARL BURKE
MIDDLEHAM, NORTH YORKSHIRE

Andesite: well thought of at Spigot Lodge

RECORD AROUND THE COURSES

	W-R	Per cent	Non-hcp 2yo	Non-hcp 3yo	Non-hcp 4yo+	Hcp 2yo	Hcp 3yo	Hcp 4yo+	£1 level stake
Newcastle (AW)	82-671	12.2	24-153	25-126	3-27	7-79	13-162	10-124	+23.69
Southwell (AW)	79-441	17.9	5-44	24-87	3-18	3-36	18-116	26-140	+97.55
Wolverhampton (AW)	62-489	12.7	17-100	12-75	0-21	7-59	15-146	11-88	-22.28
Haydock	49-429	11.4	9-121	11-57	3-23	4-19	14-131	8-78	-101.33
Carlisle	44-225	19.6	28-98	1-16	1-1	3-26	7-54	4-30	+16.19
Ayr	44-279	15.8	17-86	9-31	0-1	1-17	8-73	9-71	-8.01
Musselburgh	34-152	22.4	17-62	4-12	0-2	1-23	5-36	7-17	+2.18
York	33-345	9.6	14-123	2-34	0-26	5-28	4-72	8-62	-82.09
Nottingham	31-196	15.8	12-50	1-20	0-0	6-26	9-74	3-26	-25.98
Pontefract	31-201	15.4	15-69	2-28	0-3	3-14	4-46	7-41	-46.95
Catterick	29-148	19.6	14-51	6-20	3-4	1-22	2-31	3-20	+7.17
Thirsk	29-220	13.2	18-98	5-35	1-7	2-14	3-42	0-24	-79.92
Redcar	29-235	12.3	18-108	3-27	0-4	1-16	4-61	3-19	-75.40
Hamilton	28-205	13.7	15-76	3-21	0-1	3-21	3-51	4-35	-22.52
Doncaster	26-288	9.0	12-64	2-46	1-15	2-25	8-73	1-65	-70.00
Beverley	23-149	15.4	11-86	2-15	1-5	1-8	5-27	3-8	-47.53
Ripon	22-199	11.1	12-85	6-26	0-2	0-10	2-45	2-31	+14.41
Lingfield (AW)	21-144	14.6	2-8	1-19	8-37	0-2	3-42	7-36	-4.51
Ascot	19-162	11.7	8-45	2-34	3-18	0-0	4-37	2-28	+21.36
Kempton (AW)	17-169	10.1	1-19	4-18	2-16	0-19	4-40	6-57	-63.63
Newmarket	17-191	8.9	4-63	5-41	1-16	0-10	3-34	4-27	-85.22
Windsor	15-77	19.5	4-23	1-3	0-2	0-3	6-25	4-21	-3.32
Newmarket (July)	15-97	15.5	7-40	1-7	0-2	0-4	5-29	2-15	+1.83
Chelmsford (AW)	12-117	10.3	4-24	2-17	0-6	2-15	3-24	1-31	-55.38
Sandown	11-97	11.3	4-27	1-11	1-2	0-6	3-31	2-20	-15.25
Chester	9-82	11.0	2-20	0-5	2-5	2-7	2-29	1-16	-22.85
Goodwood	9-85	10.6	4-25	1-11	0-6	1-8	2-19	1-16	-28.17
Leicester	9-124	7.3	0-27	1-19	0-4	2-18	5-40	1-16	-79.68
Yarmouth	8-65	12.3	2-11	1-7	0-1	0-13	4-25	1-8	+6.75
Newbury	7-91	7.7	0-32	3-17	0-5	0-4	2-17	2-16	-43.50
Epsom	5-35	14.3	2-7	0-7	0-1	1-4	1-7	1-9	-13.88
Newcastle	4-13	30.8	0-4	1-2	0-1	0-0	1-3	2-3	+20.87
Brighton	4-14	28.6	1-4	0-0	0-0	1-3	2-3	0-4	+7.50
Chepstow	3-13	23.1	1-4	0-0	0-0	0-1	2-8	0-0	+3.75
Bath	3-19	15.8	0-2	0-3	1-4	1-3	1-5	0-2	+7.10
Lingfield	2-16	12.5	0-1	0-6	0-0	0-1	0-4	2-4	-6.50
Ffos Las	1-3	33.3	0-0	0-0	0-0	0-1	1-2	0-0	+1.00
Salisbury	1-4	25.0	0-3	0-0	0-0	0-0	0-0	1-1	+0.00
Wetherby	1-38	2.6	0-7	1-13	0-1	0-0	0-12	0-5	-35.25

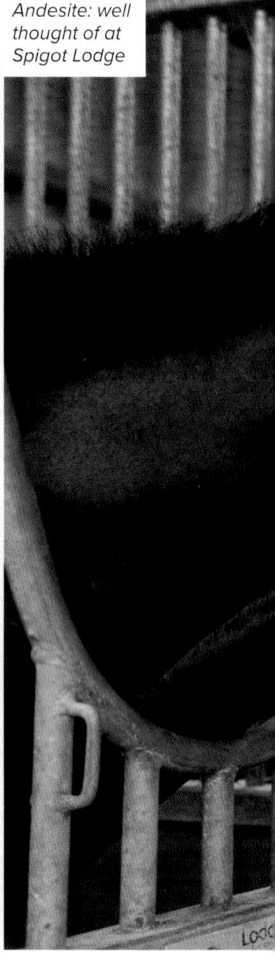

Number of horses racing for the stable **873**
Total winning prize-money **£9,754,884.31**

his debut last year, ran a race full of promise in the Group 2 Gimcrack despite being badly hampered two out when challenging.

"He's come back in looking in great shape. He's strengthened and matured really well. We'll start off low key with him but it wouldn't surprise me to see him turn into a Group horse somewhere down the line."

Flight Plan, winner of a Group 3 at Leopardstown in 2023, was disappointing last year, finishing down the field in the Group 1 Queen Anne and in four subsequent outings in Listed and Group races, but Burke reckons the five-year-old can come good.

"He's had a minor operation this winter and we'll be trying to win a little Group race somewhere with him. I think he's a genuine Group 3 horse."

Miss Lamai is in a similar vein. She won first time out at Thirsk, finished fourth in the Group 2 Queen Mary at Royal Ascot, landed a Listed race at Naas and subsequently ran down the field in the Group 2 Lowther and a Group 3 at Longchamp.

"The Listed fillies' race at Bath in April we won with White Lavender three years ago would be a good starting point for her."

GUIDE TO THE FLAT 2025

Carlisle is a happy hunting ground for Burke punters with a career strike-rate of 18% and a profit of £77.19

Burke has two entered for the Lincoln, a race he has yet to win. Last year the strongly backed Liberty Lane finished down the field. This year **Native Warrior** and **Thunder Run** are being prepared for the Doncaster straight-mile cavalry charge.

"They're both very good handicappers/Listed horses and I think Thunder Run could go there with a very good chance. He's done very well over the winter."

Liberty Lane may have failed in the Lincoln but he made no mistake next time out at Newmarket over nine furlongs, and returned in the autumn to win the Cambridgeshire over the same trip.

"He's rated 113, so he'll stick to Listed or Group races now and we'll see how high we can take him. He's wintered very well."

City Of God stepped forward from a promising first run over seven furlongs when fourth at Wolverhampton in late December, winning well over a furlong further at Southwell in January. He was then just touched off over seven again at Wolverhampton a month later, but should be winning again off his rating.

"He looks a nice prospect," says Burke. "He'll have one more run on the all-weather.

21

RACING POST

They've given him a very nice handicap mark of 77 and I think we can take advantage of that. He won over a mile but I think he'll be quick enough over seven.

"The same can be said for **Rebel's Gamble**. He won his first two races on the all-weather over six and could step up to the Listed Spring Cup at Lingfield over seven furlongs. Although his dam was quick and he doesn't look slow, I think he'll stay."

Zeus Olympios ran on well to justify long odds-on over seven furlongs on debut at Kempton in January and looks a fine prospect.

"He's a nice horse. He'll probably have one more run on the all-weather and then wait for the turf over a mile or more."

Another of Burke's all-weather winners who should be followed in the early part of the season is **The Watcher**, an easy winner over six at Newcastle, then even easier over seven at Wolverhampton. "He's a lovely horse who will definitely stay a mile later on," says his trainer.

Greydreambeliever won first time out at York over six and stepped straight into a Group 3 at Salisbury on her next outing when she ran into all sorts of problems in finishing a running-on fifth.

Burke describes her as "a nice filly" and it would be no surprise to see her performing well at Group class level this season.

The 90 two-year-olds at Spigot Lodge are "the best bunch we've ever had", says Burke.

"There are some sharp ones and some lovely ones for the second part of the season. There's a nice Showcasing filly out of Spright called **Polly Darling** who looks an early one, and there's a Twilight Son filly out of Rococoa who also looks quite sharp. There's also a nice Dandy Man colt out of Betsey Trotter."

Reporting by LAWRIE KELSEY

GUIDE TO THE FLAT **2025**

Greydreambeliever: York winner could prove to be Group class

RACING POST

OWEN BURROWS

WINNERS IN LAST FIVE YEARS 24, 23, 21, 22, 20

It's quality all the way as Lambourn trainer not chasing numbers

OWEN BURROWS accepts he won't train "hundreds of winners a season" from his 50-box yard at Farncombe Down stables in Lambourn, so he's concentrating on quality rather than quantity.

To have that intention a trainer needs strong backing from powerful owners – and that is exactly what he has.

Since becoming a public trainer in 2022 after the death of Sheikh Hamdan al Maktoum, for whom he had trained privately for six years after 12 years as assistant to Sir Michael Stoute, Burrows has carried on training for the family, which means a regular supply of top-grade bloodstock.

The sheikh's daughter, Sheikha Hissa, has continued her father's breeding legacy at Shadwell in Norfolk, albeit streamlined, and has kept Burrows as one of her trainers.

Her uncle, Sheikh Ahmed al Maktoum, whose yellow silks with black epaulettes are as recognisable as her blue and white colours, is another who has provided strong backing, as has Dubaian businessman Ahmad Al Shaikh's Green Team Racing operation.

Those powerful owners have sent Burrows 25 bred-in-the-purple two-year-olds and, not surprisingly, he is bubbling with optimism about the coming season, although topping last year's record £1.6 million domestic prize-money and £200,000 from abroad will take some doing.

He describes his operation as "a boutique yard which aims to be competitive in top races".

"I have to be realistic," he says. "With the number of horses we have I know we're not going to train hundreds of winners a season, and there's no point in suddenly taking on a hundred horses because there'd be nowhere to put them."

One of the main reasons for Burrows' optimism is an unnamed colt by Sea The Stars out of Aghareed, which makes him a brother to champions Hukum and Baaeed.

Burrows trained Hukum *(above)* to win the King George and the Coronation Cup in 2023 and, because his young brother resembles the champion, he has been sent to Farncombe Down.

He's also keen on an unnamed filly owned by Sheikh Ahmed, by Dubawi out of the Sea The Stars mare Jammrah, who is a "quality individual" for the latter part of the season.

So, with half his string made up of juveniles, Burrows will be relying on a handful of older horses and some well-bred and talented three-year-olds to fly the Farncombe flag.

Leading them will be Shadwell's seven-year-old gelding **Anmaat**, winner of the Champion Stakes in October.

"I'd be lying if I said we were going to Ascot expecting to win but I thought he would be competitive," reflects Burrows. "I thought we were a certainty in France the race before [Group 2 Prix Dollar]. That was the only time he'd been out of the frame in 15 races and, for whatever reason, things didn't go to plan.

"People discounted him after that run, but at Ascot I thought he should have been a 14-1 shot not 40-1."

This season his programme will include the likes of the Group 3 Brigadier Gerard Stakes in late May, a race Burrows won with Hukum in 2023; the Group 1 Prix Ganay at Longchamp in late April; the Juddmonte International at York in August; Royal Ascot; the Irish Champion and the British Champion Stakes.

"I'm not saying he'll go for all of them, but they'll be on his agenda. He goes on fast ground but I wouldn't want him running too many times."

Another Shadwell-owned horse expected to pay his way this season is **Alflaila**, a six-year-old who last year was beaten just under four lengths in the Group 1 Prince of Wales's Stakes by the 2023 Derby winner Auguste Rodin.

He landed the Group 2 York Stakes next time out for the second year running but disappointed in the Juddmonte International the following month after a slow start, before running fourth in the ten-furlong Bahrain International Trophy in November.

"He was staying on well but didn't quicken as well as the winner, so with his style of running I thought there's no reason why he shouldn't be getting an extra two furlongs."

With that in mind, Burrows ran Alflaila in the £2m Amir Trophy over a mile and a half on turf at Al Uqda racecourse in Doha in mid-February when he finished fifth.

"If he had run well it would have opened up more options. Unfortunately, it was a bit of a non-event," says Burrows. "He was slowly away and then very keen, so we didn't learn a lot. It's a case of back to the drawing board."

■ Pat Dobbs has a 33% strike-rate for the stable during the last five years – and a profit of £17.50

GUIDE TO THE FLAT **2025**

Anmaat: Group 1 targets again this season

It was a similar story a week later when Derby and St Leger fourth **Deira Mile** weakened into sixth in the £2 million Red Sea Turf Handicap over 1m7f at Riyadh, although he did earn £40,000 for his efforts.

"He had a break after the Leger and he's done well over the winter. We're really happy with him," says Burrows. "He's a big horse and he's really filled into his frame and is much stronger."

Fair Wind, a five-year-old gelding owned by Kennet Valley Thoroughbreds, won twice last year and was improving rapidly until refusing to leave the stalls at Goodwood.

"He was on a real upward curve until blotting his copybook," says Burrows. "I just don't know what happened. For whatever reason he didn't fancy it that day. He's rated 94 and will probably be better off running in big handicaps rather than going for stakes races.

"He's done really well for his winter break and all those five-furlong races he ran in last year will be on the agenda again. His optimum distance is five but depending on how he runs, we might explore six."

27

Two four-year-olds to follow owned by Sheikh Ahmed are the colt Jarraaf and filly Nakheel.

After landing two six-furlong sprints impressively at Ascot in the summer, **Jarraaf** returned to the course for the Group 3 Bengough Stakes in October and finished a respectable runner-up.

"I don't think he's an out-and-out sprinter. Those stiff sixes at Ascot seem to suit him down to the ground. He's a big horse who has done well over the winter. Whether that will put a bit more speed into him, we'll find out, but my gut feeling is he's a six-and-a-half or seven-furlong horse."

Nakheel won the Group 2 Park Hill at Doncaster after which she had a break and has returned in fine fettle.

"I'm thrilled with the way she's come back. We'll be trying to make her a Group 1 winner with probably more of her targets in the second half of the season. She goes on fast ground but I think she's a little better with give under foot. The cheekpieces certainly helped at Donny and she'll definitely keep them.

"She'll be aimed at the fillies' and mares' race at Ascot on Champions Day or the fillies' and mares' race at Longchamp on Arc day. We'll play it by ear before then."

Alyanaabi ended up "a bit of a headscratcher" last season after finishing fifth in the 2,000 Guineas and filling the same position in the St James's Palace at Royal Ascot after winning a Group 3 as a juvenile and finishing runner-up behind City Of Troy in the Dewhurst.

He was tried over ten and nine furlongs in his next two races but disappointed.

"We sent him back to Godolphin for a full MOT but they couldn't find anything wrong

OWEN BURROWS
LAMBOURN, BERKSHIRE

RECORD AROUND THE COURSES

	W-R	Per cent	Non-hcp 2yo	Non-hcp 3yo	Non-hcp 4yo+	Hcp 2yo	Hcp 3yo	Hcp 4yo+	£1 level stake
Chelmsford (AW)	21-98	21.4	3-22	7-36	2-2	1-1	2-19	6-18	+8.60
Ascot	17-84	20.2	0-9	2-20	5-16	0-0	8-23	2-16	+57.40
Kempton (AW)	17-120	14.2	8-54	2-25	2-5	1-1	4-26	0-9	-27.10
Nottingham	13-45	28.9	3-11	6-16	0-0	0-0	4-13	0-5	+31.42
Doncaster	12-54	22.2	3-13	4-18	1-3	0-0	3-13	1-7	+7.42
Wolverhampton (AW)	12-68	17.6	2-25	7-26	0-5	1-1	2-9	0-2	-25.85
Newbury	12-74	16.2	3-20	3-17	4-10	0-2	1-13	1-12	-11.82
Haydock	11-35	31.4	1-4	2-7	4-10	1-1	3-8	0-5	+5.99
Salisbury	11-54	20.4	5-21	2-24	0-0	0-0	3-6	1-3	-16.28
Lingfield (AW)	10-50	20.0	1-12	4-19	2-5	0-0	2-8	1-6	-9.60
York	8-34	23.5	1-2	2-10	3-7	0-1	1-8	1-6	+5.50
Newmarket (July)	8-46	17.4	2-8	0-17	0-4	0-0	6-13	0-4	-11.05
Newmarket	8-71	11.3	3-21	3-24	0-4	0-0	2-14	0-8	-10.76
Sandown	7-51	13.7	3-10	2-10	1-5	0-1	1-18	0-7	-23.75
Windsor	6-14	42.9	1-2	3-7	0-0	0-0	2-4	0-1	+29.94
Goodwood	6-28	21.4	0-3	2-11	1-3	0-0	1-4	2-7	+5.93
Yarmouth	6-28	21.4	2-13	0-2	0-0	0-1	2-8	1-3	-7.25
Leicester	6-32	18.7	2-8	1-8	0-1	0-1	3-11	0-3	+15.47
Beverley	4-6	66.7	0-1	4-4	0-0	0-0	0-1	0-0	+4.43
Epsom	4-10	40.0	1-2	0-2	1-1	0-0	2-3	0-2	+19.50
Bath	4-22	18.2	1-4	1-7	0-0	0-1	2-8	0-2	-10.68
Lingfield	3-16	18.7	0-5	1-6	1-1	0-1	1-2	0-1	-6.63
Catterick	2-4	50.0	0-0	2-3	0-0	0-0	0-0	0-1	-0.83
Ripon	2-7	28.6	2-4	0-2	0-0	0-0	0-1	0-0	-1.10
Brighton	2-11	18.2	0-2	0-2	0-0	0-2	2-5	0-0	-1.17
Ffos Las	2-16	12.5	1-9	1-6	0-0	0-0	0-1	0-0	-12.33
Chepstow	2-19	10.5	0-1	2-8	0-1	0-0	0-7	0-2	-11.25
Ayr	1-2	50.0	0-1	0-0	0-0	0-0	0-0	1-1	+4.50
Redcar	1-4	25.0	0-1	0-1	0-0	1-2	0-0	0-0	-0.50
Pontefract	1-8	12.5	0-0	1-3	0-2	0-0	0-2	0-1	-3.50
Thirsk	1-9	11.1	0-0	1-6	0-0	0-0	0-1	0-2	-7.71
Newcastle (AW)	1-14	7.1	0-1	0-4	1-4	0-0	0-2	0-3	-8.50
Wetherby	0-1	0.0	0-0	0-1	0-0	0-0	0-0	0-0	-1.00
Musselburgh	0-1	0.0	0-0	0-0	0-0	0-0	0-0	0-1	-1.00
Chester	0-7	0.0	0-0	0-3	0-0	0-0	0-2	0-2	-7.00
Southwell (AW)	0-12	0.0	0-2	0-6	0-2	0-1	0-0	0-2	-12.00

Number of horses racing for the stable 243
Total winning prize-money £4,561,447.24

Nakheel: winner of the Park Hill Stakes last season and has been pleasing her trainer at home

with him, so he's been gelded. In fact, gelding could be the making of him," says Burrows.

"I thought the Listed Paradise Stakes at Ascot at the end of April might be a nice start for him over a stiff mile and take it from there.

"He's a great work horse and I wouldn't have too many that could work with him. He was just a few pounds off top class last year."

Burrows has Classic hopes for **Gethin**, who won his only start by six lengths in October on heavy ground at Nottingham over 1m½f. He's a 66-1 shot for the Derby.

"He'd been showing up nicely at home and I thought if he went on the ground – it was very soft – he'd go very close, but I don't necessarily think he's going to need it as soft as that.

"He's a big horse and has done well through the winter and filled into his frame. He's bred to be a mile and a quarter, mile and a half horse, who'll get a Derby entry. If we're happy with how he's training, we'll have a look at one of the trials in May."

Falakeyah is also a Classic hope after winning her only outing by five and a half lengths at Wolverhampton in November. She's 25-1 for the Oaks.

RACING POST

"She was very impressive and couldn't have done it any nicer," says Burrows. "She's a big scopey filly. I'm pleased with how she's developed. She's by New Bay out of a War Front mare, so she should stay.

"There's a lot of potential there. We'll class her as a mile and a quarter filly and she'll get an entry in the Prix de Diane [French Oaks] over 1m2½f and the Epsom Oaks."

Glittering Surf is another promising filly who won her only start last year, impressing on the all-weather at Kempton in late December. "She was another big scopey filly who was taking a bit of time," says Burrows. "She'd been doing everything right at home and it was no surprise she did what she did, but I'll be honest, I didn't think she'd do as well as she did.

"I'm not sure how far she'll stay. She's out of a daughter of Frankel, but I think she takes after Oasis Dream [her sire] a bit; she's not short of speed.

"We'll start her off over a mile in a conditions race at Kempton at the end of March, depending on what the weather does, but we could drop her back to a sharp seven, which would give us more options."

Deira Storm was an eyecatching runner-up on debut over seven furlongs at Wolverhampton in December and is another full of promise.

"With a better draw we'd have gone very close," says Burrows. "We took our time with him last year. He's a decent-sized colt but still needs to fill his frame, that's why I wasn't tempted to run him again. I felt he needed a bit of a break.

"We'll get him out early and see where we are with him, but he's another with a lot of speed."

The three-year-old Wootton Bassett filly **Sea Poetry** was yet another to be successful at the backend when handed her debut over seven at Newmarket.

"She'd been showing up nice enough at home and I thought she was the type of filly to go and finish third or fourth, so it took me a bit by surprise.

"Jim [Crowley] said she showed a good attitude and really wanted it. She's had a nice break and has done well physically, although she's not the biggest, so I don't think she's the type to run with a penalty. We'll see how she's working but I think we can have a bit of fun with her."

The most expensive of Burrows' blue-bloods is **Alfareqa**, a Frankel filly who cost 1.6 million guineas, but she failed to live up to her price tag when finishing ninth at Kempton in December on her debut.

"I was very disappointed because her work had been very good," says Burrows. "She'd been working with some of the fillies who had been running well. In fact, she'd have been working better than most of them. She'd been quite a forward-going filly but with the lights and everything I think she was a bit star-struck.

"That certainly wasn't her true showing. I wouldn't read too much into it. She still looks a nice filly at home. We'll wait for the turf and start her off somewhere nice. She's done well over the winter."

Also for the notebook are **Waardah**, who will be a middle-distance filly; the unraced **El Megeeth**, a Ghaiyyath filly who cost £300,000 and had been working well with Burrows' winning fillies; **Remmooz** a £250,000 yearling who reached a good level at home but was immature and put away for the winter; **Tasalla**, a £390,000 half-brother to July Cup winner Mill Stream; and **William Walton**, a brother to 2019 Arc winner Waldgeist, who has "room to play with" on a rating of 78.

Reporting by LAWRIE KELSEY

Jarraaf: goes particularly well at Ascot

31

RACING POST

JACK CHANNON

GUIDE TO THE FLAT **2025**

WINNERS IN LAST TWO YEARS 56, 49

Jack Channon: took over the reins from father Mick

He might be eight but this Lad certainly hasn't finished winning

WHEN a horse is still winning Group races at eight years old, why retire him? That's the logic behind Jack Channon's decision to race on with **Certain Lad**.

The old boy has been a stable favourite since winning his first two races in the early summer of 2018 and has amassed almost £446,000 prize-money and won 11 races.

And last season was probably his best after running exclusively in Group races, except for taking time out to cruise to a seven-length victory in a Listed race at Compiegne.

Last season, after starting with a fourth in the John Porter at Newbury, Certain Lad *(below)* was a length second in the Brigadier Gerard at Sandown, then a neck second in the Rose of Lancaster at Haydock.

Two weeks later the Haydock result was replicated at Windsor before he rounded off his remarkable season in early September by winning at Longchamp.

"He's our stable stalwart and probably had his best season last year," says Channon, who is in his third season after taking over the licence at West Ilsley from his famous father Mick, one of the few people to make it to the pinnacle of two different sports after winning 46 caps as a striker for England's football team in the mid-70s.

"He was my first Group winner and is an

33

absolute star for me," says Channon. "He's back in full training and going really well. Now he's got a Group 3 penalty, we'll be looking at some of those Group 2s and have a couple of speculative entries in Group 1s.

"He loves soft ground and there aren't that many races early on in the Group 3 division, so we could always look at the Ganay or Prix d'Ispahan, both at Longchamp when the ground is really soft. You never know because you don't always have to be a top-class Group 1 horse to compete in those races.

"We'll have to see how he's training before deciding whether he'll have a prep run before going to France. He's a very active horse and he acts more like a two-year-old than a nine-year-old. So he's a horse that doesn't take much to get fit and I wouldn't be afraid to send him to a big race without a run."

Metal Merchant won the Spring Cup at Newbury first time out last season and ran "an absolute belter" to be seventh in the Hunt Cup at Royal Ascot, leading inside the two-pole but just fading in the last half furlong. He ran equally well to finish fourth in a valuable handicap back at Ascot over seven furlongs in July.

"He had a really positive season last year. His rating is 97 and he'll be competing in those big handicaps again this year. We might start him off in the Spring Cup again or the Lincoln if he comes to hand quick enough."

Johan, who won the Lincoln in 2022, is eight and doesn't run that often nowadays after being beset by health issues, but he manages to win a big race each season.

He could join his stablemate at Doncaster on March 29, although his rating of 109 means he's on the cusp of stakes-race standard.

"He's back in full training and I'm really happy with him," says Channon. "He's up to 109 now. He's never been that high and won a handicap. We could look at the Lincoln but you've also got the Doncaster Stakes there that day, which is a Listed race.

Johan and Metal Merchant exercise on the turf at West Ilsley stables

"It might be a case that we ply our trade early on in some stakes races or we could always look at France for him, and even Ireland. Sometimes those mile races aren't as competitive.

"If he can't quite reach the grade in stakes company, we can always look at something like the Golden Mile for him in the summer.

"He's had a lot of problems that keep holding us up and is a very hard horse to train. But when we get him right he's very good. He's got a lot of ability. He's one of those horses you don't mind putting blood, sweat and tears into because when you get it right he wins a big one."

After winning his second race as a two-year-old, then finishing unplaced in the Group 2 Superlative Stakes at Newmarket, **Metallo** missed his three-year-old career with a setback, but he's back in the groove with successive placed runs this winter.

"Because he missed the whole of his three-year-old career he was a horse we highlighted for an all-weather campaign," says Channon.

"The problem is there aren't a million races for a horse rated in the high 80s like him, but the races there are, are obviously worth the money.

"We hope to aim him at the All Weather Championships at Newcastle on Good Friday. He has very low mileage and is a horse who goes from strength to strength. He could be a real nice mile-and-a-quarter heritage handicap horse and something like the John Smith's Cup might suit him. I think he's really exciting."

RACING POST

Majestic, who won the 2022 Cambridgeshire, finished fourth in it the following year and 12th last season, is almost certain to return for another tilt in the autumn.

But it will mean he'll have had a long year because he's been in Bahrain this winter finishing second in December over ten furlongs, then winning a valuable race over the same distance in January before finishing down the field over nine furlongs at the end of January.

"He'll keep going in Bahrain until March, then he'll be competing in all the big handicaps in the summer, such as the John Smith's and the Cambridgeshire."

Rathgar had a fruitful 2024, winning a big handicap at Yarmouth after being dropped from two miles to a mile and a quarter.

"He did win over a mile-six but he did it by ability rather than it being the right trip. We've finally realised he's a very good mile-and-a-quarter handicapper.

"He'll only improve for another winter and I'm hoping he can step up to the heritage handicaps. He's a gorgeous big horse and I think that's why we got hoodwinked into thinking he was a stayer. I wouldn't be afraid to run him over nine furlongs in the Cambridgeshire."

Ferrous was brought in early and is more forward in fitness than most of Channon's string.

"He seems a horse who flourishes on the all-weather, so he'll run on all-weather trials day at Lingfield on February 28 with a view to getting a run into him before finals day at Newcastle. Then he'll be aimed at all the heritage handicaps such as the Wokingham again and Stewards' Cup."

One to definitely make a bold note of is **Galyx**, who won over a mile last year at Windsor and a mile-two at Leicester at the backend, and had only five runs in total.

"I've been very patient with him. He's the sort of horse who could either settle in the

■ Look out for Tom Marquand in the saddle for the stable – four winners and a 29% strike-rate has turned a profit of £11.50

Majestic: 2022 Cambridgeshire winner will be back for more in the big handicaps

mid-90s and be a nice heritage handicap horse or potentially go on and be a stakes horse. He's done brilliantly during the winter and is a proper horse. He's very exciting."

Hot Cash won first time out at Epsom in July and the following month was stepped up to Group 3 level at Deauville where he was fourth.

"He had a small setback after that and we thought we'd leave him for this year," says Channon. "He's a middle-distance horse who'll get a mile and two plus. He's done really well over the winter. We'll start him off in a small race and look to step him up in grade. I think he's quite smart."

JACK CHANNON
WEST ILSLEY, BERKSHIRE

RECORD AROUND THE COURSES

	W-R	Per cent	Non-hcp 2yo	Non-hcp 3yo	Non-hcp 4yo+	Hcp 2yo	Hcp 3yo	Hcp 4yo+	£1 level stake
Windsor	12-54	22.2	3-11	2-7	0-1	0-2	3-14	4-19	-1.42
Goodwood	8-55	14.5	1-12	0-4	1-2	0-2	1-15	5-20	+2.28
Wolverhampton (AW)	6-43	14.0	0-9	1-5	0-0	0-2	3-17	2-10	+12.46
Catterick	5-8	62.5	1-2	0-1	0-0	0-0	2-2	2-3	+11.58
Ffos Las	5-18	27.8	1-3	0-1	0-0	1-1	2-11	1-2	+8.25
Lingfield (AW)	5-28	17.9	0-2	1-5	0-1	0-0	1-14	3-6	+6.00
Newbury	5-42	11.9	0-11	1-5	0-1	0-0	2-14	2-11	+23.50
Ripon	4-12	33.3	1-2	1-3	0-0	1-1	0-2	1-4	+0.92
Chelmsford (AW)	4-21	19.0	0-2	3-7	0-0	0-0	1-7	0-5	-12.55
Chepstow	4-22	18.2	0-5	0-0	0-0	0-1	1-7	3-9	+0.18
Haydock	4-28	14.3	0-1	0-1	0-3	0-1	3-16	1-6	-7.50
Leicester	3-13	23.1	1-2	0-1	0-0	0-0	1-6	1-4	-2.42
Newcastle (AW)	3-14	21.4	1-1	1-5	0-0	0-0	1-2	0-6	-3.84
Nottingham	3-15	20.0	0-1	1-3	0-0	0-1	1-8	1-2	+7.00
Brighton	3-15	20.0	1-2	0-2	0-0	0-1	2-5	0-5	+3.00
Epsom	3-22	13.6	1-3	0-1	0-0	0-2	1-9	1-7	+5.50
York	3-23	13.0	0-2	0-1	0-2	0-1	1-5	2-12	+9.50
Bath	3-26	11.5	1-4	0-5	0-0	0-2	1-8	1-7	-7.38
Doncaster	3-28	10.7	0-3	0-1	0-1	0-1	0-10	3-12	+3.33
Kempton (AW)	3-36	8.3	0-7	1-8	0-0	0-0	1-11	1-10	-24.70
Pontefract	2-3	66.7	0-0	0-0	1-1	0-0	0-0	1-2	+17.50
Chester	2-7	28.6	1-2	0-0	0-0	1-1	0-3	0-1	+2.23
Hamilton	2-12	16.7	0-1	1-1	0-0	0-0	0-5	1-5	+0.87
Salisbury	2-22	9.1	2-11	0-2	0-0	0-0	0-6	0-3	+20.73
Redcar	1-4	25.0	0-1	1-1	0-0	0-0	0-1	0-0	-1.63
Musselburgh	1-6	16.7	0-1	0-0	0-0	0-0	1-4	0-1	-3.38
Lingfield	1-6	16.7	1-2	0-0	0-0	0-0	0-4	0-0	-4.00
Yarmouth	1-12	8.3	0-0	0-0	0-0	0-0	0-6	1-5	+14.00
Newmarket (July)	1-14	7.1	0-1	0-1	0-0	0-0	1-7	0-5	-10.00
Ascot	1-18	5.6	0-2	1-2	0-2	0-0	0-6	0-6	-12.00
Southwell (AW)	1-23	4.3	0-3	0-4	0-0	0-1	0-5	1-10	-20.13
Newmarket	1-31	3.2	0-4	0-2	0-1	0-1	0-10	1-13	-26.50
Wetherby	0-1	0.0	0-0	0-0	0-0	0-0	0-1	0-0	-1.00
Beverley	0-2	0.0	0-0	0-1	0-0	0-0	0-1	0-0	-2.00
Carlisle	0-3	0.0	0-1	0-1	0-0	0-0	0-1	0-0	-3.00
Thirsk	0-7	0.0	0-0	0-1	0-0	0-0	0-3	0-3	-7.00
Sandown	0-19	0.0	0-6	0-1	0-2	0-0	0-3	0-7	-19.00

Number of horses racing for the stable **90**
Total winning prize-money **£954,898.21**

Crestofdistinction is considered a fine sprinting three-year-old colt who was third first time out at Doncaster, then second on the all-weather at Kempton, both over six furlongs.

"I decided to give him a winter break rather than cracking on and winning his maiden. He's the type of horse who could go through the grades quite quickly and is exciting. He'll be out in April. He's a horse I've liked a lot for a long time. He had a setback early in his two-year-old career but came good at the backend."

Sarab Star won his maiden first time out at Salisbury from a subsequent double winner now rated 93, and the third who is rated 87 after two seconds in photo finishes.

He then ran in the Group 2 Mill Reef on heavy ground that he didn't cope with.

"He absolutely despised it," says Channon. "He's the one I think is a very, very good horse, the one that has a bit of star quality.

"We'll look at one of the Guineas trials to see if he's good enough. But regardless, he's a high quality animal and we're looking forward to his season."

Raveena had only one outing as a two-year-old but ran well until fading in the final furlong in a Goodwood six-furlong race that has produced winners, including the

37

Lowther heroine Celandine, now rated 106, who was only half a length in front of Channon's filly.

"She's quite smart and ran a very good race at Goodwood, but she was a bit immature last year and I had to be patient and take my time.

"I could probably have won a race with her at the back, but I thought giving her the winter was the best thing for her.

"She's in full work, looks good, has matured and could be out in early March with a view to breaking her maiden, then going on to bigger and better things."

Hey Boo is an unraced three-year-old to look out for. "She's a big filly who was very weak as a two-year-old, but she's strengthened over the winter and her work is really pleasing me," says Channon. "She looks a tough filly who could shed her maiden tag in the next few weeks and who knows what she could go on to after that."

Of his two-year-olds, take note of a colt by 2019 Irish Guineas winner Phoenix Of Spain out of Chicita Banana, who has "a lot of size and class and is doing everything right"; a Sands Of Mali colt out of Macau who "looks a sharp five- or six-furlong horse" and a Gregorian colt out of Princess Lahar who is also sharp.

Of the fillies, **Sukanya** by Havana Grey looks as though she could be doing well early, and so too could **Hope Horizon** by A'Ali out of Ile Deserte.

Reporting by LAWRIE KELSEY

Jack Channon keeps an eye on work at West Ilsley Stables

GUIDE TO THE FLAT **2025**

RACING POST

JAMES OWEN

Burdett Road flying the flag for stable off to a flyer

AFTER his Cheltenham Festival exertions **Burdett Road** will be prepared for a showdown with the Flat's leading stayers in the Gold Cup at Royal Ascot.

That's where he is almost certain to butt heads again with the double winner of the season's top staying race, Kyprios, who beat Burdett Road by almost eight lengths in the Long Distance Cup at Ascot on British Champions Day in October.

There's a huge discrepancy in ratings between the two, 122-111, but James Owen is planning – and hoping – to see if the handicapper has got his sums wrong.

GUIDE TO THE FLAT **2025**

WINNERS IN LAST TWO YEARS 63, 0

James Owen with East India Dock at Green Ridge Stables in Newmarket

"Burdett Road definitely goes back on the Flat and will be aimed at the Ascot Gold Cup," confirms Owen, Newmarket's pre-eminent dual purpose trainer.

"We feel he's improving as he's getting older and maturing. He'll have a little break after Cheltenham and be prepared for the Group 3 Henry II Stakes at Sandown in late May."

That was the same preparation Big Orange had when he won the Gold Cup in 2017 for Bill Gredley, who owns Burdett Road.

After Ascot, Burdett Road will be aimed at the Melbourne Cup on November 4, Australia's two-mile Group 1 race that "stops a nation".

"We do see him as a Melbourne Cup horse," says Owen. "He might have a little break [before Australia] because he'll have been on the go [all year], but he's actually a horse that thrives on racing and thrives on being trained. So we'll see after the Gold Cup where we are.

"For a yard like ours, he's a pleasure to have and to be talking about these races is fantastic."

Owen can add an even bigger race to his conversation – the Derby – which was raised, as well as the 2,000 Guineas, after **Wimbledon Hawkeye** won the Royal Lodge in the autumn over Newmarket's straight mile.

That run followed second in the Group 3 Acomb Stakes at York and third in the Group 2 Superlative Stakes at Newmarket, both over seven furlongs.

The Kameko colt, bred by Gredley and son Tim from their mare Eva Maria, ended the season outgunned in the Futurity at Doncaster by two Irish raiders, confirming the suspicion that middle-distance races rather than a mile would be his route to glory.

Jockey James Doyle said after the Royal

Wimbledon Hawkeye: Owen is happy with his progress over the winter

Lodge that Wimbledon Hawkeye had plenty of filling out to do, which is exactly what nature has done.

"He's had a nice break at the owners' stud, he's wintered well, strengthened up, looks like he's matured, and is training nicely. I couldn't be happier with him," says Owen.

"The owners and I see him as a Derby horse and we'll more than likely go for a Derby trial rather than the Guineas route.

"Plans are fluid but we'll make solid plans in the next few weeks. We haven't totally ruled the Guineas out but he's always been a horse we thought would stay.

"We'll see how he trains. I've never had a Guineas runner, so I don't really know if he's one, but it's lovely to think we might have a Derby horse.

"It's the Gredleys' dream to have a Derby winner, especially a homebred. So far he's done us proud and I don't see why he wouldn't train on."

The Gredleys' long-held Derby dream looked fleetingly as though it would become reality last year when Ambiente Friendly was cruising with just over two furlongs to go, but he couldn't cope with the finishing power of City Of Troy and had to settle for runner-up.

Trad Jazz is another inmate for whom Owen and the Gredleys have Classic aspirations. The filly could hardly have been more impressive on debut over a mile at Kempton in August, bursting clear well inside the final furlong to win going away by almost four lengths.

Owen said after the race: " I thought Trad Jazz would run well. We don't turn the screw on these two-year-olds at home and we're learning as we go along this season with it being our first year, so a lot of that was natural ability, and she was professional."

She would have run in a Listed fillies' race at Newmarket after Kempton but scoped dirty, so Owen decided to put her away for the season.

"She's wintered really well back at the Gredleys' stud and we have high hopes for her. We'd love her to be an Oaks filly and her next two runs are going to be important ones.

"She's out of a good staying mare by Sea The Moon, who I think is a fantastic sire. She's a lovely individual and to win first time out means she's fairly talented.

"She could go for an Oaks trial. We'll see how she's training before making any decisions, but we'll definitely train her that way and hope she comes up trumps."

Another outstanding member of Owen's team for the Flat being prepared at his Green Ridge stables is leading Triumph Hurdle hope **East India Dock**.

After Cheltenham, Owen hopes to take him to the festivals at either Aintree or Punchestown, then prepare him for a Flat campaign.

"He's very much a better hurdler than he has been on the Flat; we feel he comes alive when he sees a hurdle," says Owen.

That point was hammered home by the extent of his three successive wins over hurdles by an aggregate 32 lengths before going to the festival, but a handy mark of 89 on the Flat could be exploited.

"He's got a nice rating to get into some of those nice staying handicaps, something like the Copper Horse Stakes at Royal Ascot or maybe the Queen Alexandra," says Owen.

Two more staying types for the Flat are the Gredley-owned four-year-olds, **Liam Swagger** and **Lavender Hill Mob**. Owen is slightly disappointed he hasn't won on the Flat with Liam Swagger, who was placed three times in five outings last season, although he has won twice over hurdles and was fancied for the Boodles Fred Winter Juvenile handicap hurdle at the festival.

"He was quite a late maturing horse but should be more than capable of winning a staying handicap on the Flat."

He describes Lavender Hill Mob as "a talented horse with quite a nice handicap mark" who will also run in the Boodles, then switch back to the Flat.

43

"There'll be some nice staying handicaps for him and hopefully we can get him to Royal Ascot too. He's rated 96, which will get him into a lot of places."

Ambiente Amigo did well last year without winning on the Flat, but was placed in Listed races at Goodwood and Newmarket.

"It took her a while to settle but she's well capable of winning Listed races. She's also won over hurdles but she's not going to be a high-end hurdler. She's a filly with a good bit of ability and the owners want to give her one more season to get some more black type. She should more than pay her way and be ready fairly early."

Probably the most remarkable horse in Owen's yard last year was **Destinado**. He ran in 28 races and won eight times from nine and a half furlongs to one mile five furlongs. To call him tough and versatile hardly does justice to the seven-year-old, whose rating rose from 45 to 70.

"He's on a break at the moment and we'll bring him back for an apprentice race at Doncaster at the start of the season," says Owen.

Another consistent horse to follow is **Carlton**, who won four out of five last year.

"He probably should have made it five but didn't get any cover on his last outing, although that was probably one of his best runs," says Owen. "He'll have one or two more runs on the all-weather, then have a break. He's a lovely horse. He's really clicked since joining us in December."

Ammes was fourth at Chelmsford on his debut in November, and Owen predicts a bright future for him.

"This horse is going to do well this season and make a nice staying handicapper. He's done really well over the winter. He was a shell of a horse but has really filled his frame. He'll be out at the end of March-April time."

Rogue Diplomat is in a similar vein after finishing third on debut. "He was a little weak, had a nice break and has really strengthened up. I really like him. A mile to a mile and a quarter will be his distance."

So, too, is the unraced **Bethnal Green**, who showed plenty of ability in a racecourse gallop and was ready to run until a small setback curtailed his season.

"The break will have done him good," says Owen. "He's back in full training and will probably make his debut in the Wood Ditton at Newmarket for unraced three-year-olds. I

GUIDE TO THE FLAT **2025**

> Keep an eye on runners from the stable at 1m4f-1m5f – they have a strike-rate of 29% (£48.23)

Prolific winner Destinado leads home the field at Musselburgh

JAMES OWEN
NEWMARKET, SUFFOLK

RECORD AROUND THE COURSES

	W-R	Per cent	Non-hcp 2yo	Non-hcp 3yo	Non-hcp 4yo+	Hcp 2yo	Hcp 3yo	Hcp 4yo+	£1 level stake
Wolverhampton (AW)	24-84	28.6	0-2	0-3	4-5	0-1	4-11	16-62	+28.24
Southwell (AW)	13-61	21.3	1-4	0-4	3-7	0-1	1-7	8-38	+2.98
Chelmsford (AW)	6-40	15.0	0-3	0-4	0-1	0-0	0-5	6-27	-18.72
Kempton (AW)	5-29	17.2	2-6	0-2	0-1	0-0	0-5	3-15	+38.25
Lingfield (AW)	5-34	14.7	0-2	0-1	2-5	0-0	0-3	3-23	-10.65
Yarmouth	3-23	13.0	1-4	0-2	0-1	0-3	0-5	2-8	+0.00
Musselburgh	2-2	100.0	0-0	0-0	0-0	0-0	1-1	1-1	+15.62
Brighton	2-4	50.0	0-0	1-2	0-0	0-0	0-1	1-1	+5.17
Lingfield	2-5	40.0	0-1	1-1	0-1	0-0	0-1	1-1	+3.25
Leicester	2-7	28.6	0-0	0-0	0-0	0-2	1-2	1-3	+0.75
Doncaster	2-9	22.2	0-1	0-1	0-1	1-2	0-0	1-4	+0.50
Windsor	2-11	18.2	0-0	0-3	0-0	0-1	1-2	1-5	-4.09
Newmarket	2-15	13.3	1-5	0-2	1-1	0-1	0-2	0-4	+1.00
Chepstow	1-2	50.0	0-0	0-0	0-0	0-0	0-0	1-2	+5.00
Ripon	1-2	50.0	0-0	1-1	0-0	0-0	0-0	0-1	+0.25
Bath	1-6	16.7	0-0	0-0	0-0	0-0	1-3	0-3	+0.00
Sandown	1-7	14.3	0-0	0-0	0-0	0-0	0-1	1-6	+10.00
Chester	1-9	11.1	0-1	0-1	0-1	0-0	0-0	1-6	-6.50
Newmarket (July)	1-16	6.2	0-6	1-3	0-1	0-0	0-2	0-4	+10.00
Newcastle (AW)	1-16	6.2	0-1	0-1	0-1	0-0	0-1	1-12	-12.50
Thirsk	0-1	0.0	0-0	0-0	0-0	0-0	0-0	0-1	-1.00
Wetherby	0-1	0.0	0-0	0-0	0-0	0-0	0-0	0-1	-1.00
Salisbury	0-2	0.0	0-0	0-1	0-1	0-0	0-0	0-0	-2.00
Redcar	0-2	0.0	0-0	0-2	0-0	0-0	0-0	0-0	-2.00
Hamilton	0-2	0.0	0-0	0-0	0-0	0-0	0-0	0-2	-2.00
Pontefract	0-3	0.0	0-0	0-1	0-0	0-1	0-1	0-0	-3.00
Beverley	0-3	0.0	0-0	0-1	0-0	0-0	0-2	0-0	-3.00
Goodwood	0-3	0.0	0-0	0-0	0-2	0-0	0-0	0-1	-3.00
Epsom	0-3	0.0	0-0	0-0	0-0	0-0	0-1	0-2	-3.00
Haydock	0-3	0.0	0-0	0-0	0-0	0-0	0-1	0-2	-3.00
Newbury	0-3	0.0	0-0	0-0	0-0	0-0	0-0	0-3	-3.00
Ascot	0-4	0.0	0-1	0-0	0-1	0-0	0-2	0-0	-4.00
Nottingham	0-5	0.0	0-0	0-0	0-0	0-0	0-1	0-4	-5.00
York	0-8	0.0	0-2	0-1	0-1	0-0	0-2	0-2	-8.00

Number of horses racing for the stable **76**
Total winning prize-money **£428,223.75**

RACING POST

Hurdles winners The Cavern Club (above) and Charging Thunder should both be winning races on the Flat

really liked him last year and on pedigree he should be a better three-year-old. Hopefully, he's going to turn into quite a nice horse.

"**Sir Edward Lear** is another lovely horse. He won on debut at Ripon but got stuck in the mud next time at Redcar. There's plenty of room in his mark of 73."

Pellitory looked a promising type after winning at Yarmouth and Doncaster as a two-year-old. "He's a big horse with a lot of class. He's wintered really well and I have high hopes for him. We'll start him at the Craven meeting and hopefully he can turn into a Royal Ascot horse. He's better than a handicapper."

Noisy Jazz, a half-sister to Big Orange, won on debut last year as a three-year-old but was slightly disappointing in her next three races.

"She was a frame last year and a bit weak, but she's wintered really well and filled out. I think she has a bit more speed than a stayer, probably a mile to a mile and a quarter filly."

The Cavern Club is a dual-purpose horse who has won on the Flat and over hurdles. "The owners are from near Chester and he won on his first start there. There'll be some nice staying races for him, something like the Chester Plate, the consolation race for the Chester Cup."

Charging Thunder is a seven-year-old who contested Group and Listed races and once had a rating of 99 on the Flat, was bought for 20,000gns at the Tattersalls September sale and could prove a bargain.

He ran once on the Flat for Owen, winning on stable debut at Yarmouth over a mile and six, then won twice over hurdles in the autumn.

"He'll go back over hurdles and flip between that and the Flat. There are definitely more Flat races in him," says Owen. "He stays well but he's ground dependent."

From his batch of two-year-olds, Owen has selected three to follow. An unnamed filly by Acclamation out of Winter Snow is athletic and catching the eye in her canters. "She's a mid-season filly who is for sale. I really like her," says Owen.

A second one to note is the Gredleys' homebred colt by Mohaather out of Eva Maria, a half-brother to Wimbledon Hawkeye who is "very athletic and a good mover". He will also be out mid-season.

The third is a filly by Lope Y Fernandez out of She's Amazing and is likely to be his first two-year-old runner in the Brocklesby at Doncaster.

"She's a pocket rocket and well forward," he says.

Reporting by LAWRIE KELSEY

RACING POST

HUGO PALMER

Zoffee's victory in the Chester Cup was a highlight last season – and a repeat is the aim

WINNERS IN LAST FIVE YEARS 76, 56, 43, 54, 54

Chester cup repeat high on the agenda this term

HUGO PALMER won the Chester Cup last season with Zoffee and could be double-handed as he attempts to win the historic race again this season.

The race, first run in 1824, is two miles, two and a half furlongs on Chester's famous tight-turning track, and has been won by dual-purpose horses.

So **Zoffee** could be joined on the Roodee by stablemate **Roaring Legend**, winner of both his starts since joining Palmer's Manor House stables 16 miles south of Chester racecourse, at the turn of the year after a spell over jumps.

The five-year-old gelding began life in Newmarket with James Ferguson for whom he won twice and was runner-up five times.

He was sent to Olly Murphy to go hurdling and won twice and was placed four times. He even ran over fences on his final outing.

His two wins for Palmer in January – by six lengths at Wolverhampton over one mile-six and a valuable two-mile handicap at Newcastle – has seen his rating rise a stone to a mark of 96, but Palmer feels there's more to come.

"He's a very welcome new addition to the yard," says the trainer. "He's had time to strengthen up and even on his new mark of 96 he still looks pretty well handicapped.

"David Probert got a ticking off for winning as far as he did at Wolverhampton, pushing him out and hitting him! But he

RACING POST

won hands and heels at Newcastle and Dave said he was just toying with them.

"I think there's plenty more under the bonnet. How much more we'll see. He'll go to trials day at Lingfield [for the all-weather championships finals at Newcastle at the end of March], but he does have an entry for the Dubai Gold Cup and if he were to go and win well at Lingfield and be rated 103 or 104, he might just get an invitation to World Cup night [April 5].

"I'm a great believer in striking while the iron's hot, so I'm sure he'll run in the Chester Cup. You can give horses a break and they don't always come back the same, so we'll keep running him."

Would the Chester turns suit Roaring Legend? "Well, they're going so slowly that

Roaring Legend (grey): will join Zoffee for a crack at the Chester Cup

the turns aren't that tight," says Palmer.

"That's very much the plan. He's doing well. He's had a nice break and is back in cantering. I would think he'll go straight to Chester."

Seagulls Eleven had a cracking season, ending with a rating of 112 after finishing run-up in the Grade 2 Superlative Stakes at Newmarket, third in the Group 3 National Stakes at the Curragh, and fourth in the Grade 1 Dewhurst back at Newmarket. He ran in the Breeders Cup Juvenile turf but finished down the field.

"He was running a nice race at Del Mar when he got crashed into from behind and completely lost his action," says Palmer. "Luckily, he wasn't injured. He's had a good break, is back cantering and looks great.

"He's changed as much physically over the winter as his father [Galileo Gold] did. He's rated a couple of pounds higher than his father was at the same stage. Whether he can make the same jump as his father did for us [to win the 2016 Guineas], I don't know, but it's perfectly possible for a horse to improve ten or eleven pounds from two to three.

That's all he has to do to be competitive in the 2,000 Guineas, and that is where I expect he'll start his season.

"He likes top of the ground, which is strange, because his father liked a bit of cut, and he's more likely to get fast ground at Newmarket than the Curragh or in France."

The Waco Kid won the Group 3 Tattersalls Autumn Stakes and finished alongside Seagulls Eleven at Del Mar.

"He's grown outwards rather than upwards this winter and is a much stronger horse. He's a very tough horse who tries very hard.

"I'd have thought he'll likely start in either the Greenham [Newbury] or the Craven [Newmarket]. He likes cut in the ground."

Like Seagulls Eleven, he's likely to be given a Guineas, as is **Hawksbill**. He opened his account at Haydock at the third time of asking last season but was unplaced when upped to Grade 2 level in the Royal Lodge after leading to the two pole.

"He probably didn't quite achieve what I thought he might have done last year, but he still finished his two-year-old season rated in the 90s," says Palmer.

"I've told the owners we see him very much as a Royal Ascot horse. Whether that's in the Britannia, the ten-furlong Golden Gates handicap, or whether he makes that jump to something better like the Group 3 Hampton Court, we'll have to wait and see.

"He's always been a big strong horse and probably hasn't changed that much over the winter, but he looks more mature."

Palmer's fourth Guineas entry will be **Wolf Of Badenoch**, who will also start his season in the Greenham or Craven.

He won on debut last year, finished strongly to be second in the Vintage Stakes at Goodwood, but ended the season disappointingly when fourth in the Group 2 Champagne Stakes at Doncaster and last of six in the Autumn Stakes at Newmarket, after which his jockey Jamie Spencer told Palmer he thought his mount was weak.

"He's grown, done well physically and strengthened, so hopefully all that weakness has gone. The jury's still out on him but he's rated 102. After his first race we'll make a plan and take it from there. He could easily be German Guineas horse."

Grey Cuban was a consistent handicapper last season, winning four times, including twice at Chester.

"He's done really well physically over the winter. I'm hoping there's going to be a ten-furlong race for him at Doncaster on the

GUIDE TO THE FLAT **2025**

The Waco Kid (left): reported to be much stronger this season

opening weekend of the season. He's in good nick and filled out and grown and changed more than I thought he was going to. He likes a bit of cut in the ground, so after Doncaster, there's a ten-furlong handicap at Chester. After that we'll see."

He's A Gentleman ran 14 times last season from seven to ten furlongs for the Michael Owen Racing Club, winning once and finishing runner-up four times. He's already won first time out this year.

"He's such a star and is the perfect racing syndicate horse," says Palmer. "I was delighted he could win on the turf last year and I hope he can do so again. We know where he is and the handicapper knows where he is. So he'll just go up and down in the 70s and win when he can and not when he can't. He's in good shape."

Misty Sky won well over seven furlongs at Newmarket in October, had a break and came out to win twice at Kempton and Southwell over the same distance in January.

"She's been something of a revelation.

RACING POST

She's a tough filly and I'd be hopeful there'll be more races to be won with her on the all-weather. She's rated 83 and if she starts to get closer to 90, we'll probably start to think about getting some black type with her.

"She likes cut in the ground, so we might think about the Fred Darling. I don't think she's good enough to win it, but fitness and toughness might see her finishing third, which would do her value no end of good."

Stratusnine won once last year and finished a close runner-up in his three other outings.

"He's an enormous horse now. He really has done very well indeed, although he's had a few niggles. His form was good last year and he should do well this year," says Palmer.

After winning in the spring at Haydock, Nariko ended her season with victory in October at Salisbury and failing by a nose at Doncaster to make it a hat-trick of six-furlong handicaps.

"I'd like to think she'll make a black-type horse this year. She's done very well over the winter.

Seagolazo is another who has done well over the winter. He ran very well after being

He's A Gentleman: a regular runner for his stable who looks highly likely to add more victories to his cv

54

ASCOT TOP HATS
FABER CAUSIARUM ALTARUM

At **Ascot Top Hats Ltd**, we provide new felt Toppers and Vintage Silk Top Hats, as well as refurbishment and fitting services to reshape hats to heads to make them comfortable.

Ascot Top Hats Ltd

By appointment at our workshop please call:
01344 638 838 www.ascot-tophats.co.uk

Unit 24 Space Business Centre,
Molly Millars Lane, Wokingham, Berks RG41 2PQ

Ascot Top Hats Ltd is a company registered in England and Wales Incorporation Number: 5740259 Registered Office: Beechey House, 87 Church Street, Crowthorne, Berkshire, RG45 7AW

RACING POST

- Lewis Edmunds has ridden for the yard four times in the last five years and won twice (£13.50)

One Eye Jack (left) gets the verdict on his debut at Haydock

gelded last year, finishing fourth at Doncaster in the Weatherbys sales race, then second at York over a mile.

"I hope he can step forward again this year. I think his trip will be a mile and probably top of the ground conditions."

One Eye Jack won on his debut at Haydock but flopped in a big sales race in France on his next outing.

"I think we probably overfaced him by taking him to Paris. He was weak but he's done very well physically since then and is one to look forward to."

Palmer will begin the season with around 120 horses, 55 of whom will be juveniles as he attempts to beat last year's 76 winners and £1.37m prize-money.

"We have some lovely two-year-olds and I particularly like Wolf Of Badenoch's Too Darn Hot brother out of Miss Latin. He could be a very nice colt and should be early enough, probably a bit earlier than his brother [made his debut in mid-June].

"There's a very nice filly by Sergei Prokoviev out of Papaya who wasn't expensive. She looks sharp, strong and forward and has to

GUIDE TO THE FLAT **2025**

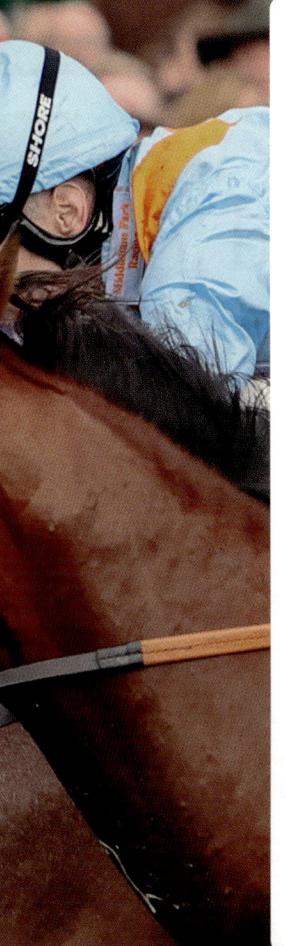

HUGO PALMER
MALPAS, CHESHIRE

RECORD AROUND THE COURSES

	W-R	Per cent	Non-hcp 2yo	Non-hcp 3yo	Non-hcp 4yo+	Hcp 2yo	Hcp 3yo	Hcp 4yo+	£1 level stake
Wolverhampton (A.W)	67-337	19.9	15-69	13-67	3-13	7-28	13-107	16-53	+33.55
Kempton (A.W)	58-374	15.5	20-130	8-62	1-17	3-24	19-101	7-40	-55.97
Newcastle (A.W)	48-277	17.3	13-57	14-60	1-7	0-24	11-69	9-60	-16.64
Chelmsford (A.W)	40-266	15.0	14-65	7-60	1-9	1-14	8-70	9-48	-94.18
Lingfield (A.W)	34-207	16.4	3-43	7-47	2-11	2-9	10-56	10-41	-13.27
Haydock	33-178	18.5	12-50	5-27	3-8	1-9	10-56	2-28	+88.68
Chester	32-178	18.0	8-40	4-12	0-5	1-9	12-61	7-51	+13.18
Doncaster	22-133	16.5	10-44	3-19	1-4	0-7	7-41	1-18	-18.09
Newmarket (July)	22-180	12.2	5-57	1-20	3-6	3-10	9-70	1-17	-63.26
Newmarket	21-206	10.2	10-75	3-46	0-8	1-10	5-50	2-17	-16.43
Windsor	20-134	14.9	3-27	7-35	0-6	4-12	3-45	3-9	-37.53
Yarmouth	18-111	16.2	5-35	4-13	0-2	0-8	8-43	1-10	-8.37
Southwell (A.W)	15-99	15.2	0-10	7-31	0-3	1-10	2-20	5-25	-16.90
Newbury	15-134	11.2	8-48	2-24	0-12	0-2	5-32	0-16	-15.28
Nottingham	13-91	14.3	5-28	1-20	1-2	1-8	5-28	0-5	+1.92
Salisbury	12-55	21.8	6-23	2-12	0-1	0-2	4-14	0-3	-1.13
Carlisle	11-38	28.9	3-9	4-8	0-0	0-4	2-11	2-6	-1.80
Ffos Las	9-28	32.1	2-5	3-6	1-1	1-2	2-9	0-5	+22.67
Leicester	9-61	14.8	3-16	1-7	3-5	0-5	0-21	2-7	-32.29
Redcar	9-68	13.2	4-21	1-14	0-1	0-3	4-26	0-3	-10.32
Goodwood	9-108	8.3	3-24	1-18	0-5	0-13	3-30	2-18	-41.67
Ascot	9-135	6.7	3-22	3-29	0-6	1-2	2-46	0-30	-97.05
Hamilton	8-37	21.6	1-9	4-5	1-1	0-1	2-15	0-6	-13.31
Thirsk	8-63	12.7	1-14	2-16	0-0	0-3	2-18	3-12	-34.12
Sandown	8-72	11.1	4-24	0-11	0-2	0-1	4-29	0-5	-29.25
Bath	7-29	24.1	2-4	0-6	1-2	0-1	4-15	0-1	+16.79
Lingfield	7-34	20.6	2-8	2-13	0-2	2-2	1-7	0-2	-11.86
Beverley	7-37	18.9	3-14	4-8	0-0	0-0	0-14	0-1	-9.45
Brighton	6-23	26.1	4-10	1-3	0-0	0-1	1-9	0-0	-6.04
Ayr	6-46	13.0	1-11	3-6	0-1	0-3	1-15	1-10	-30.87
York	5-113	4.4	1-40	1-13	0-6	0-10	3-23	0-21	-48.00
Chepstow	4-16	25.0	1-3	1-4	0-0	0-1	0-5	2-3	+29.50
Musselburgh	4-18	22.2	1-2	1-4	0-2	0-0	2-7	0-3	-0.38
Ripon	4-20	20.0	0-3	0-6	0-0	0-3	3-7	1-3	-6.68
Catterick	4-24	16.7	1-4	1-2	0-0	1-6	1-10	0-2	-9.52
Epsom	3-26	11.5	1-6	1-5	0-1	1-3	0-7	0-4	-12.55
Pontefract	3-35	8.6	0-6	1-9	0-4	0-5	2-9	0-2	-21.39
Newcastle	2-5	40.0	1-3	1-2	0-0	0-0	0-0	0-0	+0.61
Wetherby	0-13	0.0	0-2	0-3	0-0	0-0	0-3	0-5	-13.00

Number of horses racing for the stable **593**
Total winning prize-money **£5,908,037.75**

have plenty about her. She could be early.

"Probably the best bred of them all, though, is a Dream Ahead full-brother to Dream Of Dreams out of Vasilia. He looks a nice solid colt, but I'm not sure he'll be that early. If you walked into his box and didn't know he was the full-brother to a champion sprinter, you'd say he looks like he should be."

"We were delighted by last season. It was certainly the best since we moved up north [from Newmarket]. We have lots of the good horses from last season and we have a nice intake of two-year-olds. As long as we can keep them healthy and sound we'd like to think we can progress this year.

"But the big thing we desperately want to achieve is to win our first Group 1 from Manor House, although it won't be a failure if we don't win one.

"That's what I really want to achieve, not least because a friend of mine gave me an amazing bottle of wine and inside was a note saying, "not to be drunk until you've won your first Group 1 at Manor House. It was a Mouton Rothschild 1986.""

Reporting by LAWRIE KELSEY

RACING POST

KEVIN & ADAM RYAN

Inisherin leads the way for team renowned for prowess with sprinters

Kevin Ryan with his Royal Ascot winner Inisherin

WINNERS IN LAST FIVE YEARS 74, 57, 65, 79, 52

THE father-and-son team of Kevin and Adam Ryan hope ace sprinter **Inisherin** can repeat his Royal Ascot heroics and help them top the £1.8million prize-money which their Hambleton stable earned last year.

Inisherin won the Group 2 Sandy Lane at Haydock before going to Ascot to beat an elite field of sprinters in the Group 1 Commonwealth Cup for three-year-olds.

He ran well to finish fifth in the July Cup against older sprinters but ended the season with a disappointing 13th of 16 in the Betfair Sprint Cup at Haydock.

"These sprinters get better as they get older," says Adam, who is assistant to his dad. "He's done very well during the winter and hopefully he can return to the form he showed at Ascot. He'll go for all the top sprint races but we'll see how he is during the spring before making any plans."

Inisherin leads what Adam describes as "a good, strong, varied team and a handful of sprinters who could be really competitive in top handicaps".

He adds: "I'm very positive for the season ahead and very happy with the ammunition we have for all the top

RACING POST

Washington Heights (noseband): more 5f sprints on the agenda

meetings. We have nice covering of all the distances."

Washington Heights is another member of the Ryans' express team of sprinters who is expected to make his mark again this year.

He opened last season by winning the Group 3 Abernant Stakes at Newmarket and was then fourth in a blanket finish to the Group 2 Duke of York Stakes. He was stepped up to Group 1 class in the Queen Elizabeth II Jubilee but after showing speed he faded to finish unplaced.

He was brought back to five furlongs to tackle Group 1 rivals in the Nunthorpe, Flying Five at the Curragh and the Abbaye at Longchamp, running with distinction but finishing just outside the places.

"As last season went on, he showed he's a horse with a lot of natural speed and likes to hear his feet rattle," says Adam, "so quick ground will be ideal for him."

He began this year by finishing a close runner-up in the £320,000 6f Dukhan Sprint in Qatar in late February and will "be ready to rock and roll when he comes back".

"We'll look for five-furlong sprints for him," says Adam. "He ran well in Qatar and will have learned a lot mentally from running in those Group 1s last year and hopefully he can show it this year."

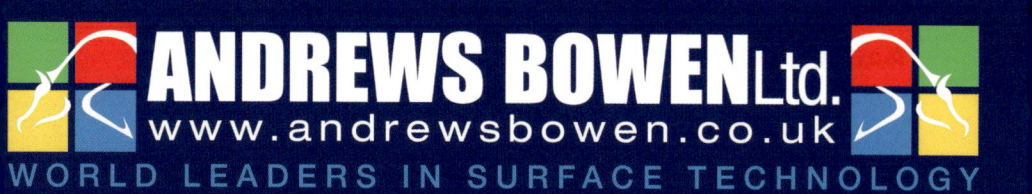

ANDREWS BOWEN Ltd.
www.andrewsbowen.co.uk
WORLD LEADERS IN SURFACE TECHNOLOGY

Delivering Excellence When Performance Is Paramount

World-leading solutions for all of your surface, facility and stabling requirements.

Providing a fully comprehensive development service for professional racing and equestrian facilities alongside international competition venues in all climates.

Finance Options Now Available

BHA BRITISH HORSERACING AUTHORITY

sales@andrewsbowen.co.uk   T: +44 (0)1995 672103

KEVIN & ADAM RYAN
HAMBLETON, NORTH YORKSHIRE

Ain't Nobody: open account at Carlisle

RECORD AROUND THE COURSES

	W-R	Per cent	Non-hcp 2yo	Non-hcp 3yo	Non-hcp 4yo+	Hcp 2yo	Hcp 3yo	Hcp 4yo+	£1 level stake
Wolverhampton (AW)	67-337	19.9	15-69	13-67	3-13	7-28	13-107	16-53	+33.55
Kempton (AW)	58-374	15.5	20-130	8-62	1-17	3-24	19-101	7-40	-55.97
Newcastle (AW)	48-277	17.3	13-57	14-60	1-7	0-24	11-69	9-60	-16.64
Chelmsford (AW)	40-266	15.0	14-65	7-60	1-9	1-14	8-70	9-48	-94.18
Lingfield (AW)	34-207	16.4	3-43	7-47	2-11	2-9	10-56	10-41	-13.27
Haydock	33-178	18.5	12-50	5-27	3-8	1-9	10-56	2-28	+88.68
Chester	32-178	18.0	8-40	4-12	0-5	1-9	12-61	7-51	+13.18
Doncaster	22-133	16.5	10-44	3-19	1-4	0-7	7-41	1-18	-18.09
Newmarket (July)	22-180	12.2	5-57	1-20	3-6	3-10	9-70	1-17	-63.26
Newmarket	21-206	10.2	10-75	3-46	0-8	1-10	5-50	2-17	-16.43
Windsor	20-134	14.9	3-27	7-35	0-6	4-12	3-45	3-9	-37.53
Yarmouth	18-111	16.2	5-35	4-13	0-2	0-8	8-43	1-10	-8.37
Southwell (AW)	15-99	15.2	0-10	7-31	0-3	1-10	2-20	5-25	-16.90
Newbury	15-134	11.2	8-48	2-24	0-12	0-2	5-32	0-16	-15.28
Nottingham	13-91	14.3	5-28	1-20	1-2	1-8	5-28	0-5	+1.92
Salisbury	12-55	21.8	6-23	2-12	0-1	0-2	4-14	0-3	-1.13
Carlisle	11-38	28.9	3-9	4-8	0-0	0-4	2-11	2-6	-1.80
Ffos Las	9-28	32.1	2-5	3-6	1-1	1-2	2-9	0-5	+22.67
Leicester	9-61	14.8	3-16	1-7	3-5	0-5	0-21	2-7	-32.29
Redcar	9-68	13.2	4-21	1-14	0-1	0-3	4-26	0-3	-10.32
Goodwood	9-108	8.3	3-24	1-18	0-5	0-13	3-30	2-18	-41.67
Ascot	9-135	6.7	3-22	3-29	0-6	1-2	2-46	0-30	-97.05
Hamilton	8-37	21.6	1-9	4-5	1-1	0-1	2-15	0-6	-13.31
Thirsk	8-63	12.7	1-14	2-16	0-0	0-3	2-18	3-12	-34.12
Sandown	8-72	11.1	4-24	0-11	0-2	0-1	4-29	0-5	-29.25
Bath	7-29	24.1	2-4	0-6	1-2	0-1	4-15	0-1	+16.79
Lingfield	7-34	20.6	2-8	2-13	0-2	2-2	1-7	0-2	-11.86
Beverley	7-37	18.9	3-14	4-8	0-0	0-0	0-14	0-1	-9.45
Brighton	6-23	26.1	4-10	1-3	0-0	0-1	1-9	0-0	-6.04
Ayr	6-46	13.0	1-11	3-6	0-1	0-3	1-15	1-10	-30.87
York	5-113	4.4	1-40	1-13	0-6	0-10	3-23	0-21	-48.00
Chepstow	4-16	25.0	1-3	1-4	0-0	0-1	0-5	2-3	+29.50
Musselburgh	4-18	22.2	1-2	1-4	0-2	0-0	2-7	0-3	-0.38
Ripon	4-20	20.0	0-3	0-4	0-0	0-3	3-7	1-3	-6.68
Catterick	4-24	16.7	1-4	1-2	0-0	1-6	1-10	0-2	-9.52
Epsom	3-26	11.5	1-6	1-5	0-1	1-3	0-7	0-4	-12.55
Pontefract	3-35	8.6	0-6	1-9	0-4	0-5	2-9	0-2	-21.39
Newcastle	2-5	40.0	1-3	1-2	0-0	0-0	0-0	0-0	+0.61
Wetherby	0-13	0.0	0-2	0-3	0-0	0-0	0-3	0-5	-13.00

Number of horses racing for the stable **593**
Total winning prize-money **£5,908,037.75**

Aint Nobody took time to come to himself as a two-year-old but when he did he won on his debut at Carlisle, then went to Royal Ascot and beat 26 rivals in the Listed Windsor Castle.

He was unplaced when stepped up to Group 2 class in the July Stakes and Flying Childers, but he is expected to reach Group standard this season.

"He's already proved himself at Listed level, has wintered well and is a horse who can only progress in time," says Adam.

The Ryans always felt there was a big race in Room Service, who proved it by winning the big Weatherbys sales race at Doncaster at the end of his two-year-old career.

After being tried at Group 3 and Listed level last season, he landed a decent handicap at Pontefract. He was unplaced in the Ayr Gold Cup but ran a cracker to be a close second in a heritage handicap at York before ending his season by winning a Listed race at Doncaster.

"He's a horse we've always liked. He was a bit unfortunate last year. The ground went against him at Ayr, he was mightily unlucky

GUIDE TO THE FLAT **2025**

■ David Egan has ridden for the yard only seven times but won three starts for a profit of £7.25

in the Coral Sprint Trophy at York but made up for it when he won at Doncaster.

"He's been finishing off his races strongly, so we'll step him up to seven furlongs this year in all those top races. He likes a bit of juice in the ground but he's not dependent on it."

Sergeant Wilko was ultra-consistent last year, winning four of his first five outings and ending the year with fifth in the Coral Sprint Trophy at York just behind stablemate Room Service.

"He's by Bungle Inthejungle, so they tend to improve for a bit of juice in the ground," says Adam. "He's a very tough and genuine sprinter and with another winter on his back he'll be ready for those top sprint handicaps."

Volterra is a four-year-old colt who book-ended last season with handicap wins at Newmarket and a valuable heritage handicap at Ascot. Between those two runs he was unplaced in the Britannia at Royal Ascot and a close second in a heritage handicap at York.

"He's a genuine sort of horse who likes to bowl along in his races. He's rated 109 now, so he'll be stepped up into Pattern company over seven furlongs and a mile. He's a lovely horse who is improving with age."

Lothlorien is a lovely filly who did very well, winning her only start at Beverley. She

63

looked a filly who would be better as three-year-old, so to win at two was a bonus. She's done well through the winter and filled out. We'll see how she does in the spring, but there are loads of options for her."

The Ryans will have plenty of runners on the all-weather in preparation for the turf season, including Apiarist, who ran well last year without getting his head in front in eight races on grass.

When he switched to the all-weather in December, it was a different story. He won at Newcastle over a mile, repeated the feat at Chelmsford and successfully dropped down to seven furlongs Southwell in February.

"We kept him in training for the all-weather and he's kept his form well," says Adam. "He's a horse who can run free but he loves a strong gallop and is a strong traveller.

"He's on a mark of 93, so he'll be aimed at some of those good mile handicaps and could be one who starts the turf season off in the Lincoln. He's a classy horse and with another winter on his back he'll be even better this year."

We Never Stop won twice last year over five and six furlongs and had been runner-up three times this winter on the all-weather.

"He's been gelded and after the application of headgear he's thrived. He'll be aimed at some of those top sprint handicaps throughout the year."

Allezdancer is another sprint handicapper rated in the 90s the Ryans hope can be found suitable openings.

"He's very good when there's juice in the ground. He won the six-furlong sprint at the Lincoln meeting and was third in it last year. He could go for it again."

Venture Capital really thrived in the

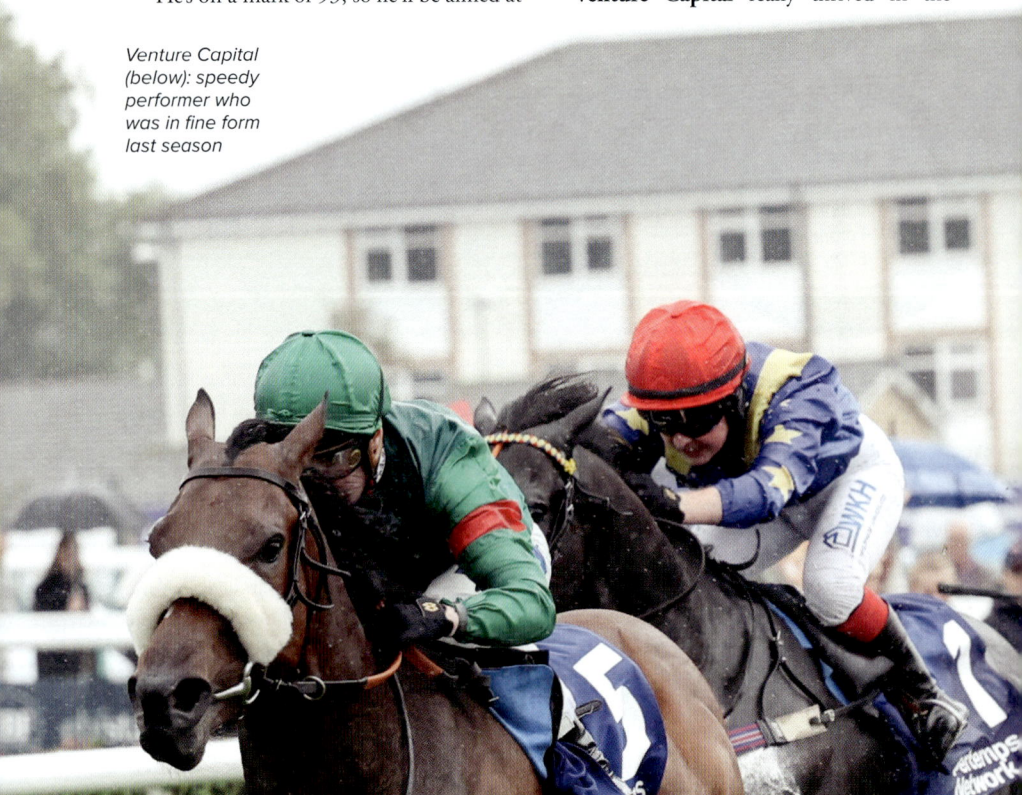

Venture Capital (below): speedy performer who was in fine form last season

second part of last season after winning twice on the all-weather as a two-year-old and twice last year at Ayr and Doncaster. He was also placed twice in Ascot sprint handicaps and finished a close fourth at Doncaster.

"As the season went on he grew, strengthened and matured," says Adam, "and got faster and faster. He has a lot of natural speed and will be another one for those top sprint handicaps over five, but I wouldn't shy away from running him over six furlongs on sharp tracks. And he's versatile as to the ground, although he wouldn't want extremes."

Sisyphean is a colt by Dubawi, a big stamp of a horse, who won over a mile on the all-weather Newcastle in February and bolted up by five lengths at York in July over the same distance. He didn't seem to see out the trip over two furlongs further at Goodwood and York, where the ground was soft.

"Another winter on his back will do him no harm," says Adam. "He's a lovely moving horse with a mark of 92 and I think there's still room for improvement over a mile or even a mile-two."

Despite a blip in the November Handicap

at Doncaster, **Dark Moon Rising** bounced back to form in the autumn and winter, winning once and being placed five times in seven outings, the last of which was on the all-weather at Newcastle.

"He ran a couple of huge races. He's a strong traveller and those mile and a quarter races or mile and a half will be on his agenda. There'll be plenty of options for him and I think he's due to pick up a big one."

Although he was unplaced in seven outings last year, the seven-year-old stayer **Forza Orta** ran some fine races in defeat.

"He's rated 82 but I think he's a far better horse than that. He ran some big races in some of those cup races like the Chester Cup [poor draw], the Northumberland Plate [wrong side of the track] and the Ebor.

"To get in those same races he'd have to go up a few more pounds again, but obviously on his best form he's starting on a very fair mark, so I think he could progress without much trouble. He'll be out fairly early so we can get him into the races he should be in."

Vantheman is a very fast horse and a strong traveller, who ran a couple of huge races at York and Royal Ascot, where he was a creditable tenth in the Palace of Holyrood House handicap.

"He's a big stamp of a horse and should get better with age," says Adam. "He's rated 91 and is another one for those big handicaps. He has a lot of natural speed but I wouldn't be afraid to try him over six if the right race came up, especially at York, where you need a lot of natural speed."

Against The Wind took a couple of runs "to learn how to race correctly" before getting off the mark at Newcastle. He then ran a huge race in the Goff's Half Million sales race at York where he led at the furlong pole but faded into fifth in the last half furlong.

"He's a very fast horse who travels for a long way. He's done well over the winter and strengthened up nicely. He's one who could really improve from his mark of 86 and will be in some nice races early doors."

Reporting by LAWRIE KELSEY

Fora Orta (centre): seven years old but could prove well treated

GUIDE TO THE FLAT **2025**

GEORGE SCOTT

Ready to hit the heights with an impressive team

GEORGE SCOTT could be poised to make a big impact this season. After finishing 36th in the trainers' championship last year, 2025 could be his annus mirabilis judged on the leading owners and their blue-blooded broods he has at his Eve Lodge stables in Newmarket.

He begins the year with a string of about 90, 40 of which are two-year-olds, many owned by the likes of Sheikh Nasser's Victorious Racing operation, Amo Racing, the Niarchos family and Al Shaqab.

It's hardly surprising, therefore, that Scott is brimming with hope. "We're in a really strong position for us," he says. "We've got lots of quality across the board: sprinters, staying horses, unexposed three-year-olds and middle-distance horses. I'm really optimistic about the year ahead.

"When you look at the stock we have compared with the stock we used to have, we're miles ahead in quality.

"Five years ago we didn't have five horses rated over 85. Now we have four horses rated over 110, and we've got a very good horse to come!

"That will be five horses rated over 110. We could never have dreamed of that. And we have some nice three-year-olds coming through who are unexposed, as well as 40 two-year-olds, 12 for Sheikh Nasser at an average of 300 grand. We spent millions and millions on them and there are some unbelievably nice ones."

Trainers are judged on Group 1 winners, as much as numbers and prize-money, and Scott's winter hopes have centred on Classic glory for his stable star **Bay City Roller**, but it will be the Irish or French Guineas rather than the English race that is the target.

The plan, hatched after the New Bay colt won the Group 2 Champagne Stakes at Doncaster, was to put him away for the winter to let him grow and mature into what connections hope will be a horse capable of repelling whatever the likes of Aidan O'Brien, Charlie Appleby and the French line up against him.

GUIDE TO THE FLAT **2025**

WINNERS IN LAST FIVE YEARS 42, 36, 37, 18, 18

Bay City Roller showed plenty of speed to hold off two O'Brien fancies at Doncaster and Scott reckons the Curragh or Longchamp's flat track and turns will suit his colt much better than Newmarket's tough, undulating, straight mile. He's also more likely to get the cut in the ground he needs away from his home course.

"He was a perfect three from three last season and had been on my radar very early on as a quality individual," says Scott.

"He's got a lovely pedigree, a great attitude and was showing up well in his homework. He'll certainly go a mile but it remains to be seen whether he'll go further than that.

"He's done particularly well over the winter and looks a beautiful horse. He's strengthened and grown and I'm as pleased as I could be with a horse over a winter period."

Scott aims to send his €320,000 colt straight to whichever Guineas he chooses without a prep race, but he's not making any plans beyond the opening race.

Another outstanding horse who helped Scott's yard reach a personal best 42 winners last season and £897,000 prize-money, was Isle Of Jura, owned, like Bay City Roller, by Sheikh Nasser.

Last year, after a winter in the owner's home country of Bahrain that reaped four victories, including the unprecedented Bahrain Triple Crown, **Isle Of Jura** opened his domestic season by winning a Listed race at Goodwood.

His next outing was in the Group 2 Hardwicke Stakes at Royal Ascot, which he won emphatically from French raider Goliath, and was promptly cut to 8-1 for the King George.

That challenge didn't materialise, however, after injury ruled him out for the rest of the season, but he's fully recovered and this year everything will revolve around the King George.

"He's an incredible horse and his win ratio is amazing," says Scott. "He beat the subsequent King George winner comfortably in the Hardwicke and we were really disappointed he picked up an injury in the race. It was a very minor tendon issue and you're never really over it until you're back racing and you know you're over it. But he's very much on the right track for his main target."

Scott aims to run Isle Of Jura in the Hardwicke again with the possibility of a prep run in the Jockey Club Stakes at Newmarket, although plans are fluid.

"I'd love to give him a prep run before the Hardwicke but I don't think he'll be ready for that. So it may be that we have to start him in the Hardwicke as preparation for the King George."

That ruled out a return trip to Bahrain and Dubai, but Scott did send a winter team to the Middle East, including Phantom Flight and City House.

Phantom Flight, who opened last season by landing a Listed race at Newbury, began this year with victory in a valuable Bahrain handicap in mid-January and followed up by winning the local Grade 1 Crown Prince Cup over 1m2f two weeks later.

He finished second in the local Grade 1 Sheikh Nasser Cup in late February before being aimed at the mile and a half King's Cup, Bahrain's most prestigious race.

"He'll then come home and we'll re-evaluate," says Scott. "He'll probably have one race and then go for something like the Wolferton at Royal Ascot.

"He's a very good horse on his day. He's very effective under the right conditions – he needs a strong pace, fast ground and a nice rhythm in the early part of his race to be able to relax and breathe. When he does he's very much capable of holding his own in most divisions."

City House was disappointing in England, so he was gelded and given a wind operation last summer, which turned him into a reformed character. After an outing at Southwell in November, when he was a close

Find your career in horseracing

Whether it's training, apprenticeships or job roles, we are here to help you understand the industry and guide you towards making the right choice.

careersinracing.com

APPRENTICESHIP & TRAINING INFORMATION • CASE STUDIES & JOB PROFILES • FREE JOB BOARD

RACING POST

Prydwen: in the winner's enclosure at Killarney after a successful trip from Newmarket

GEORGE SCOTT
NEWMARKET, SUFFOLK

RECORD AROUND THE COURSES

	W-R	Per cent	Non-hcp 2yo	Non-hcp 3yo	Non-hcp 4yo+	Hcp 2yo	Hcp 3yo	Hcp 4yo+	£1 level stake
Wolverhampton (AW)	26-178	14.6	3-37	1-29	1-8	4-16	13-58	4-30	-45.80
Chelmsford (AW)	17-145	11.7	2-28	1-25	0-4	1-11	7-38	6-39	-19.08
Southwell (AW)	14-86	16.3	3-13	2-20	1-2	0-8	4-19	4-24	-24.12
Kempton (AW)	12-133	9.0	2-30	0-21	0-4	1-12	7-41	2-25	-46.75
Lingfield (AW)	11-108	10.2	1-15	1-24	0-5	0-4	4-34	5-26	-47.55
Windsor	10-71	14.1	5-24	0-10	1-1	0-1	3-18	1-17	-34.46
Doncaster	9-78	11.5	3-29	3-6	2-3	0-4	1-18	0-18	-9.75
Yarmouth	9-95	9.5	2-27	0-3	0-1	1-12	5-31	1-21	-24.92
Brighton	8-28	28.6	2-9	0-0	0-0	1-2	5-12	0-5	+8.71
Lingfield	8-28	28.6	6-13	0-0	0-0	1-2	1-9	0-4	-1.44
Newcastle (AW)	8-65	12.3	3-7	1-6	1-3	1-7	0-20	2-22	-19.32
Redcar	7-30	23.3	0-10	1-4	3-4	0-1	3-10	0-1	-4.24
Bath	7-32	21.9	1-7	1-1	0-0	0-1	2-15	3-8	-1.26
Nottingham	7-49	14.3	3-16	0-6	0-0	1-3	2-13	1-11	-1.49
Hamilton	6-11	54.5	3-6	0-0	0-0	2-2	1-2	0-1	+11.12
Goodwood	6-41	14.6	2-12	0-2	1-2	0-4	2-14	1-7	+13.50
Ripon	5-22	22.7	3-7	0-1	0-1	1-1	1-6	0-6	-6.32
Beverley	5-25	20.0	2-9	0-1	0-1	1-1	2-9	0-4	-5.03
Thirsk	5-33	15.2	2-11	1-3	0-0	1-4	1-11	0-4	-14.35
Newbury	5-41	12.2	1-20	1-7	1-1	0-0	1-5	1-8	-6.80
Newmarket (July)	5-65	7.7	0-29	0-8	0-0	1-3	2-16	2-9	-28.63
Newmarket	5-72	6.9	1-30	1-16	0-0	1-4	1-8	1-14	+1.25
Pontefract	4-16	25.0	2-6	1-4	0-0	1-1	0-5	0-0	+3.12
Sandown	4-25	16.0	2-10	0-1	0-0	0-3	1-6	1-5	-13.25
Leicester	4-47	8.5	1-18	0-6	0-2	2-5	1-13	0-3	-27.68
Catterick	3-21	14.3	1-5	0-2	0-0	1-7	1-4	0-3	-4.25
Epsom	3-23	13.0	0-6	0-1	0-0	0-1	1-4	2-12	-5.80
Ayr	2-6	33.3	1-2	0-0	0-1	0-0	1-1	0-2	-0.42
Chester	2-13	15.4	0-0	0-0	0-1	0-2	1-4	1-6	+0.00
York	2-21	9.5	1-11	0-1	0-1	0-5	0-1	1-2	-11.75
Haydock	2-27	7.4	1-4	0-6	0-0	0-2	0-9	1-6	-16.00
Musselburgh	1-3	33.3	1-2	0-0	0-0	0-0	0-0	0-0	-1.09
Salisbury	1-11	9.1	0-3	0-3	0-0	0-0	1-4	0-1	-7.50
Chepstow	1-13	7.7	0-2	0-0	0-0	1-3	0-8	0-0	-10.63
Ffos Las	1-15	6.7	0-3	0-0	0-0	0-3	1-6	0-3	-13.50
Ascot	1-44	2.3	0-11	0-3	1-2	0-0	0-11	0-17	-27.00
Carlisle	0-7	0.0	0-3	0-0	0-0	0-2	0-1	0-1	-7.00

Number of horses racing for the stable **270**
Total winning prize-money **£1,613,805.97**

Pay close attention to stable runners at 1m6f-1m7f where there is a strike-rate of 28% (£11.73)

sixth in a bunch finish over six furlongs, he had a winter in Bahrain where he seemed to sprout wings.

"I'm very pleased with him," says Scott. "He's improving rapidly. He'd really lost his confidence but he's put in four polished displays in Bahrain [two wins, including a big handicap, and two seconds], and is a horse on the right trajectory with a lot of upside and plenty of quality.

"We'll bring him home and then work back from the Wokingham. I think he'll be tailor-made for that. He's been running over seven in Bahrain but I wouldn't mind bringing him back to six. I like this horse a lot and the wind operation has done him a world of good."

Prydwen, who won the German St Leger last season, is described by Scott as "a brilliant definition of a staying star".

He adds: "He travelled twice successfully last year to Ireland and Germany. On his day he's a very good performer when conditions suit him. He loves to get his toe in and loves a strong pace to run at. He's a horse you want to catch on the right day.

"But he's caught between a rock and a hard place because he's very high in the handicap and probably lacks that little bit of quality for domestic Group races. As a result we sent

73

him to Dubai, where he was fourth in a Group 3 at Meydan at the end of January.

"We'll be imaginative with his placing, as we were last year, and choose races in which he can be competitive."

West Acre looks a future star judged on his stunning acceleration to win the Group 2 Blue Point Sprint in record time at Meydan in January.

"It was an extraordinary performance. He's now rated 114 after just six starts," says Scott. "He's an out-and-out speed horse with a huge engine."

West Acre will take in the Nad Al Sheba Turf Sprint at Meydan on Super Saturday, then the Al Quoz in April, before returning to Newmarket to be trained for the King Charles III [former King's Stand] at Royal Ascot after which connections will consider all subsequent five and six-furlong Group 1 races as well as possible trips to the Breeders' Cup and Hong Kong.

After her first three indifferent races **Modern Utopia** had 11 weeks off and returned a different animal, coasting home on the bridle in her last two races of the season to earn a rating of 88 and high praise from Scott.

"She couldn't have been more impressive. She might start in a handicap but could end up in an Oaks trial. She's not very big but she's got an engine. She loves soft ground and we'll definitely be going for some black type at some stage."

King Of Bears, a lightly raced horse formerly trained by Paul and Oliver Cole, was bought at Tattersalls Horses in Training sale in October for Harry Redknapp for 200,000 guineas.

"We gelded him and gave him a wind operation," says Scott. "I'm really pleased with him. He's rated 94 and could run in the Listed Spring Cup we won with Watch My Tracer last year. He's a horse I like very much."

Bryant finished fourth on his only start in an above-average maiden over a mile at York and the form has worked out quite well.

"He's a lovely, big, raw horse by Wootton Bassett owned by Kia Joorabchian's Amo Racing. He's got an Irish Derby entry and, although that's a little lofty at this stage, I like the horse very much. He's got a great mind, is very easy to train and very straightforward. He'll go for a maiden because he is getting very bored and I want to get some more experience into him. I would expect him to win his maiden and go on from there."

He did everything but win over 1m1½f at Wolverhampton in late February, finishing a head second with the rest of the field five lengths away, but showed he's a winner in waiting.

Bragbor is a four-year-old Saxon Warrior gelding who was "a very expensive" breeze-up purchase after going through the ring at Arqana unsold at €400,000 in May 2023.

"He came with a lot of quality and I was very hopeful he would win first time out," says Scott, which is what he did at Newcastle in early January, beating another debut winner in a nodding finish over a mile.

"He'll go for a novice and we're thinking of one of the handicaps at Royal Ascot for him. I like him a lot."

GUIDE TO THE FLAT 2025

Caballo De Mar (orange colours): not a good worker at home but has turned a corner on the track over staying trips

Caballo De Mar has won his last two starts, progressing as he went up in trip from a mile to one mile six furlongs, and is in the same ownership as Prydwen.

"He's really taken us by surprise because he can hardly lift a leg at home but on the track he seems to come alive. He's definitely a stayer in the making. We only started to get to the bottom of him when we rode him more positively. He'll be very busy because he takes his racing particularly well."

Dopamine won second time out over seven furlongs at Southwell after "coming alive" between her first two runs.

"It was a nice surprise," says Scott. "There's plenty of mileage left with her and we won't be in a rush. She has a lovely pedigree and is a filly with plenty of scope."

Zubaru was second on his debut in a Newmarket maiden towards the end of the season from which the third horse has come out and won easily.

"His work improved steadily through the autumn but we were surprised by him. He's got a lot of scope. We'll start him off on the all-weather and we'll look to win a maiden and then make plans. He was a shell of a horse last year but he's done well over the winter. He's grown and filled out."

Touch The Moon is a Sea The Stars half-brother to Group 1 winner Blond Me, and won his first two starts in Bahrain this winter.

"We were a little disappointed with him at first," admits Scott. "His attitude was a little suspect and he wasn't too in love with the game, but I always felt that if we took him to Bahrain he might come alive, and he really has.

"He's been very impressive the way he's gone about things. He's rated 92 now and we'll aim him at the King's Cup in Bahrain in March, a race we won last year with Isle Of Jura.

"He's got a little way to go yet but the system out there suits him well. When he matures a bit I think he could be a nice staying horse."

The final one to note is Force And Valour, third of 16 over seven furlongs on turf at Meydan in mid-February, and whom Scott thinks is still well handicapped off 85.

"He has plenty in hand under the right circumstances," he says. "He's worth keeping an eye on. He'll pop up in a nice race one day, I have no doubt about it."

Reporting by LAWRIE KELSEY

RACING POST

RACING POST RATINGS: LAST SEASON'S LEADING TWO-YEAR-OLDS

KEY: Horse name, best RPR figure, finishing position when earning figure, (details of race where figure was earned)

Shadow Of Light 117 [1] (7f, Newm, Sft, Oct 12)
Delacroix (IRE) 116 [2] (1m, Donc, Sft, Oct 26)
Hotazhell 116 [1] (1m, Donc, Sft, Oct 26)
Lake Victoria (IRE) 116 [1] (6f, Newm, Sft, Sep 28)
The Lion In Winter (IRE) 116 [1] (7f, York, GF, Aug 21)
Desert Flower (IRE) 115 [1] (1m, Newm, GS, Oct 11)
Expanded (IRE) 113 [2] (7f, Newm, Sft, Oct 12)
Ancient Truth (IRE) 112 [3] (7f, Newm, Sft, Oct 12)
Scorthy Champ (IRE) 112 [1] (7f, Curr, Gd, Sep 15)
Babouche 111 [1] (6f, Curr, GF, Aug 10)
Henri Matisse (IRE) 110 [2] (7f, Curr, Gd, Sep 15)
Wimbledon Hawkeye 110 [1] (1m, Newm, Sft, Sep 28)
Exactly (IRE) 109 [1] (7f 30y, Leop, Sft, Oct 19)
Fairy Godmother (IRE) 109 [1] (6f, Asco, GF, Jun 21)
Aesterius (IRE) 108 [1] (5f 3y, Donc, Gd, Sep 13)
Bedtime Story (IRE) 108 [1] (7f, Asco, GF, Jun 22)
Cool Hoof Luke 108 [1] (6f, York, Gd, Aug 23)
Seagulls Eleven (IRE) 108 [3] (7f, Curr, Gd, Sep 15)
Whistlejacket (IRE) 108 [2] (6f, Curr, GF, Aug 10)
Bay City Roller (IRE) 107 [1] (7f 6y, Donc, Gd, Sep 14)
Big Mojo (IRE) 107 [2] (5f 3y, Donc, Gd, Sep 13)
Coto De Caza (IRE) 107 [1] (5f, Newm, GS, Oct 11)
Ides Of March (IRE) 107 [1] (6f, Curr, Gd, Aug 31)
Starzintheireyes 107 [1] (1m 2f, Newm, GS, Oct 12)
La Bellota (IRE) 106 [1] (6f 2y, Donc, Sft, Aug 24)
Powerful Glory (IRE) 106 [1] (6f, Newb, Hvy, Sep 21)
Royal Playwright 106 [2] (1m, Newm, Sft, Sep 28)
Ruling Court (USA) 106 [3] (7f, York, GF, Aug 21)
Simmering 106 [2] (7f, Curr, Gd, Sep 15)
The Waco Kid (IRE) 106 [1] (7f, Newm, Sft, Sep 26)
Daylight (FR) 105 [2] (6f, Newm, Sft, Sep 28)
Diego Ventura (IRE) 105 [2] (6f 2y, Donc, Sft, Oct 26)
Field Of Gold (IRE) 105 [1] (7f, Sand, Gd, Aug 31)
Merrily (USA) 105 [1] (7f, Newm, GS, Oct 11)
Monumental (IRE) 105 [2] (7f 6y, Donc, Gd, Sep 14)
Red Letter 105 [4] (7f, Curr, Gd, Sep 15)
Stanhope Gardens (IRE) 105 [2] (1m, Newm, GS, Oct 12)
Bubbling (IRE) 104 [1] (7f, Newm, Sft, Sep 27)
Cathedral 104 [2] (7f, Newm, GS, Oct 11)
Grande Marques (IRE) 104 [2] (5f, Newm, GS, Oct 11)
Green Impact (IRE) 104 [1] (1m, Leop, Gd, Sep 14)
Make You Smile (IRE) 104 [1] (7f, Newb, Hvy, Oct 26)
Shareholder (USA) 104 [1] (5f, Asco, GF, Jun 20)
Symbol Of Strength (IRE) 104 [3] (6f, York, Gd, Aug 23)
Tennessee Stud (IRE) 104 [2] (1m, Curr, Yld, Sep 28)
Aomori City (FR) 103 [1] (7f, Good, Gd, Jul 30)
Arabian Dusk 103 [3] (6f, Newm, Sft, Sep 28)
Benevento (IRE) 103 [1] (7f 6y, Donc, Gd, Sep 13)
Black Forza (IRE) 103 [1] (6f, Good, GF, Aug 1)
Detain (IRE) 103 [1] (7f, Kemw, SS, Oct 9)
Green Storm (IRE) 103 [2] (1m 2f, Newm, GS, Oct 12)
Jungle Drums (IRE) 103 [1] (6f, York, Sft, Oct 12)
Luther 103 [1] (1m 37y, Hayd, Gd, Sep 7)
Magnum Force (IRE) 103 [3] (5f 3y, Donc, Gd, Sep 13)
Rashabar (IRE) 103 [1] (6f, Asco, GF, Jun 18)
The Strikin Viking (IRE) 103 [2] (6f, Curr, Yld, Jun 30)
Windlord 103 [3] (1m, Curr, Yld, Sep 28)
Yaroogh (IRE) 103 [2] (7f, Newb, Hvy, Oct 26)
Al Qudra 102 [1] (7f, Asco, GF, Jul 27)
Angelo Buonarroti (USA) 102 [3] (1m, Newm, Sft, Sep 28)
Arizona Blaze 102 [3] (6f, Curr, GF, Aug 10)
January (IRE) 102 [2] (1m, Newm, GS, Oct 11)
Puppet Master (IRE) 102 [4] (1m, Newm, Sft, Sep 28)
Seaplane 102 [4] (1m, Donc, Sft, Aug 24)
Soldier's Heart 102 [1] (6f, Ripo, Gd, Aug 26)
Symbol Of Honour 102 [2] (7f 6y, Donc, Gd, Sep 13)
Trinity College (IRE) 102 [4] (1m, Curr, Yld, Sep 28)
Tropical Storm 102 [1] (5f, York, GF, Aug 24)
Apples And Bananas (IRE) 101 [1] (7f, Curr, Yld, Sep 28)
Ballet Slippers (IRE) 101 [3] (1m, Newm, GS, Oct 11)
Cowardofthecounty (IRE) 101 [5] (7f, Curr, Gd, Sep 15)
Fiery Lucy 101 [2] (7f, Curr, Gd, Sep 29)
Heavens Gate (IRE) 101 [1] (7f, Curr, Gd, Sep 29)
Matauri Bay (IRE) 101 [2] (7f, Sand, Gd, Aug 31)
New Century 101 [1] (1m, Sali, GF, Aug 14)
Sky Majesty (IRE) 101 [1] (6f, Ayr, GF, Sep 21)
Tabiti 101 [1] (6f, Sali, GS, Sep 13)
Aftermath (IRE) 100 [1] (7f, Curr, Gd, Sep 29)
Ain't Nobody (IRE) 100 [1] (5f, Asco, GF, Jun 19)
Antelope Canyon (IRE) 100 [2] (7f, Curr, Yld, Sep 28)
Camille Pissarro (IRE) 100 [2] (6f 63y, Curr, Gd, Jul 21)
Celandine 100 [1] (6f, York, GF, Aug 22)
Dreamy (IRE) 100 [1] (1m, Curr, Gd, Aug 31)
Leovanni (IRE) 100 [1] (5f, Asco, GF, Jun 19)
Mr Lightside (IRE) 100 [3] (5f, Good, GF, Jul 31)
Northern Ticker (IRE) 100 [3] (5f 217y, Redc, Sft, Oct 5)
Sigh No More (IRE) 100 [1] (1m 1f, Leop, Sft, Oct 19)
Treasure Isle (IRE) 100 [1] (5f, Curr, Gd, Aug 17)
Tunbridge Wells (IRE) 100 [1] (6f, Curr, Gd, Jun 5)
Tuscan Hills (FR) 100 [1] (1m 6y, Pont, Sft, Oct 21)
Age Of Gold (IRE) 99 [2] (7f, York, GF, Aug 22)
Anno Domini 99 [5] (1m, Donc, Sft, Oct 26)
Brian (IRE) 99 [1] (6f, Newj, Sft, Aug 24)
Candy 99 [1] (5f 217y, Redc, Sft, Oct 5)
Centigrade (IRE) 99 [1] (1m 7y, Newb, Hvy, Oct 25)
Cosmic Year 99 [1] (7f, Sand, Gd, Sep 18)
Dash Dizzy (IRE) 99 [3] (6f, Newm, Sft, Sep 28)
Electrolyte (IRE) 99 [2] (6f, Asco, GF, Jun 18)
Flight 99 [3] (1m, Donc, Gd, Sep 12)
Francisco's Piece 99 [2] (5f, Hayd, Sft, Sep 27)
Hallasan 99 [1] (6f 111y, Donc, Gd, Sep 12)
Hopewell Rock (IRE) 99 [1] (1m, Bath, Hvy, Oct 1)
Jouncy 99 [2] (6f, Kemw, SS, Sep 7)
Miss Fascinator (IRE) 99 [2] (6f, Sali, GS, Sep 13)
Powerful Nation (IRE) 99 [2] (5f, Dunw, SD, Oct 25)
Star Anthem (IRE) 99 [3] (7f, Newb, Hvy, Oct 26)
Time For Sandals (IRE) 99 [2] (6f, York, GF, Aug 22)
Uncle Don 99 [2] (5f, Ayr, Gd, Sep 20)
Anniversary 98 [2] (1m 2f, Newm, Sft, Oct 23)
Bolo Neighs (IRE) 98 [1] (6f, Curr, Yld, Sep 28)
Columnist 98 [3] (6f, Asco, GF, Jun 18)
Intrusively 98 [3] (6f, Good, GF, Aug 1)
Miss Tonnerre (IRE) 98 [4] (1m, Donc, Gd, Sep 12)
Rebel Diamond (IRE) 98 [1] (6f, Fair, Gd, Sep 23)
Right And True (IRE) 98 [1] (7f, Dunw, SD, Oct 4)
Serving With Style 98 [2] (7f, Newm, Sft, Sep 27)
Star Of Mehmas (IRE) 98 [1] (5f, Ayr, Gd, Sep 20)
Wolf Of Badenoch 98 [2] (7f, Good, Gd, Jul 30)
Anshoda (IRE) 97 [1] (6f, Good, Sft, Aug 24)
Barnavara (IRE) 97 [3] (7f, Curr, Gd, Sep 29)
Bernard Shaw (USA) 97 [3] (1m, Leop, Gd, Sep 14)
Billboard Star 97 [3] (6f, Newb, Hvy, Sep 21)
Chancellor 97 [1] (7f 6y, Donc, GF, Aug 17)
Ellaria Sand 97 [1] (7f, Newb, Hvy, Oct 26)
Eternal Elixir (IRE) 97 [3] (1m 37y, Hayd, Gd, Sep 7)
Gabalonso (USA) 97 [2] (5f, Asco, GF, Jun 19)
Glittering Legend 97 [1] (1m, Donc, Sft, Oct 25)
Kodilicious (IRE) 97 [2] (6f, Cork, Yld, Oct 1)
Maw Lam (IRE) 97 [2] (6f, Ayr, GF, Sep 21)
Milford 97 [3] (6f, York, Sft, Oct 12)
Mountain Breeze (IRE) 97 [2] (7f, Newj, GF, Aug 10)
Rock Of Cashel (IRE) 97 [5] (7f, Newm, Sft, Oct 12)
Rudi's Apple (IRE) 97 [1] (6f, Curr, Gd, Jul 20)
Seagolazo (IRE) 97 [2] (7f 192y, York, Sft, Oct 12)

GUIDE TO THE FLAT 2025

RACING POST RATINGS: LAST SEASON'S LEADING TWO-YEAR-OLDS

KEY: Horse name, best RPR figure, finishing position when earning figure, (details of race where figure was earned)

Shackleton (IRE) 97 [3] (1m 2f, Newm, GS, Oct 12)
Shadow Army 97 [4] (6f, Curr, GF, Aug 10)
Truly Enchanting (IRE) 97 [1] (6f, Curr, Gd, Jun 29)
Zayer (IRE) 97 [5] (5f 3y, Donc, Gd, Sep 13)
Attack 96 [2] (1m, Donc, Sft, Oct 25)
Bounty (IRE) 96 [3] (6f 2y, Donc, Sft, Oct 26)
Caburn (IRE) 96 [5] (6f, York, Gd, Aug 23)
California Dreamer 96 [4] (7f, Curr, Gd, Sep 29)
Celestial Orbit 96 [1] (7f, Sand, Gd, Jul 25)
First Instinct 96 [1] (6f, Hayd, GS, Sep 6)
King Of Light 96 [4] (5f, Ayr, Gd, Sep 20)
Kullazain 96 [3] (5f, Newm, GS, Oct 11)
Midnight Thunder 96 [1] (6f 3y, Yarm, Gd, Sep 17)
Nightwalker 96 [3] (1m, Newm, GS, Oct 12)
One Smack Mac (IRE) 96 [2] (6f, Fair, Gd, Sep 23)
Shout (IRE) 96 [1] (6f 2y, Donc, Gd, Sep 13)
Sir Yoshi (IRE) 96 [3] (5f, York, GF, Aug 24)
Too Soon 96 [4] (1m 2f, Newm, GS, Oct 12)
Wemightakedlongway (IRE) 96 [3] (1m 1f, Leop, Sft, Oct 19)
Yah Mo Be There 96 [1] (6f, Newb, Gd, Jul 19)
Betty Clover 95 [2] (6f, Asco, GF, Jul 27)
Comanche Brave (IRE) 95 [2] (7f, Dunw, SD, Oct 4)
Distant Seas 95 [1] (6f, Curr, Gd, Aug 17)
Green Triangle (IRE) 95 (1m 40y, Kill, Gd, Jul 17)
King's Call (IRE) 95 [2] (5f, York, Sft, Oct 11)
Last Encore (IRE) 95 [1] (5f 205y, Naas, Yld, Oct 12)
Majestic Wave 95 [1] (5f 180y, Nava, Yld, Oct 9)
Mandurah (IRE) 95 [4] (6f, Asco, GF, Jul 27)
Mirabeau 95 [5] (7f, Newb, Hvy, Oct 26)
Morning Vietnam 95 [5] (5f, Dunw, SD, Oct 4)
Mr Chaplin 95 [4] (7f 6y, Donc, Gd, Sep 13)
Rajeko (IRE) 95 [1] (1m, Chmf, SD, Dec 7)
Thrice (IRE) 95 [4] (1m 1f, Leop, Sft, Oct 19)
Twain (IRE) 95 [1] (7f 30y, Leop, Sft, Oct 19)
Angel Hunter 94 [1] (7f, York, GF, Aug 22)
Bodhi Bear (IRE) 94 [1] (5f 180y, Nava, Yld, Oct 23)
Bountiful 94 [4] (6f, Newj, Gd, Jul 12)
Ecstatic (JPN) 94 [5] (1m, Donc, Gd, Sep 12)
Elsie's Ruan (IRE) 94 [3] (7f, Newj, GF, Aug 10)
Flaming Stone 94 [4] (7f, Newj, GF, Aug 10)
Hawksbill 94 [4] (1m 37y, Hayd, GF, Sep 7)
Invictus Gold (IRE) 94 [5] (6f, York, Sft, Oct 12)
It Ain't Two 94 [1] (6f 17y, Ches, Gd, Aug 31)
Lady With The Lamp (IRE) 94 [1] (5f, Dunw, SD, Oct 4)
Mighty Eriu (IRE) 94 [2] (5f, Asco, GF, Jun 19)
Nebras 94 [7] (1m, Donc, Sft, Oct 26)
Port Light (IRE) 94 [2] (1m, Chmf, SD, Dec 19)
Saracen (FR) 94 [1] (6f, Curr, Sft, Oct 22)
Smoken 94 [1] (1m, Newm, Sft, Nov 2)
Spirit D'or (IRE) 94 [1] (6f 63y, Curr, Gd, Sep 15)
Swagman (GER) 94 [2] (7f 32y, Leop, Yld, Jul 25)
Tiger Mask (IRE) 94 [4] (7f, Sand, Gd, Aug 31)
Usdi Atohi (IRE) 94 [1] (5f, Tipp, GF, Jul 3)
Verse Of Love 94 [1] (7f, Newm, GS, Oct 11)
Vingegaard (IRE) 94 [2] (5f 34y, Newb, GF, Jul 20)
West Acre (IRE) 94 [1] (4f 214y, Souw, SD, Oct 24)
Acapulco Bay (IRE) 93 [1] (1m, Curr, Gd, Aug 31)
Alla Stella 93 [3] (1m, Curr, Gd, Aug 31)
Bright Times Ahead (IRE) 93 [1] (7f, Newm, GS, Nov 2)
Chantez (IRE) 93 [1] (7f, Leop, Gd, Sep 14)
Defence Minister 93 [1] (6f, Hayd, GS, Sep 5)
El Burhan (IRE) 93 [3] (7f, Good, GF, Aug 1)
Falakeyah 93 [1] (1m 142y, Wolw, SD, Nov 21)
Hazdann (IRE) 93 [1] (7f, Curr, Gd, Jun 29)
Linwood (IRE) 93 [5] (1m 37y, Hayd, Gd, Sep 7)
Magic Mild 93 [3] (6f, Sali, GS, Sep 13)

Miss Lamai (IRE) 93 [1] (5f, Naas, Yld, Jul 24)
Noble Champion (IRE) 93 [1] (7f 1y, Linw, SD, Nov 21)
Olympus Point (IRE) 93 [2] (7f, Newm, Sft, Oct 12)
Qilin Queen (IRE) 93 [2] (1m 37y, Hayd, Gd, Sep 7)
Revoke 93 [2] (5f, Dunw, SD, Oct 4)
Saqqara Sands 93 [2] (7f, Newb, Hvy, Oct 26)
Silver Peak (FR) 93 [4] (1m, Newm, GS, Oct 12)
Square D'alboni (FR) 93 [1] (1m, Sali, GS, Sep 13)
Tales Of The Heart (IRE) 93 [3] (6f, Asco, GF, Jul 27)
The Parthenon (IRE) 93 [8] (5f 205y, Naas, Yld, Oct 12)
Whirl (IRE) 93 [1] (1m, Curr, Sft, Oct 22)
Wild Nature 93 [1] (1m, Kemw, SS, Dec 11)
And So To Bed (IRE) 92 [2] (1m, Curr, Sft, Oct 22)
Andesite 92 [1] (6f, York, Gd, May 16)
Arctic Voyage 92 [1] (6f 18y, Nott, Hvy, Oct 9)
Big Cyril (IRE) 92 [6] (6f, Good, GF, Aug 1)
Binadham (IRE) 92 [6] (5f, Asco, GF, Jun 20)
Castle Gates 92 [1] (1m 1f 11y, Good, Hvy, Oct 13)
Convergent (IRE) 92 [1] (7f 219y, Redc, Sft, Oct 18)
Devil's Advocate 92 [1] (1m 2f, Chmf, SD, Oct 17)
Duty First 92 [2] (7f, Good, Sft, Aug 24)
End Of Story (IRE) 92 [1] (5f, York, Sft, Oct 11)
Fearless Freddy 92 [1] (7f 192y, York, Sft, Oct 11)
Giselle (IRE) 92 [4] (1m, Curr, Sft, Oct 22)
God Of War 92 [5] (7f 6y, Donc, Gd, Sep 13)
Good Banter (IRE) 92 [2] (6f 20y, Wolw, SD, Nov 18)
I Am I Said 92 [1] (1m, Newm, Sft, Oct 23)
Jareth (IRE) 92 [1] (1m 44y, Thur, Gd, Oct 10)
Jonquil 92 [1] (7f, Sand, Gd, Aug 30)
Kibris (IRE) 92 [1] (1m, Curr, Sft, Nov 3)
King Of Bears (IRE) 92 [7] (6f, Good, GF, Aug 1)
Magical Trail 92 [1] (6f, Kemw, SS, Sep 25)
Moving Force (IRE) 92 [5] (6f, York, GF, Aug 21)
Righthere Rightnow (FR) 92 [1] (7f, Newj, Gd, Aug 9)
Shah 92 [1] (7f, York, GF, Aug 23)
Sparkling Sea (IRE) 92 [2] (5f 205y, Naas, Gd, May 19)
Surpass (IRE) 92 [1] (7f 100y, Tipp, GF, Jul 3)
Troia 92 [4] (7f, Newm, GS, Oct 11)
Almeraq 91 [1] (6f 3y, Yarm, Sft, Oct 15)
Alobayyah 91 [1] (1m 3y, Yarm, Sft, Oct 22)
Amiloc 91 [1] (1m, Kemw, SS, Sep 6)
Beauty Queen (IRE) 91 [1] (4f 214y, Souw, SD, Oct 24)
Bob Mali (IRE) 91 [1] (6f, Sali, Hvy, Oct 3)
Bowmark 91 [1] (1m, Kemw, SS, Dec 4)
Brooklyn (IRE) 91 [1] (7f 14y, Ncsw, SD, Nov 22)
Damysus 91 [1] (7f 14y, Souw, SD, Dec 10)
Emit (IRE) 91 [5] (1m 1f, Leop, Sft, Oct 19)
Englemere (IRE) 91 [1] (5f 34y, Newb, Gd, Aug 16)
Game Point (IRE) 91 [2] (1m, Curr, Sft, Nov 3)
Garden Of Eden (IRE) 91 [2] (7f, Leop, Gd, Sep 14)
Genealogy 91 [1] (1m 30y, Punc, Gd, Sep 17)
Leonardo Dax (IRE) 91 [1] (6f, Hayd, Gd, Aug 4)
Loch Tay 91 [1] (7f 94y, Rosc, Sft, Sep 2)
Officer (IRE) 91 [1] (7f, Curr, Gd, Aug 24)
Principality (IRE) 91 [1] (6f, Good, Gd, Jun 9)
Royalty Bay (IRE) 91 [1] (7f, York, GS, Jul 12)
Scandinavia (USA) 91 [2] (1m, Newj, Gd, Aug 16)
Sir Dinadan (IRE) 91 [1] (1m 2f 5y, Pont, Sft, Oct 7)
Spell Master 91 [2] (7f 6y, Donc, Gd, Sep 13)
The Dragon King (IRE) 91 [1] (6f, Newm, GS, Oct 5)
Adrestia 90 [1] (5f 10y, Sand, GF, Jul 31)
Artagnan 90 [2] (6f 2y, Donc, Gd, Sep 13)
Asuka 90 [1] (6f, Newj, Gd, Aug 9)
Aviation Time (IRE) 90 [3] (5f, Asco, GF, Jun 19)
Back In Black (IRE) 90 [3] (7f 6y, Donc, Gd, Sep 12)
Beckman (IRE) 90 [1] (7f, Dunw, SD, Oct 4)
Brighton Boy (IRE) 90 [2] (6f, Newm, GS, Oct 5)
Celtic Motif (IRE) 90 [3] (1m, Curr, Sft, Oct 22)

77

RACING POST

RACING POST RATINGS: LAST SEASON'S LEADING TWO-YEAR-OLDS

KEY: Horse name, best RPR figure, finishing position when earning figure, (details of race where figure was earned)

Chester Nimitz (IRE) 90 [2] (5f 180y, Nava, Yld, Oct 9)
Dark Ace (IRE) 90 [1] (6f, Dunw, SD, Nov 15)
Deetee 90 [2] (1m 1f, Curr, Gd, Sep 29)
Double Vision (IRE) 90 [3] (1m, Curr, Sft, Nov 3)
Falling Snow (IRE) 90 [1] (7f, Curr, GF, Aug 10)
Gethin (IRE) 90 [1] (1m 75y, Nott, Hvy, Oct 9)
Gold Star Hero (IRE) 90 [7] (5f, Ayr, Gd, Sep 20)
Greydreambeliever (IRE) 90 [1] (6f, York, GF, Jul 27)
Handcuffed 90 [4] (6f, York, GF, Aug 21)
Havana Blast 90 [6] (6f, Kemw, SS, Sep 7)
Hott Shott 90 [1] (7f, Kemw, SS, Oct 16)
Itsatenfromlen 90 [4] (5f, Fair, Gd, Sep 23)
Janey Mackers (IRE) 90 [1] (1m, Donc, Sft, Oct 25)
Kaadi (IRE) 90 [5] (5f, Ayr, Gd, Sep 20)
Loom (IRE) 90 [7] (5f, Asco, GF, Jun 20)
Love Talk (IRE) 90 [1] (7f, Good, Hvy, Sep 25)
Midnight Strike (IRE) 90 [3] (6f, Curr, Gd, May 25)
Pellitory 90 [1] (7f 6y, Donc, Sft, Oct 26)
Pinhole 90 [1] (1m 13y, Souw, SD, Dec 14)
Saratoga Special (IRE) 90 [2] (5f, Curr, Gd, Aug 17)
Secret Of Love 90 [2] (1m, Newm, Sft, Nov 2)
Serengeti (FR) 90 [1] (7f, Dunw, SD, Oct 30)
Spirit Of Farhh (IRE) 90 [1] (6f 110y, Newb, Hvy, Oct 25)
Spirit Of Leros 90 [1] (6f, Newb, Gd, Aug 16)
That's Amore (IRE) 90 [1] (1m 6y, Newb, Hvy, Oct 26)
The Lost King 90 [6] (1m 37y, Hayd, Gd, Sep 7)
Weissmuller (IRE) 90 [4] (5f, Asco, GF, Jun 19)
Addison Grey 89 [1] (6f 16y, Souw, SD, Nov 7)
Al Misbar (IRE) 89 [2] (7f, Newm, Sft, Oct 23)
Assertively (IRE) 89 [5] (7f, Newj, Gd, Jul 13)
Calla Lagoon 89 [2] (1m 6y, Pont, Sft, Oct 21)
Consolidation 89 [1] (7f, Kemw, SS, Oct 5)
Corolla Point (IRE) 89 [1] (5f 42y, Yarm, Sft, Oct 22)
Dante's Lad (IRE) 89 [1] (1m, Kemw, SS, Nov 20)
Do It Now 89 [5] (5f 34y, Newb, GF, Jul 20)
Easy Mover (IRE) 89 [4] (7f, Leop, Gd, Sep 14)
Galveston 89 [1] (1m, Naas, Yld, Oct 12)
High Season 89 [1] (7f, Redc, Gd, Sep 25)
Hornsea Bay 89 [2] (1m, Ayr, Gd, Oct 10)
Island Hopping (IRE) 89 [5] (1m, Curr, Sft, Oct 22)
King Of Cities (IRE) 89 [2] (1m, Newb, Sft, Sep 20)
Law Of Design (IRE) 89 [1] (7f, Asco, Sft, Sep 7)
Layla Liz (IRE) 89 [1] (5f 21y, Wolw, SD, Dec 26)
Mojave River (FR) 89 [6] (7f, Curr, Gd, Sep 29)
Red Sand (IRE) 89 [1] (6f, Good, Gd, May 24)
Regal Gem 89 [5] (6f 63y, Curr, Gd, Jul 21)
River Seine (IRE) 89 [1] (5f 3y, Pont, GF, Jul 28)
Rogue Allegiance (IRE) 89 [1] (6f, Ncsw, SD, Dec 6)
Sallaal (IRE) 89 [1] (7f 3y, Yarm, Sft, Oct 15)
Sea Baaeed 89 [1] (7f 36y, Wolw, SD, Oct 7)
Seacruiser (IRE) 89 [1] (1m, Newm, GS, Sep 26)
Seraph Gabriel (IRE) 89 [2] (7f, Redc, Sft, Oct 5)
Sixtygeesbaby (IRE) 89 [1] (6f, Newm, Gd, Nov 1)
Snapdragon (IRE) 89 [4] (5f 205y, Naas, Yld, Oct 12)
Stormy Impact 89 [1] (5f 1y, Muss, Gd, Oct 2)
Swelter 89 [1] (1m, Leop, Gd, Jul 18)
Tundra Rose (IRE) 89 [3] (1m, Newm, Sft, Nov 2)
Wiltshire Lad (IRE) 89 [1] (1m 13y, Souw, SD, Oct 5)
Wise Men Say (IRE) 89 [4] (6f, Curr, Gd, Aug 31)
Afentiko (IRE) 88 [1] (7f, Kemw, SS, Sep 6)
Anna Swan 88 [1] (7f 3y, Yarm, GF, Aug 8)
Arabian Sun (IRE) 88 [1] (6f, Sali, GF, Jun 11)
Archivali 88 [2] (1m 75y, Nott, Hvy, Oct 16)
Beccali (IRE) 88 [2] (1m, Kemw, SS, Jan 8)
Belgrave 88 [1] (6f, Leic, Hvy, Oct 28)
Brindavan (IRE) 88 [2] (1m 13y, Souw, SD, Oct 5)

Cap Saint Martin (FR) 88 [1] (1m, Curr, Sft, Oct 17)
County Mayo (IRE) 88 [1] (1m, Gowr, Gd, Sep 21)
Currawood (IRE) 88 [2] (7f, Curr, Gd, Jul 20)
Cyclonite (USA) 88 [1] (6f, Kemw, SS, Dec 4)
Diablo Rojo (IRE) 88 [1] (5f 217y, Redc, GF, Jul 31)
Eclairage (IRE) 88 [1] (5f, Dunw, SD, Dec 13)
End Of Romance (IRE) 88 [1] (7f 14y, Souw, SD, Oct 21)
Falconer 88 [1] (1m 75y, Nott, Sft, Oct 30)
Fuji Mountain (IRE) 88 [1] (5f 15y, Ches, Sft, Sep 14)
Gallant (FR) 88 [1] (6f, Kemw, SS, Oct 2)
Hill Road (USA) 88 [7] (7f, Curr, Gd, Sep 15)
Huscal (IRE) 88 [1] (6f, Thir, GF, Sep 7)
Kuwaitya (IRE) 88 [3] (5f 34y, Newb, Gd, Aug 16)
Lambourn (IRE) 88 [5] (1m, Curr, Yld, Sep 28)
Li Ban (IRE) 88 [5] (6f, Kemw, SS, Sep 7)
Likedbymike (IRE) 88 [1] (5f, Cork, Yld, Oct 1)
Local Lad (IRE) 88 [4] (6f, Curr, Gd, May 25)
Make Haste 88 [1] (5f, Naas, Gd, May 11)
Mathan (IRE) 88 [2] (5f 180y, Nava, Yld, Oct 23)
Miss Rascal 88 [1] (5f, Asco, Gd, May 10)
Mission Command (IRE) 88 [1] (5f, Beve, GF, Aug 25)
Modern Utopia (IRE) 88 [1] (1m 1f, Newm, Sft, Nov 2)
Nardra (IRE) 88 [1] (6f, Hayd, Sft, Sep 27)
Nascimento (IRE) 88 (6f, Asco, GF, Jun 18)
Perfect Pacemaker (IRE) 88 [1] (5f, Dunw, SD, Nov 1)
Perfect Part (IRE) 88 [5] (7f, York, GF, Aug 22)
Protest 88 [4] (1m, Newm, Sft, Nov 2)
Sky Advocate (IRE) 88 [2] (7f 36y, Wolw, SD, Oct 7)
Stem (IRE) 88 [1] (7f, Newb, Hvy, Sep 21)
Storm Piece 88 [2] (1m 30y, Punc, Gd, Sep 17)
Supreme Sovereign (IRE) 88 [1] (7f 14y, Souw, SD, Nov 2)
Timescape 88 [2] (5f 1y, Muss, Gd, Oct 2)
Treble Tee (IRE) 88 [1] (7f, Newm, Sft, Oct 23)
Tremorgio 88 [1] (1m 4f 14y, Souw, SD, Feb 7)
Vecu (IRE) 88 [4] (1m, Newj, Gd, Aug 16)
Viking Invasion (IRE) 88 [1] (1m 75y, Gowr, Hvy, Oct 21)
Yamal (IRE) 88 [1] (1m, Leop, Sft, Oct 19)
Against The Wind 87 [1] (5f, Ncsw, SS, Jun 29)
Al Hussar 87 [1] (4f 214y, Souw, SD, Oct 28)
Almeric 87 [1] (7f 192y, York, Sft, Oct 12)
Amestris 87 [7] (5f, Good, GF, Jul 31)
Biniorella Bay 87 [4] (7f, Good, Sft, Aug 24)
Brave Mission 87 [1] (7f, Kemw, SS, Sep 6)
Brosay 87 [2] (6f 1y, Linw, SS, Jan 9)
Catalyse (IRE) 87 [1] (6f 6y, Hami, Gd, Jun 2)
Cavallo Bay 87 [1] (6f 212y, Hayd, Gd, Jul 4)
Char (IRE) 87 [1] (7f, Kemw, SS, Oct 23)
Dakota Blue (FR) 87 [2] (1m, Dunw, SD, Oct 25)
Definitive 87 [5] (6f, Asco, GF, Jul 27)
Diligently 87 [1] (6f, York, GF, Aug 22)
Dividend 87 [1] (1m, Kemw, SS, Sep 25)
Evening Saigon (IRE) 87 [2] (6f, Newj, GS, Aug 24)
Fast Track Harry 87 [1] (6f, Newb, Sft, Sep 20)
Glenderry 87 [1] (1m, Dunw, SD, Oct 25)
Isambard Brunel (USA) 87 [1] (1m 10y, Nava, Yld, Oct 9)
Kassaya 87 [2] (5f, Asco, GF, Jun 19)
Lesley's Boy 87 [3] (7f 14y, Ncsw, SD, Oct 4)
Liberalised 87 [5] (7f, Newj, GF, Aug 10)
Lightning Bear (IRE) 87 [1] (7f, Dowr, Gd, Sep 6)
Mano Chicago (IRE) 87 [5] (7f, Curr, Yld, Sep 28)
Marhaba Ghaiyyath (IRE) 87 [1] (1m 1y, Linw, SD, Dec 3)
Nancy J (IRE) 87 [5] (7f, Leop, Gd, Sep 14)
Pearl Of Windsor 87 [6] (5f, Ayr, Gd, Sep 20)
Pentle Bay (IRE) 87 [2] (7f, Asco, GF, Jun 22)
Praetorian (IRE) 87 [2] (7f, York, GF, Jul 26)
Pride Of Arras (IRE) 87 [1] (1m, Sand, Gd, Aug 8)
Prince Of The Seas (IRE) 87 [1] (1m, Sand, SD, Sep 18)
Push The Limit (FR) 87 [1] (1m, Kemw, SS, Oct 14)

… GUIDE TO THE FLAT **2025**

RACING POST RATINGS: LAST SEASON'S LEADING TWO-YEAR-OLDS

KEY: Horse name, best RPR figure, finishing position when earning figure, (details of race where figure was earned)

Rayevka (IRE) 87 [6] (6f, Newm, Sft, Sep 28)
Regal Ulixes 87 [1] (1m, Newb, Sft, Sep 20)
Running Queen 87 [3] (6f, Newm, Gd, Nov 1)
Sex On Fire (IRE) 87 [2] (6f, Hayd, Gd, Jul 6)
Sounds Like A Plan 87 [1] (5f 180y, Nava, Gd, May 18)
Tangapour (IRE) 87 [1] (1m 30y, Kill, Hvy, Oct 7)
Teej A (IRE) 87 [2] (5f 15y, Ches, Sft, Sep 14)
The Watcher (IRE) 87 [1] (7f 36y, Wolw, SD, Feb 8)
Tremolo 87 [1] (7f 14y, Souw, SD, Dec 10)
Tribal Nation 87 [1] (7f, Galw, Hvy, Oct 28)
Twafeeg 87 [1] (6f 111y, Donc, Gd, Jun 1)
Winnebago (IRE) 87 [1] (7f 1y, Linw, SD, Feb 16)
Yankee Dude (IRE) 87 [1] (7f, Kemw, SS, Oct 9)
Alice Fairfax 86 [6] (6f, Asco, GF, Jul 27)
An Outlaw's Grace (IRE) 86 [5] (7f, Good, Gd, Jul 30)
Antonin Dvorak (IRE) 86 [1] (7f, Chmf, SD, Oct 12)
Ardennes (IRE) 86 [2] (6f, Kemw, SS, Jan 29)
Bold Impact (IRE) 86 [1] (7f 3y, Epso, Sft, Sep 12)
Cabelleroso 86 [1] (7f, Chmf, SD, Dec 12)
Circus Of Rome 86 [2] (1m 1y, Linw, SD, Dec 3)
Continuite 86 [2] (1m, Gowr, Gd, Sep 21)
First Wave (FR) 86 [2] (7f, Dunw, SD, Oct 30)
Fregada (IRE) 86 [1] (6f, Curr, Yld, Sep 28)
Ghost Run 86 [1] (6f 111y, Donc, Gd, Sep 12)
Glitterati 86 [2] (6f 3y, Yarm, GF, Sep 19)
Hawaiian 86 [1] (5f 34y, Newb, GS, Apr 19)
Honeysuckle Rose 86 [1] (7f, Dunw, SD, Dec 13)
Humam (IRE) 86 [1] (6f 16y, Souw, SD, Feb 7)
Iron Fist (IRE) 86 [2] (1m, Curr, Sft, Oct 17)
Jakarta 86 [1] (7f, Newm, Sft, Oct 23)
Jewelry (IRE) 86 [1] (6f, Newb, Gd, Aug 16)
Lexington Blitz (IRE) 86 [1] (5f 16y, Chep, Gd, Sep 2)
Lothlorien (IRE) 86 [1] (5f, Beve, GF, Aug 15)
Magic Basma (IRE) 86 [2] (6f, Ncsw, SS, Sep 17)
Mearall (IRE) 86 [1] (6f, Ripo, Gd, Aug 11)
Miss El Fundi 86 [7] (6f, Kemw, SS, Sep 7)
Miss Nightfall 86 [3] (6f 111y, Donc, Gd, Sep 12)
Mr Fantastic 86 [1] (7f 14y, Ncsw, SD, Sep 24)
Original Outlaw 86 [2] (7f, Good, GF, Aug 1)
Present Times 86 [2] (1m, Newm, GS, Sep 26)
Qetaifan (IRE) 86 [1] (6f, Good, Hvy, Oct 13)
Remaat 86 [1] (7f, Newj, GF, Jun 29)
Rock Hunter 86 [2] (5f 10y, Sand, Sft, May 23)
Sandtrap (IRE) 86 [1] (6f 213y, Sali, GS, Sep 13)
Sayidah Dariyan (IRE) 86 [1] (6f 1y, Linw, SD, Sep 10)
Secret Theory (IRE) 86 [1] (7f, Newm, GS, Oct 5)
Serious Contender (IRE) 86 [1] (1m, Leop, Sft, Oct 19)
Smoke Them Out (IRE) 86 [2] (5f 205y, Naas, Yld, Oct 12)

So Darn Hot 86 [1] (6f, Ncsw, SD, Jan 7)
Spherical 86 [1] (6f, Kemw, SS, Oct 11)
Station X 86 [1] (6f 2y, Donc, Sft, Nov 9)
Territorial Knight 86 [1] (6f, Pont, Gd, Jul 19)
The Actor (IRE) 86 [1] (5f, Newm, Gd, May 5)
Too Much Heaven 86 [1] (7f, Newb, Sep 5)
Tornado Alert (IRE) 86 [1] (1m 5y, Ncsw, SD, Oct 3)
Trad Jazz 86 [1] (1m, Kemw, SS, Aug 20)
Violet Love 86 [1] (6f, Ripo, Gd, Jul 8)
Waardah (IRE) 86 [1] (1m, Sand, Sft, Sep 13)
Watching Stars 86 [1] (7f, Thir, GS, Sep 16)
Zanzoun 86 [1] (7f 14y, Souw, SD, Nov 18)
Arabie 85 [1] (6f, York, GS, May 25)
Aviatrice (IRE) 85 [1] (6f, Dunw, SD, Nov 29)
Aysgarth 85 [1] (7f, Newb, Sft, Sep 20)
Bermuda Longtail (FR) 85 [1] (7f, Kemw, SS, Oct 30)
Blue Pinatubo 85 [1] (6f, Ayr, GD, Oct 1)
Blue Zodiac (IRE) 85 [1] (5f, Beve, Gd, Sep 18)
Boxtel (IRE) 85 [2] (6f, Newb, Sft, Sep 5)
Cairdeas 85 [1] (7f, Newj, Gd, Aug 16)
Carbine Harvester (FR) 85 [1] (6f 1y, Linw, SS, Jan 9)
Castle Stuart (IRE) 85 [1] (1m 68y, Hami, Sft, Aug 23)
Cercene (IRE) 85 [1] (7f, Naas, Gd, Sep 19)
Dark Cloud Rising 85 [3] (6f, Hayd, GS, Sep 5)
Dignam (IRE) 85 [1] (7f 110y, Tipp, Gd, Sep 1)
Don Pacifico (IRE) 85 [1] (6f 16y, Souw, SD, Dec 19)
Dubai Bling (IRE) 85 [5] (6f, Newb, Gd, Jul 19)
Dunamase (IRE) 85 [5] (1m 2f, Newm, GS, Oct 12)
Educating Rita 85 [2] (5f, Beve, GF, Aug 25)
El Matador (IRE) 85 [2] (1m 75y, Nott, Sft, Oct 30)
Elements Of Fire 85 [1] (7f, Chmf, SD, Nov 9)
Elouise's Prince (IRE) 85 [1] (5f 21y, Wolw, SD, Nov 21)
Elwateen (IRE) 85 [1] (7f, Kemw, SS, Aug 14)
Griselda (IRE) 85 [3] (6f 111y, Donc, Gd, Sep 12)
Hold A Dream (IRE) 85 [1] (6f 3y, Yarm, GF, Sep 18)
Hyperchromatic (IRE) 85 [1] (7f, Newm, Sft, Oct 12)
Kilcrea Rock (IRE) 85 [2] (1m, Leop, Sft, Oct 19)
King's Charter (IRE) 85 [3] (7f, Sand, GF, Jul 31)
Lady Mairen (IRE) 85 [4] (1m, Curr, Gd, Aug 31)
Lady O (IRE) 85 [1] (7f, Galw, Sft, Aug 3)
Line Of Force (IRE) 85 [2] (6f, Ripo, Gd, Aug 17)
Manhattan Chute (IRE) 85 [3] (5f 205y, Naas, Yld, Oct 12)
Marchogion 85 [1] (6f 16y, Souw, SD, Jan 31)
Medici Venus (USA) 85 [1] (1m, List, Yld, Sep 24)
Mister Adam 85 [4] (1m, Curr, Sft, Nov 3)
Motawahij (USA) 85 [1] (5f, Ncsw, SD, Jan 25)
Mukaber (IRE) 85 [1] (7f, Newb, GF, Aug 17)
Music Of Time 85 [1] (7f 6y, Donc, Sft, Oct 25)
Mythical Composer 85 [7] (5f 34y, Newb, GF, Jul 20)
Naina 85 [1] (7f, Newm, Sft, Sep 28)

RACING POST

RACING POST RATINGS: LAST SEASON'S TOP PERFORMERS 3YO+

KEY: Horse name, best RPR figure, finishing position when earning figure, (details of race where figure was earned)

City Of Troy (USA) 129 [1] (1m 2f 56y, York, GF, Aug 21)
Calandagan (IRE) 127 [2] (1m 2f 56y, York, GF, Aug 21)
Charyn (IRE) 127 [1] (1m, Asco, Sft, Oct 19)
Goliath (GER) 127 [1] (1m 3f 211y, Asco, GF, Jul 27)
Auguste Rodin (IRE) 125 [1] (1m 1f 212y, Asco, GF, Jun 19)
White Birch 125 [1] (1m 2f 110y, Curr, Yld, May 26)
Anmaat (IRE) 124 [1] (1m 2f, Asco, Sft, Oct 19)
Bradsell 124 [1] (5f, Curr, Gd, Sep 15)
Economics 124 [1] (1m 2f, Leop, Gd, Sep 14)
Luxembourg (IRE) 124 [1] (1m 4f 6y, Epso, GS, May 31)
Notable Speech 124 [1] (1m, Good, GF, Jul 31)
Rosallion (IRE) 124 [1] (7f 213y, Asco, GF, Jun 18)
Audience 123 [1] (1m, Newb, Gd, May 18)
Henry Longfellow (IRE) 123 [2] (7f 213y, Asco, GF, Jun 18)
Asfoora (AUS) 122 [2] (5f, Good, GF, Aug 2)
Facteur Cheval (IRE) 122 [2] (1m, Asco, Sft, Oct 19)
Giavellotto (IRE) 122 [1] (1m 4f, Newj, GS, Jul 11)
Kyprios (IRE) 122 [1] (2m, Good, Gd, Jul 30)
Lead Artist 122 [1] (1m 1f, Newm, GS, Oct 12)
Shin Emperor (FR) 122 [3] (1m 2f, Leop, Gd, Sep 14)
Zarakem (FR) 122 [2] (1m 1f 212y, Asco, GF, Jun 19)
Hamish 121 [2] (1m 4f 6y, Epso, GS, May 31)
Kind Of Blue 121 [1] (6f, Asco, Sft, Oct 19)
Kinross 121 [1] (7f 6y, Donc, Gd, Sep 14)
Los Angeles (IRE) 121 [4] (1m 2f, Leop, Gd, Sep 14)
Maljoom (IRE) 121 [2] (1m, Good, GF, Jul 31)
Passenger (USA) 121 [1] (1m 2f 70y, Ches, GF, May 10)
Alflaila 120 [1] (1m 2f 56y, York, GF, Jul 27)
Ambiente Friendly (IRE) 120 [1] (1m 4f 6y, Epso, GS, Jun 1)
Big Evs (IRE) 120 [1] (5f, Good, GF, Aug 2)
Ghostwriter (IRE) 120 [5] (1m 2f, Leop, Gd, Sep 14)
Horizon Dore (FR) 120 [3] (1m 1f 212y, Asco, GF, Jun 19)
Inisherin 120 [1] (6f, Asco, GF, Jun 21)
Isle Of Jura 120 [1] (1m 3f 211y, Asco, GF, Jun 22)
Israr 120 [1] (1m 1f 212y, Asco, GF, Jun 18)
Jan Brueghel (IRE) 120 [1] (1m 6f 115y, Donc, Gd, Sep 14)
Mill Stream (IRE) 120 [1] (6f, Newj, Gd, Jul 13)
Night Raider (IRE) 120 [1] (6f, Ncsw, SD, Nov 16)
Poet Master (IRE) 120 [1] (7f, Curr, Gd, Jul 21)
Starlust 120 [3] (5f, York, GF, Aug 23)
Tamfana (GER) 120 [1] (1m, Newm, GS, Oct 5)
Topgear (FR) 120 [1] (7f, Newm, GS, Oct 11)
Trawlerman (IRE) 120 [2] (2m 3f 210y, Asco, GF, Jun 20)
Bluestocking 119 [2] (1m 3f 211y, Asco, GF, Jul 27)
Dear My Friend 119 [1] (1m 1y, Linw, SD, Mar 1)
Dubai Honour (IRE) 119 [1] (1m 1f 219y, Kemw, SS, Apr 1)
Elegant Man (USA) 119 [1] (1m 2f 42y, Ncsw, SD, Mar 29)
Elite Status 119 [1] (6f, Newb, GF, Jul 20)
Illinois (IRE) 119 [2] (1m 6f 115y, Donc, Gd, Sep 14)
Khaadem (IRE) 119 [1] (6f, Asco, GF, Jun 22)
King's Gambit (IRE) 119 [2] (1m 2f 56y, York, GF, Jul 27)
Montassib 119 [1] (6f, Hayd, GF, Sep 7)
Regional 119 [2] (5f, Asco, GF, Jun 18)
Royal Rhyme (IRE) 119 [3] (1m 2f, Asco, Sft, Oct 19)
Sonny Liston (IRE) 119 [2] (1m, Asco, GF, Jun 19)
Tower Of London (IRE) 119 [1] (1m 6f 16y, Curr, Gd, Jul 20)
Al Aasy (IRE) 118 [1] (1m 5f 61y, Newb, GF, Aug 17)
Al Riffa (FR) 118 [2] (1m 1f 209y, Sand, Sft, Jul 6)
Believing (IRE) 118 [2] (5f, Asco, GF, Aug 23)
Diego Velazquez (IRE) 118 [1] (1m, Leop, Gd, Sep 14)
Docklands 118 [2] (1m, Asco, GF, Jun 18)
Iresine (FR) 118 [4] (1m 2f, Asco, Sft, Oct 19)
Kalpana 118 [1] (1m 3f 133y, Asco, Sft, Oct 19)
Noble Dynasty 118 [1] (7f, Newj, GF, Jun 29)
Okeechobee 118 [1] (1m 1f 209y, Sand, GF, Apr 26)
Porta Fortuna (IRE) 118 [1] (1m, Newj, Gd, Jul 12)
Prague (IRE) 118 [1] (1m, Newm, Sft, Sep 27)
Quddwah 118 [1] (7f 213y, Asco, Gd, Jul 13)
Sunway (FR) 118 [2] (1m 4f, Curr, Gd, Jun 30)
Sweet William (IRE) 118 [2] (1m 7f 127y, Asco, Sft, Oct 19)
Beauvatier (FR) 117 [4] (6f, Asco, Sft, Oct 19)
Botanical (IRE) 117 [2] (1m 1f 197y, Good, Hvy, Sep 25)
Content (IRE) 117 [1] (1m 3f 188y, York, GF, Aug 22)
Deira Mile (IRE) 117 [3] (1m 6f 115y, Donc, Gd, Sep 14)
Emily Upjohn 117 [2] (1m 2f, Curr, Sft, Jun 29)
Enfjaar (IRE) 117 [2] (1m 1f 197y, Good, Gd, Jul 30)
Haatem (IRE) 117 [1] (7f, Asco, GF, Jun 22)
Kerdos (IRE) 117 [1] (5f, Hayd, Sft, May 25)
King Of Conquest 117 [1] (1m 3f 218y, Good, Gd, Jun 9)
Liberty Lane (IRE) 117 [1] (1m, Newm, Sft, Sep 28)
Matsuri 117 [4] (1m 4f, Curr, Gd, Jun 30)
Middle Earth 117 [1] (1m 4f, Newb, Gd, May 18)
Opera Singer (USA) 117 [1] (1m 1f 197y, Good, GF, Aug 1)
Ottoman Fleet 117 [1] (1m 1f, Newm, Gd, Apr 17)
Rebel's Romance (IRE) 117 [3] (1m 3f 211y, Asco, GF, Jul 27)
Royal Scotsman (IRE) 117 [1] (1m 113y, Epso, GS, Jun 1)
Shouldvebeenaring 117 [2] (6f, York, Gd, May 15)
Swingalong (IRE) 117 [2] (6f, Asco, Sft, Oct 19)
Washington Heights 117 [1] (6f, Newm, Gd, Apr 18)
Yosemite Valley 117 [1] (7f, Curr, Hvy, Apr 21)
Al Nayyir 116 [2] (2m 56y, York, Gd, Aug 23)
Al Qareem (IRE) 116 [1] (1m 3f 211y, Asco, Sft, Oct 5)
Annaf (IRE) 116 [2] (6f 1y, Linw, SD, Feb 4)
Clarendon House 116 [1] (5f, Cork, Yld, Jun 14)
Crystal Black (IRE) 116 [1] (1m 4f, Leop, Gd, Aug 8)
Desert Hero 116 [2] (1m 1f 209y, Sand, GS, Apr 26)
Diligent Harry 116 [3] (6f, York, Gd, May 15)
Fallen Angel 116 [1] (1m, Curr, Yld, May 26)
Flora Of Bermuda (IRE) 116 [3] (6f, Asco, Sft, Oct 19)
Gregory 116 [3] (2m, Good, Gd, Jul 30)
Grey's Monument 116 [1] (7f, Asco, Sft, Sep 7)
Grosvenor Square (IRE) 116 [1] (1m 6f, Curr, Gd, Aug 17)
Inspiral 116 [2] (1m, Newm, GS, Oct 5)
Lake Forest 116 [2] (6f, Newb, GF, Jul 20)
Metropolitan (FR) 116 [3] (7f 213y, Asco, GF, Jun 18)
Mutasarref 116 [1] (1m, Cork, Yld, Oct 1)
My Prospero (IRE) 116 [1] (1m 2f, Wind, Sft, Aug 24)
Nostrum 116 [2] (7f, Newj, GF, Jun 29)
Poker Face (IRE) 116 [2] (1m, Sand, GS, Apr 26)
Quinault (GER) 116 [1] (6f, York, GS, Sep 8)
Royal Champion (IRE) 116 [1] (1m 2f, Linw, SD, Dec 31)
See The Fire 116 [2] (1m 1f 197y, Good, GF, Aug 1)
Sir Busker (IRE) 116 [1] (1m 2f 56y, York, GF, Aug 24)
Tiber Flow (IRE) 116 [1] (7f 37y, Hayd, Gd, Jun 8)
Vauban (FR) 116 [2] (1m 6f, Curr, Gd, Sep 15)
Witness Stand 116 [1] (7f, Newb, Sft, Sep 20)
You Got To Me 116 [2] (1m 3f 188y, York, GF, Aug 22)
Absurde (FR) 115 [1] (1m 6f 87y, Ches, Gd, Aug 31)
Al Mubhir 115 [1] (1m 1f 209y, Sand, Gd, Jul 5)
Art Power (IRE) 115 [5] (6f, York, Gd, May 15)
Bolster 115 [1] (1m 2f 56y, York, Sft, Oct 12)
Carrytheone 115 [1] (1m, Asco, Sft, Oct 19)
Certain Lad 115 [2] (1m 2f, Wind, Sft, Aug 24)
Commanche Falls 115 [3] (6f, York, GF, Aug 24)
Continuous (JPN) 115 [1] (1m 2f, Curr, Gd, Aug 17)
Ezeliya (FR) 115 [1] (1m 4f 6y, Epso, GS, May 31)
James's Delight (IRE) 115 [1] (6f, York, GS, Jun 15)
Johan 115 [1] (1m, Donc, Gd, Sep 14)
Lethal Levi 115 [1] (6f, Ayr, GF, Sep 21)
Live In The Dream (IRE) 115 [2] (5f, Hayd, Sft, May 25)
Marshman 115 [1] (6f 1y, Linw, SD, Feb 2)
Military Academy 115 [1] (1m 3f 219y, Kemw, SS, Nov 4)
Military Order (IRE) 115 [1] (1m 3f 23y, Souw, SD, Feb 24)
Passion And Glory (IRE) 115 [1] (1m 3f 211y, Asco, Gd, Jul 13)

GUIDE TO THE FLAT 2025

RACING POST RATINGS: LAST SEASON'S TOP PERFORMERS 3YO+

KEY: Horse name, best RPR figure, finishing position when earning figure, (details of race where figure was earned)

Persica (IRE) 115[1] (1m 2f, Ayr, GF, Sep 21)
Point Lynas (IRE) 115[1] (1m 6y, Pont, GF, Jul 28)
Queen Of The Pride 115[1] (1m 3f 175y, Hayd, Gd, Jul 6)
Room Service (IRE) 115[2] (6f, York, Sft, Oct 12)
Sparkling Plenty (FR) 115[3] (1m 1f 197y, Good, GF, Aug 1)
Spycatcher (IRE) 115[3] (6f, Newm, Gd, Apr 18)
Stay Alert 115[1] (1m 1f, Newm, Gd, May 5)
The Euphrates 115[1] (2m 170y, Curr, Gd, Sep 29)
The Foxes (IRE) 115[1] (1m 2f 42y, Ncsw, SD, Nov 16)
Trueshan (FR) 115[2] (2m 1f 197y, Donc, GS, Sep 13)
Tyrrhenian Sea (IRE) 115[1] (1m 1y, Linw, SD, Feb 1)
Willem Twee 115[1] (6f 20y, Wolw, SD, Aug 1)
Albasheer (IRE) 114[1] (5f, Ncsw, SD, Mar 15)
Almaqam 114[1] (1m, Sand, Sft, May 23)
Ancient Rome (USA) 114[2] (7f 213y, Asco, Gd, Jul 13)
Apollo One 114[1] (6f, Asco, Sft, Oct 5)
Arrest (IRE) 114[2] (1m 4f, Newj, GS, Jul 11)
Astro King (IRE) 114[2] (1m 1f, Newm, Gd, Apr 17)
Beshtani (FR) 114[2] (1m 113y, Epso, GS, May 31)
Caius Chorister (FR) 114[2] (2m 50y, Sand, Sft, May 23)
Cicero's Gift 114[1] (1m, Sand, Sft, Jul 6)
Coltrane (IRE) 114[1] (1m 7f 209y, Asco, GS, May 1)
Enemy 114[2] (2m 56y, Ncsw, SD, Jan 1)
English Oak 114[1] (7f, Asco, GF, Jun 20)
Equality 114[1] (5f 1y, Muss, GS, Apr 21)
Eydon (IRE) 114[2] (1m 2f, Ayr, GF, Sep 21)
Hidden Law (IRE) 114[1] (1m 4f 63y, Ches, Gd, May 8)
Ice Max 114[1] (1m, Good, Sft, Aug 24)
Jasour 114[3] (6f, Asco, GF, Jun 21)
Jayarebe (FR) 114[1] (1m 1f 212y, Asco, GF, Jun 20)
Make Me King (FR) 114[1] (7f 14y, Ncsw, SS, Jun 29)
Max Vega (IRE) 114[1] (1m 4f 51y, Wolw, SD, Feb 17)
Mitbaahy (IRE) 114[1] (6f, Curr, Gd, May 25)
Moss Tucker (IRE) 114[1] (5f, Naas, Yld, Sep 29)
My Mate Alfie (IRE) 114[1] (6f, Curr, Gd, Sep 29)
Prydwen (IRE) 114[1] (1m 6f 80y, Kill, Sft, Aug 23)
Ramazan (IRE) 114[2] (6f, Ripo, Gd, Aug 17)
Relentless Voyager 114[2] (1m 3f 218y, Good, GF, Aug 3)
River Tiber (IRE) 114[3] (1m, Curr, Gd, May 25)
Running Lion 114[1] (7f 213y, Asco, GF, Jun 19)
Shartash (IRE) 114[1] (6f 212y, Hayd, GF, May 11)
Unequal Love 114[1] (6f, Asco, GF, Jun 22)
Wingspan (IRE) 114[2] (1m 3f 133y, Asco, Sft, Oct 19)
Al Musmak (IRE) 113[1] (1m, Newj, GS, Jul 11)
Alsakib 113[1] (1m 5f 188y, York, GS, Jul 13)
Arabian Crown (FR) 113[1] (1m 1f 209y, Sand, GS, Apr 26)
Burdett Road 113[1] (1m 4f, Newm, Sft, Sep 27)
Cemhaan 113[1] (2m 2f 219y, Kemw, SS, Apr 6)
Checkandchallenge 113[3] (1m 177y, York, GF, Jun 24)
Democracy Dilemma (IRE) 113[1] (5f, Beve, GF, Aug 31)
Desperate Hero 113[1] (5f 7y, Hami, Gd, Jun 2)
Elmalka 113[1] (1m, Newm, GS, Oct 5)
Embesto 113[3] (7f 213y, Asco, Gd, Jul 13)
Fast Raaj (FR) 113[4] (1m 5oy, Ncsw, SD, Mar 29)
Haunted Dream (IRE) 113[1] (1m 1f 11y, Good, GF, Aug 2)
Hi Royal (IRE) 113[3] (1m 1f, Newm, Gd, Apr 17)
Holloway Boy 113[1] (1m 37y, Hayd, Gd, Sep 7)
Jarraaf 113[1] (6f, Asco, GF, Aug 10)
Kikkuli 113[2] (7f, Asco, GF, Jun 22)
Kingdom Come (IRE) 113[2] (1m 5y, Ncsw, SD, Mar 29)
Klondike 113[1] (1m 5f 188y, York, GS, Jul 13)
Lord North (IRE) 113[2] (1m 3f 23y, Souw, SD, Feb 24)
Mountain Bear (IRE) 113[3] (1m, Leop, Gd, Sep 14)
Novus (IRE) 113[1] (1m 1f 197y, Good, Hvy, Sep 25)
Peace Man 113[2] (1m 2f, Newm, Sft, Nov 2)
Phantom Flight 113[2] (1m 177y, York, GF, Jun 24)

Pogo (IRE) 113[2] (6f 212y, Hayd, GF, May 11)
Point Lonsdale (IRE) 113[3] (2m 1f 197y, Donc, GS, Sep 13)
Raadobarg 113[3] (1m, Curr, Hvy, Mar 18)
Royal Dubai (FR) 113[4] (7f 213y, Asco, Gd, Jul 13)
Sardinian Warrior (IRE) 113[1] (1m 13y, Souw, SD, Nov 2)
Savvy Victory (IRE) 113[1] (1m 2f 42y, Ncsw, SD, Dec 6)
Sean (GER) 113[3] (1m 2f, Wind, GF, Aug 15)
Strobe (USA) 113[2] (7f, Kemw, SS, Nov 4)
Time Lock 113[1] (1m 4f, Newm, Sft, Sep 27)
Torito 113[3] (1m 1f 212y, Asco, GF, Jun 18)
Unquestionable (FR) 113[4] (7f 213y, Asco, GF, Jun 18)
Wiltshire 113[2] (5f, Hayd, Sft, Sep 28)
Zoum Zoum 113[1] (6f 2y, Donc, Sft, Oct 25)
Aimeric 112[1] (1m 4f, Newj, GF, Jun 29)
Alyanaabi (IRE) 112[5] (7f 213y, Asco, GF, Jun 18)
Bellum Justum (IRE) 112[2] (1m 3f 218y, Good, GF, Aug 1)
Blue Storm 112[1] (5f, Hayd, Sft, Sep 28)
Crystal Delight 112[1] (1m 3f 188y, York, Gd, May 15)
Dark Trooper (IRE) 112[2] (6f, Asco, GF, Jun 22)
Emaraaty Ana 112[3] (5f, Beve, GF, Aug 31)
Fivethousandtoone (IRE) 112[1] (6f, Ncsw, SD, Mar 29)
Flight Plan 112[5] (7f 37y, Hayd, Gd, Jun 8)
Givemethebeatboys (IRE) 112[1] (6f, Curr, GF, Aug 10)
Harbour Wind (IRE) 112[1] (1m 4f 110y, Lime, Gd, Jun 22)
Hooking 112[3] (1m 2f 42y, Ncsw, SD, Mar 29)
La Yakel 112[1] (1m 4f 15y, Hami, Hvy, Aug 23)
Layfayette (IRE) 112[3] (1m 3f 211y, Asco, Sft, Oct 5)
Lion's Pride 112[3] (1m 1f 219y, Kemw, SS, Apr 1)
Lord Massusus (IRE) 112[5] (1m, Leop, Gd, Sep 14)
Magical Zoe (IRE) 112[1] (1m 5f 188y, York, GF, Aug 24)
Makarova 112[3] (5f, Curr, Gd, Sep 15)
Maxux (IRE) 112[2] (1m 2f, Curr, Hvy, Apr 20)
Misty Grey (IRE) 112[1] (6f 3y, Epso, GS, Jun 1)
Mount Athos 112[1] (7f, Kemw, SS, Mar 27)
Mujtaba 112[2] (1m 1f 197y, Good, Gd, May 24)
No Half Measures 112[1] (5f 34y, Newb, Hvy, Sep 21)
Northern Express (IRE) 112[1] (7f, Asco, GF, Jul 27)
Outbox 112[1] (1m 4f, Newm, Gd, May 3)
Purosangue 112[2] (6f, York, GS, Sep 8)
Ramatuelle (USA) 112[3] (1m, Newm, Gd, May 5)
Roberto Escobarr (IRE) 112[4] (2m 56y, Ncsw, SD, Jan 1)
Roi De France (IRE) 112[2] (1m, Kemw, SS, Dec 4)
Royal Dress (IRE) 112[1] (1m 1f, Curr, Gd, Jul 21)
Rumsta 112[1] (5f, Asco, Sft, Oct 5)
Salt Bay (GER) 112[1] (1m 5f 188y, York, GS, Jul 15)
Sayedaty Sadaty (IRE) 112[5] (1m 4f 6y, Epso, GS, Jun 1)
Space Legend (IRE) 112[4] (1m 3f 188y, York, GF, Aug 21)
Sparks Fly 112[1] (1m 75y, Nott, Sft, Oct 30)
Trustyourinstinct (IRE) 112[1] (1m 4f, Leop, Sep 14)
Uxmal (IRE) 112[1] (1m 4f 5143y, Asco, GF, Jul 22)
Vandeek 112[2] (6f, Newj, Gd, Jul 13)
Witch Hunter (FR) 112[3] (1m, Asco, Sft, Oct 19)
Ancient Wisdom (FR) 111[1] (1m 5f, Newj, GS, Jul 11)
Big Gossey (IRE) 111[2] (6f, Curr, Gd, Sep 29)
Breege 111[1] (7f, York, GF, Aug 24)
Bucanero Fuerte 111[1] (5f 205y, Naas, Gd, May 19)
Candleford (IRE) 111[4] (1m 3f 211y, Asco, GF, Jun 22)
Chief Little Rock (IRE) 111[1] (1m 2f, Curr, Yld, May 26)
Dancing Gemini (IRE) 111[6] (1m 4f 6y, Epso, GS, Jun 1)
Darnation (IRE) 111[2] (1m 2f 42y, Ncsw, SS, Jun 28)
Easy (IRE) 111[1] (6f, Cork, Hvy, Mar 30)
Equilateral 111[1] (4f 214y, Souw, SD, Dec 10)
Falcon Eight (IRE) 111[1] (2m 2f 140y, Ches, GF, May 10)
Feed The Flame 111[3] (1m 4f 6y, Epso, GS, May 31)
Get It 111[1] (6f, Good, GF, Aug 3)
Go Daddy (IRE) 111[3] (1m 5f 61y, Newb, GF, Aug 17)
Great Generation (IRE) 111[1] (7f 6y, Donc, Sft, Sep 15)
Highbury (FR) 111[3] (1m 6f 34y, Asco, GF, Jun 19)

81

RACING POST

RACING POST RATINGS: LAST SEASON'S TOP PERFORMERS 3YO+

KEY: Horse name, best RPR figure, finishing position when earning figure, (details of race where figure was earned)

Highland Avenue (IRE) 111[3] (1m 113y, Epso, GS, Jun 1)
Jordan Electrics 111[2] (5f 89y, York, GF, Aug 21)
Jumby (IRE) 111[3] (7f, Newb, GF, Aug 17)
King's Gamble (IRE) 111[2] (1m, Good, GF, Aug 2)
Kylian (IRE) 111[1] (5f 21y, Wolw, SD, Jan 25)
Naqeeb (IRE) 111[2] (2m 110y, Newb, GF, Jul 20)
Popmaster (IRE) 111[7] (7f, Asco, Gd, May 11)
Quickthorn 111[1] (1m 6f 44y, Sali, GS, Sep 13)
Real Dream (IRE) 111[2] (1m 4f, Newm, Gd, May 4)
Regal Reality 111[3] (1m 2f 100y, Hayd, GF, Aug 10)
Rogue Lightning (IRE) 111[2] (5f, York, GS, Jul 13)
Rogue Millennium (IRE) 111[3] (1m, Newj, Gd, Jul 12)
Romantic Thor (USA) 111[1] (1m 2f 70y, Ches, Gd, May 9)
She's Quality (IRE) 111[1] (5f, Tipp, Gd, Sep 1)
Significantly 111[6] (5f, Newm, Gd, May 4)
Sirona (GER) 111[5] (1m, Newj, Gd, Jul 12)
Tiffany (IRE) 111[1] (1m 2f 42y, Ncsw, SS, Jun 28)
Vafortino (IRE) 111[6] (6f, Asco, GF, Jun 22)
Village Voice 111[3] (1m 2f, Curr, Hvy, Apr 20)
Volterra (IRE) 111[1] (7f, Asco, Sft, Oct 5)
Al Shabab Storm 110[2] (6f 17y, Ches, GS, Aug 4)
Birdman (IRE) 110[3] (1m 6f 34y, Asco, GF, Jun 19)
Bracken's Laugh (IRE) 110[2] (1m 2f 70y, Ches, Gd, May 9)
Cambridge (IRE) 110[2] (1m 1f 212y, Asco, GF, Jun 22)
Cash (IRE) 110[3] (1m, Sand, Gd, Sep 18)
Caviar Heights (IRE) 110[1] (1m 2f, Newm, Gd, May 3)
Chicago Critic 110[3] (7f, Asco, GF, Jun 22)
Dance Sequence 110[2] (1m 4f 6y, Epso, GS, May 31)
Elnajmm 110[1] (1m, Asco, GF, Jul 27)
Epic Poet (IRE) 110[1] (1m 6f 1y, Hayd, Gd, Sep 7)
Galen 110[1] (1m 20y, Kill, Gd, Jul 15)
Hanalia (IRE) 110[1] (1m 2f, Curr, Gd, Sep 15)
Killybegs Warrior (IRE) 110[2] (1m 2f 219y, Kemw, SS, Apr 6)
Korker (IRE) 110[4] (5f, York, Gd, May 16)
Mistral Star 110[1] (1m 4f, Newj, GF, Jul 20)
Nakheel (FR) 110[1] (1m 6f 115y, Donc, GS, Sep 12)
Norwalk Havoc 110[1] (1m, Leop, Hvy, Oct 20)
Power Under Me (IRE) 110[1] (1m 4f 100y, Tipp, Sft, Oct 6)
Real Appeal (GER) 110[1] (1m, Dunw, SD, Mar 8)
Russet Gold 110[3] (6f, Asco, Sft, Oct 5)
Samui 110[2] (2m 56y, York, GF, Aug 21)
Soprano (IRE) 110[1] (1m, Asco, GF, Jun 21)
Task Force 110[3] (1m, Good, GF, Aug 2)
Twilight Calls 110[5] (6f, Newb, GF, Jul 20)
Vadream 110[4] (6f, Hayd, Gd, Sep 7)
Ylang Ylang 110[5] (1m, Newm, Gd, May 5)
A Lilac Rolla (IRE) 109[3] (1m 2f 150y, Newj, Gd, Jul 12)
Adaay In Devon 109[4] (5f, Asco, Gd, Aug 10)
Agenda (IRE) 109[2] (1m 4f 63y, Ches, Gd, May 8)
Alfa Kellenic 109[1] (6f, Ayr, GF, Sep 21)
Asian Daze (IRE) 109[1] (7f, Newj, Gd, Jul 13)
Awaal (IRE) 109[2] (1m, Asco, Sft, Sep 6)
Base Note 109[7] (1m 2f, Linw, SD, Mar 1)
Battle Cry (IRE) 109[1] (7f 30y, Leop, Hvy, Apr 7)
Bold Discovery (USA) 109[1] (1m, Leop, Gd, May 12)
Bright Stripes (IRE) 109[7] (1m, Leop, Gd, Sep 14)
Cairo (IRE) 109[2] (1m 1f 11y, Good, GF, Aug 2)
Champagne Prince 109[1] (1m 3f 23y, Souw, SD, Jan 31)
Claymore (FR) 109[4] (1m 3f 23y, Souw, SD, Feb 24)
Cover Up (IRE) 109[1] (5f, Ncsw, SD, Feb 24)
Endless Victory 109[1] (1m 2f 23y, Yarm, GS, Aug 25)
Friendly Soul 109[1] (7f 213y, Asco, GF, Jul 27)
Jabaara (IRE) 109[2] (1m, Newj, Gd, Jul 12)
Juan Les Pins 109[2] (4f 214y, Souw, SD, Feb 24)
Kinesiology 109[2] (1m 4f, Leop, Gd, Sep 14)
Lady Boba 109[1] (1m 2f, Newm, GS, Oct 11)
Laurel 109[2] (7f 213y, Asco, GF, Jun 19)
London City (USA) 109[1] (1m 3f 188y, York, Gd, May 16)
Marine Wave (IRE) 109[2] (6f, Newm, Sft, Oct 12)
Ocean Jewel (IRE) 109[1] (1m, Curr, Gd, May 26)
Orazio (IRE) 109[3] (6f, Asco, GF, Jun 22)
Paborus 109[1] (7f 14y, Souw, SD, Oct 17)
Real Force 109[1] (5f, Curr, Hvy, Mar 18)
Rohaan (IRE) 109[5] (6f 1y, Linw, SD, Mar 1)
Royal Power (FR) 109[2] (1m 2f, Newj, Gd, Jul 12)
Run For Oscar (IRE) 109[4] (2m 2f, Newm, Sft, Oct 12)
Seven Questions (IRE) 109[1] (5f, Newm, Gd, May 4)
Sons And Lovers 109[3] (1m 2f, Newb, GF, Jul 20)
Tempus 109[4] (1m 5y, Ncsw, SD, Jan 7)
Term Of Endearment 109[1] (1m 6f, Newj, Gd, Aug 3)
Teumessias Fox (IRE) 109[1] (1m 3f 219y, Kemw, SS, Jan 27)
The Equator (IRE) 109[2] (1m 5f 188y, York, GF, Aug 24)
Torivega (IRE) 109[3] (5f, Curr, Gd, Sep 29)
Wild Tiger 109[1] (7f, Good, Gd, May 24)
Wild Waves (IRE) 109[6] (1m 6f 115y, Donc, Gd, Sep 14)
Wise Eagle (IRE) 109[3] (1m 5f 188y, York, GS, Jul 13)
American Sonja 108[3] (1m 1f, Curr, Gd, Jul 21)
Ano Syra (IRE) 108[3] (6f, Curr, Gd, May 25)
Belloccio (FR) 108[1] (1m 6f 34y, Asco, GF, Jun 18)
Danielle 108[2] (1m 4f, Newm, Hvy, Oct 26)
Dawn Rising (IRE) 108[1] (2m 71y, Curr, Yld, Nov 3)
Doctor Khan Junior 108[1] (7f 36y, Wolw, SD, Feb 17)
Drawn To Dream (IRE) 108[6] (1m 6f 34y, Asco, GF, Jun 18)
Dublin (IRE) 108[2] (1m, Cork, Yld, Oct 1)
Durezza (JPN) 108[5] (1m 2f 56y, York, GF, Aug 21)
Freescape 108[2] (1m, Dunw, SD, Mar 8)
Involvement 108[3] (1m 1f 209y, Sand, Gd, Aug 31)
Jancis (IRE) 108[1] (7f 35y, Leop, Gd, Jul 11)
Je Zous (IRE) 108[1] (1m 1f 100y, Gowr, Gd, Sep 21)
Mandoob 108[5] (1m 3f 211y, Asco, GF, Jun 21)
Midnight Gun 108[2] (1m, Donc, Sft, Oct 25)
Mostabshir 108[4] (6f, Good, GF, Aug 3)
Mums Tipple (IRE) 108[2] (7f, Kemw, SS, Mar 27)
Night Sparkle (IRE) 108[2] (1m 6f 115y, Donc, GS, Sep 12)
Nine Tenths (IRE) 108[2] (7f 14y, Ncsw, SD, Jan 7)
Not So Sleepy 108[1] (1m 5f 61y, Newb, Hvy, Sep 21)
Ouzo 108[5] (7f, Good, GS, Aug 25)
Ponntos (IRE) 108[5] (5f, York, GF, Aug 23)
Port Fairy (IRE) 108[1] (1m 3f 211y, Asco, GF, Jun 20)
Rage Of Bamby (IRE) 108[1] (6f, York, GF, Jul 27)
Royal Supremacy (IRE) 108[2] (1m 5f, Newj, GS, Jul 11)
Scenic (FR) 108[1] (1m 3f 188y, York, GF, Aug 22)
Shadow Dance 108[3] (1m 6f 115y, Donc, GS, Sep 13)
Shagraan (IRE) 108[1] (5f, Hayd, Gd, Sep 7)
Star Harbour (IRE) 108[2] (1m 2f 150y, Dunw, SD, Aug 15)
Star Of Lady M 108[1] (5f 110y, Ayr, Gd, Sep 20)
Streets Of Gold (IRE) 108[3] (7f 16y, Chep, GS, Aug 8)
Sumiha (IRE) 108[4] (1m 4f, Leop, Gd, Sep 14)
Tashkhan (IRE) 108[1] (7f 196y, Ches, Sft, Sep 14)
The Wizard Of Eye (IRE) 108[1] (7f, Asco, Gd, May 11)
Thunderbear (IRE) 108[3] (6f 2y, Donc, Sft, Nov 9)
Tyson Fury 108[1] (1m 6f, Curr, Gd, Jun 5)
War Chimes (FR) 108[3] (1m 4f 6y, Epso, GS, May 31)
Align The Stars (IRE) 107[1] (1m 6f, Good, GF, Aug 3)
Balmacara 107[2] (1m 1f 209y, Sand, Gd, Aug 31)
Beautiful Diamond 107[2] (5f, Curr, Gd, Jul 20)
Calling The Wind (IRE) 107[2] (2m, Good, GS, Sep 3)
Crown Board (IRE) 107[1] (1m, Sand, Gd, Sep 18)
Divine Comedy (IRE) 107[5] (2m 56y, York, GF, Aug 21)
Doha 107[5] (1m 1f 197y, Good, GF, Aug 1)
Dunum (IRE) 107[3] (7f, Galw, Hvy, Aug 4)
Esquire 107[1] (7f, Newb, GS, Apr 20)
Evade (FR) 107[1] (7f 3y, Epso, GS, May 31)
Fairbanks 107[4] (1m 6f 87y, Ches, Gd, Aug 31)

GUIDE TO THE FLAT 2025

RACING POST RATINGS: LAST SEASON'S TOP PERFORMERS 3YO+

KEY: Horse name, best RPR figure, finishing position when earning figure, (details of race where figure was earned)

French Duke (IRE) 107 [2] (1m 3f 211y, Asco, Sft, Sep 7)
Gather Ye Rosebuds 107 [1] (1m 3f 218y, Good, Sft, May 4)
God's Window 107 [3] (1m 3f 219y, Kemw, SS, Sep 7)
Greenland (IRE) 107 [3] (1m 2f, Curr, Sft, May 6)
Harper's Ferry 107 [1] (1m, Donc, Sft, Oct 25)
Jakajaro (IRE) 107 [4] (5f, Curr, Gd, Jul 20)
Keeper's Heart (IRE) 107 [5] (1m 4f, Curr, Gd, Jun 30)
Kolossal (GER) 107 [8] (1m 3f 211y, Asco, GF, Jun 21)
Lava Stream (IRE) 107 [2] (1m 3f 211y, Asco, GF, Jun 20)
Mashhoor 107 [4] (1m 2f 70y, Ches, GF, May 10)
Notre Belle Bete 107 [4] (1m 113y, Epso, GS, May 31)
Old Harrovian 107 [1] (1m 2f 42y, Ncsw, SD, Jan 17)
Perotto 107 [3] (1m, Sand, Sft, Jul 6)
Purple Lily (IRE) 107 [3] (1m 2f, Curr, Gd, Sep 15)
Rebel Territory 107 [6] (7f, Good, GS, Aug 25)
Relief Rally (IRE) 107 [2] (5f 34y, Newb, Hvy, Sep 21)
Rhoscolyn 107 [2] (1m, Good, Hvy, Oct 12)
River Of Stars (IRE) 107 [3] (1m 6f, Good, GF, Aug 3)
Sea Of Roses 107 [1] (1m 3f 99y, Wind, Sft, Aug 24)
Serious Challenge (IRE) 107 [3] (1m 6f, Curr, Gd, Jun 5)
Silky Wilkie (IRE) 107 [2] (6f 6y, Hami, Gd, Jul 19)
Skellet (IRE) 107 [1] (1m, Sand, Gd, Sep 18)
Sound Angela 107 [2] (1m 2f, Newm, GS, Oct 11)
Special Wan (IRE) 107 [2] (7f 47y, Leop, Yld, Jun 13)
Spiritual (IRE) 107 [3] (1m, Newm, Hvy, Sep 27)
Stromberg 107 [3] (1m 2f, Leop, Hvy, Oct 20)
Subsequent (IRE) 107 [1] (1m 6f 34y, Asco, Sft, Oct 4)
Sunchart 107 [1] (1m 2f 98y, Naas, Hvy, Mar 24)
Symbol Of Light 107 [1] (1m 13y, Souw, SD, Feb 7)
Tacarib Bay 107 [5] (6f, Ncsw, SD, Jan 1)
Tarawa (IRE) 107 [1] (1m 1f, Leop, Gd, Jun 6)
Woodhay Wonder 107 [4] (5f, Asco, GF, Jun 21)
Artistic Star (IRE) 106 [4] (1m 1f 209y, Asco, GF, Apr 26)
Beamish (FR) 106 [2] (1m 7f 209y, Asco, Gd, Aug 10)
Beechwood (IRE) 106 [1] (1m 4f, Galw, Yld, Sep 10)
Bless Him (IRE) 106 [3] (7f, Asco, Gd, May 11)
Blue For You (IRE) 106 [1] (7f 192y, York, GS, Jul 13)
Boiling Point (IRE) 106 [4] (1m, Good, GF, Aug 2)
Brewing 106 [1] (7f, Kemw, SS, Jan 31)
Chipstead 106 [1] (6f 1y, Linw, SD, Mar 1)
Choisya 106 [1] (1m 37y, Hayd, GF, Aug 10)
Coeur D'or (IRE) 106 [4] (1m, Curr, Gd, Aug 31)
Dancing Tango (IRE) 106 [2] (1m 4f 110y, Lime, Gd, Jun 22)
Deauville Legend (IRE) 106 [4] (1m 3f 218y, Good, Gd, Jun 9)
Diamond Rain 106 [1] (1m 2f, Newb, Gd, May 18)
Dream Composer (FR) 106 [1] (5f 3y, Pont, Gd, Aug 18)
Dual Identity (IRE) 106 [2] (1m 2f 56y, York, GF, Aug 24)
Eben Shaddad (USA) 106 [2] (1m, Newm, Gd, Apr 18)
Elim (IRE) 106 [2] (7f 6y, Donc, Sft, Sep 15)
Fair Point 106 [2] (1m, Newm, Hvy, Sep 27)
Ferrous (IRE) 106 [1] (6f, Kemw, SS, Apr 6)
First Look (IRE) 106 [4] (1m 1f 212y, Asco, GF, Jun 20)
Forest Of Dean 106 [5] (1m 3f 23y, Souw, SD, Feb 24)
Free Wind (IRE) 106 [2] (1m 2f 56y, York, Gd, May 16)
Funny Story 106 [3] (6f, Newm, Sft, Oct 12)
Golden Mind (IRE) 106 [1] (6f, Kemw, SS, Feb 12)
Hand Of God 106 [1] (1m 1f 212y, Asco, GF, Jun 22)
Hans Andersen 106 [5] (1m 2f 70y, Ches, GF, May 10)
Higher Leaves (IRE) 106 [3] (1m 2f, Newm, GS, Oct 11)
Hipop De Loire (FR) 106 [5] (1m 5f 188y, York, GF, Aug 24)
Holkham Bay 106 [1] (6f, Asco, Sft, Oct 4)
Imperial Quarter (IRE) 106 [3] (1m, Sand, Gd, Aug 31)
Jubilee Walk 106 [1] (5f, York, Gd, May 17)
Kihavah 106 [1] (1m 5f 26y, Ayr, GF, Sep 21)
Little Queenie (IRE) 106 [1] (6f, Dunw, SD, Aug 15)
Macduff 106 [2] (1m 1f 209y, Sand, GS, Apr 26)
Maxi King (IRE) 106 [4] (1m 4f, Newb, Gd, May 18)
Nashwa 106 [5] (1m, Newm, GS, Oct 5)
Native American (IRE) 106 [2] (7f 3y, Epso, GS, May 31)
Naval Force (IRE) 106 [1] (1m 2f 40y, Nava, GF, Jul 13)
Paradias (GER) 106 [1] (1m 2f 219y, Kemw, SS, Jan 22)
Pilgrim 106 [1] (5f, Asco, GF, Jun 21)
Portland (IRE) 106 [3] (1m 5f, Newj, GS, Jul 11)
Queenstown (IRE) 106 [2] (1m 6f, Leop, Gd, May 17)
Remaadd (IRE) 106 [7] (1m 2f 56y, York, GS, Jul 13)
Safecracker 106 [5] (1m 2f, Curr, Gd, May 25)
Samuel Colt (IRE) 106 [2] (7f 30y, Leop, Hvy, Apr 7)
Sea King 106 [3] (1m 4f 10y, Ripo, Gd, Jul 20)
Sea Theme (IRE) 106 [5] (1m 3f 188y, York, GF, Aug 22)
Secret Satire 106 [1] (1m 2f 56y, York, Gd, May 15)
Storm Catcher (IRE) 106 [2] (1m 2f 42y, Ncsw, SD, Jan 1)
Super Sox 106 [1] (7f, Cork, GF, Aug 16)
Talis Evolvere (IRE) 106 [1] (7f, Chmf, SD, Dec 19)
Tasman Bay (FR) 106 [1] (1m 2f 37y, Bath, Hvy, Apr 7)
Ten Bob Tony (IRE) 106 [1] (7f, Newm, Gd, Apr 16)
Ten Pounds (IRE) 106 [1] (7f 14y, Ncsw, SS, Aug 2)
Thunder Moor (IRE) 106 [1] (4f 214y, Souw, SD, Aug 29)
Twilight Jet (IRE) 106 [2] (5f, Naas, Gd, May 19)
Valiant Force (USA) 106 [1] (6f, Dunw, SD, Feb 7)
War Rooms (IRE) 106 [2] (1m 2f 56y, York, Gd, May 16)
Without Words (USA) 106 [1] (7f 110y, Tipp, Gd, Sep 1)
Yashin (IRE) 106 [6] (1m 4f, Leop, Gd, Sep 14)
A Piece Of Heaven (FR) 105 [2] (2m 170y, Curr, Gd, Sep 29)
American Affair 105 [1] (5f 143y, Donc, Gd, Sep 14)
Azure Blue (IRE) 105 [1] (5f, Ayr, Gd, Jun 22)
Caernarfon 105 [1] (1m 6y, Pont, Sft, Jul 9)
Chantilly (IRE) 105 [3] (1m 2f, Newb, Gd, May 18)
Chazzesmee (IRE) 105 [1] (1m, Curr, Hvy, Mar 18)

RACING POST

TOPSPEED: LAST SEASON'S LEADING TWO-YEAR-OLDS

KEY: Horse name, best Topspeed figure, finishing position when earning figure, (details of race where figure was earned)

Desert Flower (IRE) 106[1] (1m, Newm, GS, Oct 11)
Hotazhell 105[1] (1m, Donc, Sft, Oct 26)
Delacroix (IRE) 104[2] (1m, Donc, Sft, Oct 26)
Babouche 102[1] (6f, Curr, GF, Aug 10)
The Lion In Winter (IRE) 101[1] (7f, York, GF, Aug 21)
Bedtime Story (IRE) 100[1] (7f, Asco, GF, Jun 22)
Whistlejacket (IRE) 100[2] (6f, Curr, GF, Aug 10)
Wimbledon Hawkeye 100[1] (1m, Newm, Sft, Sep 28)
Lake Victoria (IRE) 98[1] (6f, Newm, Sft, Sep 28)
Powerful Glory (IRE) 96[1] (6f, Newb, Hvy, Sep 21)
Royal Playwright 96[2] (1m, Newm, Sft, Sep 28)
Ruling Court (USA) 96[3] (7f, York, GF, Aug 21)
Seaplane 96[1] (7f, Newm, Sft, Sep 27)
Ain't Nobody (IRE) 95[1] (5f, Asco, GF, Jun 19)
Arizona Blaze 95[3] (6f, Curr, GF, Aug 10)
Coto De Caza (IRE) 95[1] (5f, Newm, GS, Oct 11)
La Bellota (IRE) 95[2] (6f, Newb, Hvy, Sep 21)
Simmering 95[2] (7f, Curr, Gd, Sep 15)
Benevento (IRE) 94[1] (7f, 6y, Donc, Gd, Sep 13)
Exactly (IRE) 94[3] (7f, Curr, Gd, Sep 15)
Fairy Godmother (IRE) 94[1] (6f, Asco, GF, Jun 21)
Henri Matisse (IRE) 94[1] (7f, Curr, Gd, Aug 24)
January (IRE) 94[2] (1m, Newm, GS, Oct 11)
Red Letter 94[4] (7f, Curr, Gd, Sep 15)
Tennessee Stud (IRE) 94[2] (1m, Curr, Yld, Sep 28)
Ballet Slippers (IRE) 93[3] (1m, Newm, GS, Oct 11)
Brian (IRE) 93[1] (6f, Newj, Sft, Aug 24)
Grande Marques (IRE) 93[2] (5f, Newm, GS, Oct 11)
Shareholder (USA) 93[1] (5f, Asco, GF, Jun 20)
Symbol Of Honour 93[2] (7f 6y, Donc, Gd, Sep 13)
Windlord 93[3] (1m, Curr, Yld, Sep 28)
Aesterius (IRE) 92[1] (5f 10y, Sand, Gd, Jul 5)
Age Of Gold (IRE) 92[2] (7f, York, GF, Aug 22)
Angelo Buonarroti (IRE) 92[3] (1m, Newm, Sft, Sep 28)
Big Mojo (IRE) 92[1] (5f, Good, GF, Jul 31)
Green Impact (IRE) 92[1] (1m, Leop, Gd, Sep 14)
Magnum Force (IRE) 92[2] (5f, York, GF, Aug 24)
Puppet Master (IRE) 92[4] (1m, Newm, Sft, Sep 28)
Shadow Of Light 92[1] (6f, Newm, Sft, Sep 28)
Sky Majesty (IRE) 92[1] (6f, Ayr, GF, Sep 21)
Starzintheireyes 92[1] (1m 2f, Newm, GS, Oct 12)
Trinity College (IRE) 92[4] (1m, Curr, Yld, Sep 28)
Tropical Storm 92[1] (5f, York, GF, Aug 24)
Arabian Dusk 91[1] (6f, Newj, Gd, Jul 12)
Black Forza (USA) 91[1] (6f, Good, GF, Aug 1)
Caburn (IRE) 91[1] (5f 34y, Newb, GF, Jul 20)
Gabaldon (USA) 91[2] (5f, Asco, GF, Jun 19)
Maw Lam (IRE) 91[2] (6f, Ayr, GF, Sep 21)
The Waco Kid (IRE) 91[3] (7f 6y, Donc, Gd, Sep 13)
Vingegaard (IRE) 91[2] (5f 34y, Newb, GF, Jul 20)
Aftermath (IRE) 90[1] (7f, Curr, Gd, Sep 29)
Ancient Truth (IRE) 90[1] (7f, Newj, Gd, Jul 13)
Anniversary 90[2] (1m 2f, Newm, Sft, Oct 23)
Barnavara (IRE) 90[3] (7f, Curr, Gd, Aug 24)
Celandine 90[1] (6f, Newj, GF, Jun 29)
Centigrade (IRE) 90[1] (1m 7y, Newb, Hvy, Oct 25)
Green Storm (IRE) 90[2] (1m 2f, Newm, GS, Oct 12)
Heavens Gate (IRE) 90[3] (6f, Asco, GF, Jun 21)
Ides Of March (IRE) 90[1] (6f, Curr, Gd, Aug 31)
Loch Tay 90[1] (7f 94y, Rosc, Sft, Sep 2)
Shadow Army 90[4] (6f, Curr, GF, Aug 10)
Sigh No More (IRE) 90[1] (1m 1f, Leop, Sft, Oct 19)
Square D'alboni (FR) 90[1] (1m, Sali, Gd, Sep 13)
The Actor (IRE) 90[1] (5f, Newm, Gd, May 5)
Bernard Shaw (USA) 89[3] (1m, Leop, Gd, Sep 14)
Daylight (FR) 89[2] (6f, Newm, Sft, Sep 28)

Flight 89[3] (1m, Donc, Gd, Sep 12)
Mr Lightside (IRE) 89[3] (5f, Good, GF, Jul 31)
The Strikin Viking (IRE) 89[2] (6f, Good, GF, Aug 1)
Billboard Star 88[3] (6f, Newb, Hvy, Sep 21)
Cool Hoof Luke 88[1] (6f, York, Gd, Aug 23)
Englemere (IRE) 88[1] (5f 34y, Newb, Gd, Aug 16)
Merrily (USA) 88[1] (7f, Newm, GS, Oct 11)
Miss Tonnerre (IRE) 88[4] (1m, Donc, Gd, Sep 12)
Mountain Breeze (IRE) 88[2] (6f, Newj, Gd, Jul 12)
Scandinavia (USA) 88[2] (1m, Newj, Gd, Aug 16)
That's Amore (IRE) 88[1] (1m 7y, Newb, Hvy, Oct 26)
Al Qudra (IRE) 87[1] (7f, Asco, GF, Jul 27)
Angel Hunter 87[1] (7f, York, GF, Aug 22)
Anno Domini 87[5] (1m, Donc, Sft, Oct 26)
Camille Pissarro (IRE) 87[2] (6f 63y, Curr, Gd, Aug 21)
Cathedral 87[2] (7f, Newm, GS, Oct 11)
Intrusively 87[3] (6f, Good, GF, Aug 1)
Kaadi (IRE) 87[2] (5f 34y, Newb, Gd, Aug 16)
Right And True (IRE) 87[1] (1m, List, Gd, Sep 23)
Sir Yoshi (IRE) 87[3] (5f, York, GF, Aug 24)
Smoken 87[1] (1m 75y, Nott, Hvy, Oct 16)
Star Anthem (IRE) 87[4] (6f, Newb, Hvy, Sep 21)
The Dragon King (IRE) 87[1] (6f, Newm, GS, Oct 5)
Archivist 86[2] (1m 75y, Nott, Hvy, Oct 16)
Brighton Boy (IRE) 86[2] (6f, Newm, GS, Oct 5)
Chantez (IRE) 86[3] (7f 35y, Leop, Gd, Jul 11)
Detain (IRE) 86[1] (7f, Kemw, SS, Oct 9)
First Instinct 86[1] (6f, Hayd, GS, Sep 6)
Leovanni (IRE) 86[1] (5f, Asco, GF, Jun 19)
Mr Chaplin 86[4] (7f 6y, Donc, Gd, Sep 13)
Snapdragon (IRE) 86[2] (6f, Curr, Gd, Aug 17)
Soldier's Heart 86[1] (6f, Ripo, Gd, Aug 26)
Symbol Of Strength (IRE) 86[3] (6f, York, Gd, Aug 23)
Thrice (IRE) 86[1] (7f 15y, List, Gd, Sep 24)
Wemightakedlongway (IRE) 86[3] (1m 1f, Leop, Sft, Oct 19)
Beckman (IRE) 85[1] (6f, Curr, Gd, Jun 28)
Do It Now 85[5] (5f 34y, Newb, GF, Jul 20)
Eclairage (IRE) 85[1] (5f, Dunw, SD, Dec 13)
Ecstatic (JPN) 85[5] (1m, Donc, Gd, Sep 12)
Greydreambeliever (IRE) 85[1] (6f, York, GF, Jul 27)
Hazdann (IRE) 85[1] (7f, Curr, Gd, Jun 29)
It Ain't Two 85[2] (6f, Newj, GF, Aug 3)
Kuwaitya (IRE) 85[1] (5f 34y, Newb, Gd, Aug 16)
Magic Mild 85[1] (6f, Newj, GF, Aug 3)
Powerful Nation (IRE) 85[2] (5f, Dunw, SD, Oct 25)
Rajeko (IRE) 85[1] (1m, Chmf, SD, Dec 19)
Ride The Thunder (IRE) 85[2] (1m, Donc, Gd, Sep 14)
Scorthy Champ (IRE) 85[3] (7f, Curr, Gd, Aug 24)
Seagulls Eleven (IRE) 85[2] (7f, Newj, Gd, Jul 13)
Seraph Gabriel (IRE) 85[2] (7f, Redc, Sft, Oct 5)
Time For Sandals (IRE) 85[2] (6f, York, GF, Aug 22)
Yah Mo Be There 85[1] (6f, Newb, Gd, Jul 19)
Attack 84[2] (1m, Donc, Sft, Oct 25)
Aviation Time (IRE) 84[3] (5f, Asco, GF, Jun 19)
Bountiful 84[4] (6f, Newj, Gd, Jul 12)
Dark Cloud Rising 84[3] (7f, Thir, Gd, Aug 16)
Expanded (IRE) 84[2] (7f, Newm, Sft, Oct 12)
Fuji Mountain (IRE) 84[1] (5f 15y, Ches, Sft, Sep 14)
Glittering Legend 84[1] (1m, Donc, Sft, Oct 25)
King Of Cities (IRE) 84[3] (1m, Newj, Gd, Aug 16)
Kullazain 84[3] (5f, Newm, GS, Oct 11)
Port Light (IRE) 84[2] (1m, Chmf, SD, Dec 19)
Principality (IRE) 84[1] (6f, Curr, Gd, Jun 9)
Seacruiser (IRE) 84[1] (1m, Newm, GS, Sep 26)
Seagolazo (IRE) 84[2] (7f 192y, York, Sft, Oct 12)
Shackleton (IRE) 84[1] (1m 2f, Newm, GS, Oct 13)
Shah (IRE) 84[2] (7f, York, GF, Aug 23)
Spirit Of Leros 84[1] (6f, Newb, Gd, Aug 16)

TOPSPEED: LAST SEASON'S LEADING TWO-YEAR-OLDS

Stormy Impact 84[5] (6f, Ayr, GF, Sep 21)
Tales Of The Heart (IRE) 84[2] (6f, Newj, GF, Jun 29)
Yaroogh (IRE) 84[1] (7f 6y, Donc, Gd, Sep 12)
Adrestia 83[1] (5f 10y, Sand, GF, Jul 31)
Blue Zodiac (IRE) 83[1] (5f, Beve, Gd, Sep 18)
Convergent (IRE) 83[1] (7f 219y, Redc, Sft, Oct 18)
Francisco's Piece 83[2] (5f, York, Gd, May 15)
God Of War 83[5] (7f 6y, Donc, Gd, Sep 13)
Invictus Gold (IRE) 83[1] (6f, Newj, GS, Aug 24)
Jewelry (IRE) 83[1] (6f, Newb, Gd, Aug 16)
Kodilicious (IRE) 83[2] (6f, Cork, Yld, Oct 1)
Luther 83[1] (1m 37y, Hayd, Gd, Sep 7)
Masubi 83[4] (1m, Donc, Gd, Sep 14)
River Seine (IRE) 83[4] (5f 34y, Newb, Gd, Aug 16)
Rudi's Apple (IRE) 83[5] (6f, Curr, GF, Aug 10)
Sparkling Sea (IRE) 83[2] (5f 205y, Naas, Gd, May 19)
Spell Master 83[4] (7f, York, GF, Aug 22)
Teej A (IRE) 83[2] (5f 15y, Ches, Sft, Sep 14)
Too Soon 83[4] (1m 2f, Newm, GS, Oct 12)
Vecu (IRE) 83[4] (1m, Newj, Gd, Aug 16)
Weissmuller (IRE) 83[4] (5f, Asco, GF, Jun 19)
Big Cyril (IRE) 82[6] (6f, Good, GF, Aug 1)
Bodhi Bear (IRE) 82[1] (5f 180y, Nava, Yld, Oct 23)
Circus Of Rome 82[2] (1m 1y, Linw, SD, Dec 3)
Cyclonite (USA) 82[1] (6f, Kemw, SS, Dec 4)
Distant Seas 82[2] (6f, Curr, Gd, Jun 28)
Dreamy (IRE) 82[1] (1m, Curr, Gd, Aug 31)
End Of Story (IRE) 82[2] (6f, York, GS, Sep 8)
Jouncy 82[2] (6f, Kemw, SS, Sep 7)
Jungle Drums (IRE) 82[1] (6f, York, Sft, Oct 12)
King Of Bears (IRE) 82[7] (6f, Good, GF, Aug 1)
King's Call (IRE) 82[2] (5f, York, Sft, Oct 11)
Linwood (IRE) 82[1] (7f, Newb, Gd, Jul 19)
Marhaba Ghaiyyath (IRE) 82[1] (1m 1y, Linw, SD, Dec 3)
Modern Utopia (IRE) 82[1] (1m 1f, Newm, Sft, Nov 2)
Nebras 82[7] (1m, Donc, Sft, Oct 26)
Toomuchforme 82[2] (6f, Newb, Gd, Aug 16)
Yabher 82[1] (1m, Donc, Gd, Sep 14)
Zayer (IRE) 82[1] (5f, Ripo, GF, Aug 27)
Anshoda (IRE) 81[1] (7f, Good, Sft, Aug 24)
Arctic Voyage 81[1] (6f 18y, Nott, Hvy, Oct 9)
Aysgarth 81[1] (7f, Newb, Sft, Sep 20)
Bay City Roller (IRE) 81[1] (7f 6y, Donc, Gd, Sep 14)
Bolo Neighs (IRE) 81[1] (6f, Curr, Yld, Sep 28)
Bonnie's Boy 81[2] (6f, Thir, Gd, Aug 16)
Bounty (IRE) 81[1] (5f 205y, Naas, Yld, Oct 13)
Cressida Wildes 81[5] (5f 34y, Newb, Gd, Aug 16)
Emit (IRE) 81[5] (1m 1f, Leop, Sft, Oct 19)
Girl Like You (USA) 81[1] (6f, Curr, Gd, Aug 17)
Hill Road (USA) 81[1] (1m, Leop, Gd, Aug 8)
Hott Shott 81[1] (7f, Good, GF, Aug 3)
Mythical Composer 81[7] (5f 34y, Newb, GF, Jul 20)
Present Times 81[2] (1m, Newm, GS, Sep 26)
Qetaifan (IRE) 81[1] (6f 17y, Ches, Hvy, Sep 13)
Rashabar (IRE) 81[1] (6f, Asco, GF, Jun 18)
Spirit Of Farhh (IRE) 81[1] (6f 110y, Newb, Hvy, Oct 25)
Storm Call (IRE) 81[2] (5f, Good, GF, Jul 31)
Tabiti 81[1] (7f, Newj, GF, Aug 10)
The Lost King 81[1] (7f, Newj, Gd, Aug 23)
Tommy Mcjohn (IRE) 81[1] (5f, Naas, Gd, Sep 19)
Twafeeg (IRE) 81[1] (6f 111y, Donc, Gd, Jun 1)
Valedictory 81[3] (1m, Donc, Gd, Sep 14)
Verse Of Love 81[1] (7f, Newm, GS, Oct 11)

Desert Flower: last season's leading juvenile performer based on Topsoil figures

RACING POST

TOPSPEED: LAST SEASON'S TOP PERFORMERS 3YO+

KEY: Horse name, best Topspeed figure, finishing position when earning figure, (details of race where figure was earned)

Goliath (GER) 123 [1] (1m 3f 211y, Asco, GF, Jul 27)
Kyprios (IRE) 119 [1] (2m, Good, Gd, Jul 30)
City Of Troy (USA) 118 [1] (1m 2f 56y, York, GF, Aug 21)
Bluestocking 117 [2] (1m 3f 211y, Asco, GF, Jul 27)
Calandagan (FR) 116 [2] (1m 2f 56y, York, GF, Aug 21)
Rebel's Romance (IRE) 115 [3] (1m 3f 211y, Asco, GF, Jul 27)
Sweet William (IRE) 115 [2] (2m, Good, Gd, Jul 30)
Gregory 114 [3] (2m, Good, Gd, Jul 30)
Rosallion (IRE) 114 [1] (7f 213y, Asco, GF, Jun 18)
Henry Longfellow (IRE) 113 [2] (7f 213y, Asco, GF, Jun 18)
Anmaat (IRE) 112 [1] (1m 2f, Asco, Sft, Oct 19)
Asfoora (AUS) 112 [1] (5f, Asco, GF, Jun 18)
Regional 111 [2] (5f, Asco, GF, Jun 18)
Trawlerman (IRE) 111 [3] (1m 7f 127y, Asco, GF, Oct 19)
Vauban (FR) 111 [1] (2m 56y, York, Gd, Aug 23)
Al Nayyir 110 [2] (2m 56y, York, Gd, Aug 23)
Ghostwriter (IRE) 110 [3] (1m 2f 56y, York, GF, Aug 21)
Israr 110 [1] (1m 1f 212y, Asco, GF, Jun 18)
Los Angeles (IRE) 110 [1] (1m 4f, Curr, Gd, Jun 30)
White Birch 110 [1] (1m 2f 110y, Curr, Yld, May 26)
Royal Rhyme (IRE) 109 [3] (1m 2f, Asco, Sft, Oct 19)
Trueshan (FR) 109 [4] (2m, Good, Gd, Jul 30)
Al Qareem (IRE) 108 [5] (2m, Good, Gd, Jul 30)
Elite Status 108 [1] (6f, Newb, GF, Jul 20)
Iresine (FR) 108 [4] (1m 2f, Asco, Sft, Oct 19)
Liberty Lane (IRE) 108 [1] (1m 1f, Newm, Sft, Sep 28)
Sunway (FR) 108 [2] (1m 4f, Curr, Gd, Jun 30)
Ambiente Friendly (IRE) 107 [3] (1m 4f, Curr, Gd, Jun 30)
Hamish 107 [1] (1m 4f, Curr, Yld, Nov 3)
Illinois (IRE) 107 [1] (1m 6f 34y, Asco, GF, Jun 19)
Kind Of Blue 107 [1] (6f, Asco, Sft, Oct 19)
Okeechobee 107 [1] (1m 1f 209y, Sand, GS, Apr 26)
Big Evs (IRE) 106 [3] (5f, Asco, Sft, Oct 19)
Botanical (IRE) 106 [2] (1m 2f 56y, York, GS, Jul 13)
Burdett Road 106 [6] (1m 7f 127y, Asco, Sft, Oct 19)
Caius Chorister (FR) 106 [4] (1m 7f 127y, Asco, Sft, Oct 19)
Desert Hero 106 [2] (1m 1f 209y, Sand, GS, Apr 26)
Economics 106 [6] (1m 2f, Asco, Sft, Oct 19)
Ezeliya (FR) 106 [1] (1m 4f 6y, Epso, GS, May 31)
Jan Brueghel (IRE) 106 [1] (1m 6f 115y, Donc, Gd, Sep 14)
Kalpana 106 [1] (1m 3f 133y, Asco, Sft, Oct 19)
Khaadem (IRE) 106 [1] (6f, Asco, GF, Jun 22)
Lake Forest 106 [2] (6f, Newb, GF, Jul 20)
Matsuri 106 [4] (1m 4f, Curr, Gd, Jun 30)
You Got To Me 106 [1] (1m 4f, Curr, Gd, Jul 20)
Auguste Rodin (IRE) 105 [5] (1m 3f 211y, Asco, GF, Jul 27)
Believing (IRE) 105 [4] (5f, Asco, GF, Jun 18)
King Of Conquest 105 [1] (1m 4f, Newj, GF, Jun 29)
Point Lonsdale (IRE) 105 [1] (1m 5f 84y, Ches, Gd, May 9)
Al Musmak (IRE) 104 [1] (1m, Newj, GS, Jul 11)
Annaf (IRE) 104 [2] (6f 1y, Linw, SD, Feb 4)
Apollo One 104 [2] (6f, Good, GF, Aug 3)
Beauvatier (FR) 104 [4] (6f, Asco, Sft, Oct 19)
Caviar Heights (IRE) 104 [1] (1m 2f, Newm, GF, May 3)
Charyn (IRE) 104 [1] (1m, Asco, GF, Jun 18)
Content (IRE) 104 [2] (1m 4f, Curr, Gd, Jun 30)
Deira Mile (IRE) 104 [3] (1m 6f 115y, Donc, Gd, Sep 14)
Highbury (FR) 104 [2] (1m 6f 34y, Asco, GF, Jun 19)
Metropolitan (FR) 104 [3] (7f 213y, Asco, GF, Jun 18)
Montassib 104 [1] (6f, Hayd, Gd, Sep 7)
Royal Scotsman (IRE) 104 [1] (1m 113y, Epso, GS, Jun 1)
See The Fire 104 [5] (1m 4f, Curr, Gd, Jul 20)
Swingalong (IRE) 104 [2] (6f, Asco, Sft, Oct 19)
Tashkhan (IRE) 104 [3] (1m 7f 196y, Ches, Sft, Sep 14)
Alsakib 103 [1] (1m 5f 188y, York, GS, Jul 13)
Diligent Harry 103 [1] (6f 1y, Linw, SD, Feb 4)

Flora Of Bermuda (IRE) 103 [3] (6f, Asco, Sft, Oct 19)
Haunted Dream (IRE) 103 [2] (1m 1f 212y, Asco, GF, Jun 18)
Night Sparkle (IRE) 103 [4] (2m 56y, York, Gd, Aug 23)
Notable Speech 103 [1] (1m, Newm, Gd, May 4)
Queen Of The Pride 103 [1] (1m 3f 175y, Hayd, Gd, Jul 6)
Albasheer (IRE) 102 [1] (6f, Ncsw, SD, Jan 1)
Belloccio (FR) 102 [1] (1m 6f 34y, Asco, GF, Jun 18)
Birdman (IRE) 102 [3] (1m 6f 34y, Asco, GF, Jun 19)
Enfjaar (IRE) 102 [1] (1m 2f 56y, York, GS, Jul 13)
Get It 102 [1] (6f, Good, GF, Aug 3)
Giavellotto (IRE) 102 [1] (1m 4f, Newj, GS, Jul 11)
Hidden Law (IRE) 102 [1] (1m 4f 63y, Ches, Gd, May 8)
Port Fairy (IRE) 102 [1] (1m 3f 211y, Asco, GF, Jun 20)
Quickthorn 102 [6] (2m 56y, York, Gd, Aug 23)
The Equator (IRE) 102 [2] (1m 5f 188y, York, GF, Aug 24)
Torito 102 [3] (1m 1f 212y, Asco, GF, Jun 18)
Wingspan (IRE) 102 [2] (1m 3f 133y, Asco, Sft, Oct 19)
Aimeric 101 [2] (1m 4f, Newj, GF, Jun 29)
Al Aasy (IRE) 101 [1] (1m 5f 61y, Newb, GF, Aug 17)
Bradsell 101 [1] (5f, York, GF, Aug 23)
Kerdos (IRE) 101 [5] (5f, Asco, GF, Jun 18)
King's Gambit (IRE) 101 [7] (1m 2f, Asco, Sft, Oct 19)
Lava Stream (IRE) 101 [2] (1m 3f 211y, Asco, GF, Jun 20)
Luxembourg (IRE) 101 [6] (1m 3f 211y, Asco, GF, Jul 27)
Purple Lily (IRE) 101 [3] (1m 4f, Curr, Gd, Jul 20)
Bolster 100 [1] (1m 2f 56y, York, Sft, Oct 12)
Cambridge (IRE) 100 [2] (1m 1f 212y, Asco, GF, Jun 22)
Certain Lad 100 [2] (1m 2f, Wind, Sft, Aug 24)
Dance Sequence 100 [2] (1m 4f 6y, Epso, GS, May 31)
Durezza (JPN) 100 [5] (1m 2f 56y, York, GF, Aug 21)
English Oak 100 [1] (7f, Asco, GF, Jun 20)
Military Academy 100 [1] (1m 3f 219y, Kemw, SS, Nov 4)
Misty Grey (IRE) 100 [1] (6f, Ncsw, SD, May 12)
My Prospero (IRE) 100 [1] (1m 2f, Wind, Sft, Aug 24)
Spycatcher (IRE) 100 [1] (6f, Asco, GF, Jun 22)
The Euphrates 100 [1] (2m 170y, Curr, Gd, Sep 29)
Twilight Calls 100 [5] (5f, Asco, GF, Jun 18)
Unquestionable (IRE) 100 [4] (7f 213y, Asco, GF, Jun 18)
Vadream 100 [2] (5f, Newm, Gd, May 4)
Alyanaabi (IRE) 99 [5] (7f 213y, Asco, GF, Jun 18)
Beshtani (FR) 99 [2] (1m 113y, Epso, GS, May 31)
Dubai Honour (IRE) 99 [2] (1m 2f 42y, Ncsw, SD, Nov 16)
Emily Upjohn 99 [2] (1m 2f, Curr, Sft, Jun 29)
Endless Victory 99 [1] (1m 2f 23y, Yarm, GS, Aug 25)
Inisherin 99 [1] (6f, Asco, GF, Jun 21)
Kylian (IRE) 99 [1] (5f 6y, Linw, SD, Dec 31)
Lead Artist 99 [1] (1m, Good, GF, Aug 2)
Mill Stream (IRE) 99 [1] (6f, Asco, GF, Jun 22)
Mostabshir 99 [4] (6f, Good, GF, Aug 3)
Persica (IRE) 99 [8] (1m 2f, Asco, Sft, Oct 19)
Prydwen (IRE) 99 [1] (2m 56y, Ncsw, SD, Mar 29)
Rumstar 99 [2] (6f, Newb, Gd, May 18)
Seven Questions (IRE) 99 [1] (5f, Newm, Gd, May 4)
Shin Emperor (FR) 99 [3] (1m 2f, Leop, Gd, Sep 14)
Subsequent (IRE) 99 [1] (1m 6f 34y, Asco, Sft, Oct 4)
Tamfana (GER) 99 [1] (1m, Sand, Gd, Aug 31)
Tower Of London (IRE) 99 [1] (1m 6f 16y, Curr, Gd, Jul 20)
Trustyourinstinct (IRE) 99 [2] (1m 2f, Curr, Sft, Jun 29)
Verbier (IRE) 99 [1] (1m 2f 56y, York, GF, Jul 26)
Washington Heights 99 [1] (6f, Newm, Gd, Apr 18)
Coltrane (IRE) 98 [2] (2m 1f 197y, Donc, GS, Sep 13)
Docklands 98 [7] (1m 2f 56y, York, GF, Aug 21)
Drawn To Dream (IRE) 98 [6] (1m 6f 34y, Asco, GF, Jun 18)
Elizabeth Jane (IRE) 98 [4] (1m 4f, Curr, Gd, Jul 20)
Friendly Soul 98 [1] (1m 2f, Newm, Gd, May 5)
Grosvenor Square (IRE) 98 [5] (1m 6f 115y, Donc, Gd, Sep 14)
Haatem (IRE) 98 [1] (1m, Newm, Gd, Apr 18)
King's Gamble (IRE) 98 [2] (1m, Good, GF, Aug 2)

GUIDE TO THE FLAT 2025

TOPSPEED: LAST SEASON'S TOP PERFORMERS 3YO+

KEY: Horse name, best Topspeed figure, finishing position when earning figure, (details of race where figure was earned)

Live In The Dream (IRE) 98 [2] (5f, Hayd, Sft, May 25)
Maxi King (IRE) 98 [8] (1m 3f 197y, Donc, Sft, Nov 9)
My Mate Alfie (IRE) 98 [1] (6f, Curr, Gd, Sep 15)
Night Raider (IRE) 98 [1] (6f, Ncsw, SD, Nov 16)
Quinault (GER) 98 [1] (6f, York, GS, Sep 8)
Ramazan (IRE) 98 [8] (6f, Good, GF, Aug 3)
Roi De France (IRE) 98 [2] (1m 1f 21y, Yarm, GF, Sep 18)
Sean (GER) 98 [4] (1m 1f 209y, Sand, Gd, Aug 31)
Shartash (IRE) 98 [1] (6f 212y, Hayd, GF, May 11)
Significantly 98 [6] (5f, Newm, Gd, May 4)
Starlust 98 [3] (5f, York, GF, Aug 23)
Tabletalk (IRE) 98 [1] (1m 5f 188y, York, GF, Aug 24)
The Foxes (IRE) 98 [1] (1m 2f 42y, Ncsw, SD, Nov 16)
Tiffany (IRE) 98 [3] (1m 3f 133y, Asco, Sft, Oct 19)
Unequal Love 98 [3] (6f, Hayd, Gd, Sep 7)
Witness Stand 98 [1] (7f, Good, GF, Aug 3)
Zarakem (FR) 98 [2] (1m 1f 212y, Asco, GF, Jun 19)
Absurde (FR) 97 [1] (1m 6f 87y, Ches, Gd, Aug 31)
Al Mubhir 97 [1] (1m 1f 209y, Sand, Gd, Jul 5)
Alfa Kellenic 97 [1] (6f, Ayr, GF, Sep 21)
Almaqam 97 [6] (7f 213y, Asco, GF, Jun 18)
Brewing 97 [1] (7f, Kemw, SS, Jan 31)
Caught U Looking (IRE) 97 [5] (1m 4f, Curr, Gd, Jul 20)
Dream Composer (FR) 97 [1] (5f 3y, Pont, GF, Aug 18)
Facteur Cheval (IRE) 97 [2] (1m, Asco, Sft, Oct 19)
Highland Avenue (IRE) 97 [3] (1m 113y, Epso, GS, Jun 1)
Karmology 97 [2] (1m 2f 56y, York, GF, Jul 26)
Maljoom (IRE) 97 [8] (1m 2f 56y, York, GF, Aug 21)
Max Vega (IRE) 97 [8] (2m 56y, Ncsw, SD, Mar 29)
Mitbaahy (IRE) 97 [7] (5f, Newm, Gd, May 4)
Northern Express (IRE) 97 [1] (7f, Asco, GF, Jul 27)
Onesmoothoperator (USA) 97 [1] (2m 56y, Ncsw, SS, Jun 29)
Poet Master (IRE) 97 [1] (7f, Newm, Gd, Apr 18)
Pogo (IRE) 97 [2] (6f 212y, Hayd, GF, May 11)
Royal Champion (IRE) 97 [1] (1m 2f, Linw, SD, Dec 31)
Royal Dubai (FR) 97 [2] (1m 113y, Epso, GS, Jun 1)
Scenic (FR) 97 [1] (1m 3f 188y, York, GF, Aug 22)
Shagraan (IRE) 97 [1] (5f, Hayd, Gd, Sep 7)
Silky Wilkie (IRE) 97 [2] (6f 6y, Hami, Gd, Jul 19)
Space Legend (IRE) 97 [2] (1m 3f 211y, Asco, GF, Jun 21)
Sparks Fly 97 [5] (6f 212y, Hayd, Sft, Apr 27)
Task Force 97 [3] (1m, Good, GF, Aug 2)
Thunderbear (IRE) 97 [2] (5f, Curr, Gd, Oct 5)
Valvano (IRE) 97 [5] (1m 3f 197y, Donc, Sft, Nov 9)
War Chimes (FR) 97 [3] (1m 4f 6y, Epso, GS, May 31)
Wild Waves (IRE) 97 [6] (1m 6f 115y, Donc, GF, Sep 14)
Wise Eagle (IRE) 97 [3] (1m 5f 188y, York, GS, Jul 13)
Agenda (IRE) 96 [2] (1m 4f 63y, Ches, Gd, May 8)
Blue Storm 96 [2] (5f, Asco, GF, Jun 21)
Candleford (IRE) 96 [1] (1m 4f, Curr, Gd, May 25)
Commanche Falls 96 [5] (6f, Asco, Sft, Oct 4)
Continuous (JPN) 96 (1m 2f, Asco, Sft, Oct 19)
Cover Up (IRE) 96 [5] (6f, Good, GF, Aug 3)
Crystal Delight 96 [1] (1m 3f 188y, York, Gd, May 15)
Dance Night Andday (IRE) 96 [1] (7f, Leop, Gd, Sep 14)
Hanalia (IRE) 96 [6] (1m 4f, Curr, Gd, Jul 20)
Harper's Ferry 96 [1] (1m, Donc, Sft, Oct 25)
Horizon Dore (FR) 96 [3] (1m 1f 212y, Asco, GF, Jun 19)
Involvement 96 [3] (1m 1f 209y, Sand, Gd, Aug 31)
Jayarebe (FR) 96 [1] (1m 1f, Newm, Gd, Apr 17)
Lady Boba 96 [3] (1m 3f 175y, Hayd, Gd, Jul 6)
Lethal Levi 96 [1] (6f, Ayr, GF, Sep 21)
Midnight Gun 96 [2] (1m, Donc, Sft, Oct 25)
Miller Spirit (IRE) 96 [6] (1m 3f 197y, Donc, Gd, Nov 9)
Mistral Star 96 [1] (1m 4f, Newj, GF, Jul 20)
Norwalk Havoc 96 [1] (1m, Leop, Hvy, Oct 20)
Pilgrim 96 [1] (5f, Asco, GF, Jun 21)
Rahmi (IRE) 96 [1] (7f, Naas, Yld, Oct 12)
Rhoscolyn 96 [1] (7f 3y, Epso, GS, May 31)
Sayedaty Sadaty (IRE) 96 [2] (1m 2f, Newm, Gd, May 3)
Star Of Lady M 96 [1] (5f 110y, Ayr, Gd, Sep 20)
Woodhay Wonder 96 [4] (5f, Asco, GF, Jun 21)
A Piece Of Heaven (FR) 95 [2] (2m 170y, Curr, Gd, Sep 29)
Artistic Star (IRE) 95 [4] (1m 1f 209y, Sand, GS, Apr 26)
Auld Toon Loon (IRE) 95 [4] (1m 3f 197y, Donc, Sft, Nov 9)
Balmacara 95 [2] (1m 1f 209y, Sand, Gd, Aug 31)
Beechwood (IRE) 95 [1] (1m 4f, Galw, Yld, Sep 10)
Blue Lemons (IRE) 95 [2] (1m, Sand, GS, Apr 26)
Clarendon House 95 [1] (5f, Cork, Yld, Jun 14)
Desperate Hero 95 [1] (5f 7y, Hami, Gd, Jun 2)
Divina Grace (IRE) 95 [1] (1m 4f, Newj, GF, Aug 3)
Divine Comedy (IRE) 95 [2] (2m 3f 210y, Asco, GF, Jun 18)
First Conquest 95 [1] (1m, Newj, Gd, Jul 13)
Follow Me (FR) 95 [1] (7f, Curr, Gd, May 25)
French Duke (IRE) 95 [2] (1m 3f 211y, Asco, Sft, Sep 7)
Hand Of God 95 [1] (1m 1f 212y, Asco, GF, Jun 22)
Holkham Bay 95 [1] (6f, Asco, Sft, Oct 4)
Kinross 95 [7] (6f, Asco, Sft, Oct 19)
Lmay (IRE) 95 [2] (1m 6f 34y, Asco, GF, Jun 18)
Makarova 95 [7] (5f, Asco, GF, Jun 18)
Make Me King (FR) 95 [6] (7f, Asco, GF, Jul 27)
Mr Professor (IRE) 95 [1] (1m, Donc, Sft, Mar 23)
Sonny Liston (IRE) 95 [2] (1m, Asco, GF, Jun 19)
Sumiha (IRE) 95 [1] (1m 4f, Cork, Gd, Jun 14)
Tarawa (IRE) 95 [1] (1m 1f, Curr, Gd, Aug 31)
Term Of Endearment 95 [1] (1m 6f, Good, GF, Aug 3)
Volterra (IRE) 95 [1] (7f, Asco, Sft, Oct 5)
Yashin (IRE) 95 (2m 56y, Ncsw, SS, Jun 29)
Ancient Wisdom (FR) 94 [2] (1m 2f 56y, York, Gd, May 16)
Aramis Grey (IRE) 94 [2] (6f, Hayd, Gd, Jun 8)
Astro King 94 (1m 2f 56y, York, GS, Jul 13)
Atlantic Coast (IRE) 94 [9] (7f, Leop, Gd, Sep 14)
Beautiful Diamond 94 [3] (5f, Newm, Gd, May 4)
Carrytheone 94 [1] (1m, Asco, Sft, Oct 19)
Dark Trooper (IRE) 94 (6f, Good, GF, Aug 3)
Doha 94 [2] (1m, Sand, Gd, Aug 31)
Fakhama (IRE) 94 [3] (1m 2f 56y, York, GF, Jul 26)
Ferrous (IRE) 94 [1] (6f, Kemw, SS, Apr 6)
Great Generation (IRE) 94 [4] (6f, York, GS, Jul 12)
Imperial Quarter (IRE) 94 [3] (1m, Sand, Gd, Aug 31)
Insanity 94 [1] (1m 3f 211y, Asco, Gd, Aug 10)
Jarraaf 94 [1] (6f, Asco, GF, Aug 10)
Je Zous (IRE) 94 [5] (1m 3f 211y, Asco, GF, Jun 20)
Jordan Electrics 94 [1] (6f 6y, Hami, Gd, Jul 19)
Jubilee Walk 94 [1] (5f, York, Gd, May 17)
Keeper's Heart (IRE) 94 [5] (1m 4f, Curr, Gd, Jun 30)
Lord Melbourne (IRE) 94 [1] (1m 3f 197y, Donc, Sft, Nov 9)
My Mate Mozzie (IRE) 94 [3] (1m 6f 34y, Asco, GF, Jun 18)
No Half Measures 94 [1] (5f 34y, Newb, Hvy, Sep 21)
Old Harrovian 94 [1] (1m 2f 42y, Ncsw, SD, Jan 17)
Paborus 94 [1] (7f 14y, Souw, SD, Oct 17)
Paradias (GER) 94 [1] (1m 1f 11y, Good, GF, Aug 3)
Purosangue 94 [2] (6f, York, GS, Sep 8)
Remaadd (IRE) 94 [7] (1m 2f 56y, York, GS, Jul 13)
Tacarib Bay 94 [5] (6f, Ncsw, SD, Jan 1)
Tees Spirit 94 [1] (5f, Newm, Gd, Apr 18)
Tyrrhenian Sea (IRE) 94 [2] (1m 2f, Linw, SD, Dec 31)
Vintage Clarets 94 [1] (5f, Catt, Sft, Oct 19)
Willem Twee 94 [3] (6f 1y, Linw, SD, Feb 4)
Wonder Legend (IRE) 94 [2] (1m 3f 219y, Kemw, SS, Sep 7)
Adaay In Devon 93 [2] (6f, York, GS, Jul 12)
Arctic Mountain (IRE) 93 [3] (1m 1f 21y, Yarm, GF, Sep 18)
Asian Daze (IRE) 93 [1] (7f, Newj, Gd, Jul 13)
Big Gossey (IRE) 93 [4] (6f, Curr, GF, Aug 17)

87

RACING POST

TOPSPEED: LAST SEASON'S TOP PERFORMERS 3YO+

KEY: Horse name, best Topspeed figure, finishing position when earning figure, (details of race where figure was earned)

Billyjoh 93[3] (6f, Good, GF, Aug 3)
Boiling Point (IRE) 93[4] (1m, Good, GF, Aug 2)
Cerulean Bay (IRE) 93[7] (7f, Leop, Gd, Sep 14)
Crystal Black (IRE) 93[1] (1m 3f 211y, Asco, GF, Jun 21)
Dancing Gemini (IRE) 93[6] (1m 4f 6y, Epso, GS, Jun 1)
Dare To Dream (FR) 93[7] (1m 4f, Curr, Gd, Jul 20)
Elmalka 93[1] (1m, Newm, Gd, May 5)
Enfranchise (IRE) 93[5] (2m 179y, Galw, Yld, Jul 29)
Entrancement (FR) 93[1] (1m 6f, Bath, Hvy, Oct 10)
Evade (FR) 93[1] (7f 3y, Epso, GS, May 31)
Garfield Shadow (IRE) 93[2] (6f, Asco, Sft, Oct 4)
Givemethebeatboys (IRE) 93[1] (6f, Curr, GF, Aug 10)
Glenfinnan (IRE) 93[1] (7f, Sand, Gd, Aug 31)
Go Daddy (IRE) 93[3] (1m 5f 61y, Newb, GF, Aug 17)
Going The Distance (IRE) 93[1] (1m 3f 211y, Asco, GF, Jun 20)
Got To Love A Grey 93[2] (5f, Good, GF, Aug 1)
Grey's Monument 93[1] (7f, Asco, Sft, Sep 7)
James's Delight (IRE) 93[8] (6f, Asco, Sft, Oct 19)
Kingfisher King 93[4] (1m 2f 56y, York, GS, Jul 13)
Kyle Of Lochalsh 93[4] (2m 4f 97y, Good, GF, Aug 2)
La Yakel 93[1] (1m 4f 15y, Hami, Hvy, Aug 23)
Lattam (IRE) 93[2] (1m, Donc, Sft, Mar 23)
Layfayette (IRE) 93[3] (1m 3f 211y, Asco, Sft, Oct 5)
Meydaan (IRE) 93[4] (1m 6f 34y, Asco, GF, Jun 19)
Mount Teide (IRE) 93[1] (1m, Newj, GF, Aug 10)
Onethegutter 93[3] (1m 3f 197y, Donc, Sft, Nov 9)
Poker Face (IRE) 93[1] (1m, Kemw, SS, Dec 4)
Porta Fortuna (IRE) 93[1] (1m, Newj, Gd, Jul 12)
Rainbow Fire (IRE) 93[3] (6f 212y, Hayd, Sft, Apr 27)
River Of Stars (IRE) 93[3] (1m 6f, Good, GF, Aug 3)
Royal Supremacy (IRE) 93[3] (1m 3f 211y, Asco, GF, Jun 21)
Russet Gold 93[2] (6f, Newj, Sft, Aug 24)
Savvy Victory (IRE) 93[2] (1m 1f 209y, Sand, Gd, Jul 5)
She's Quality (IRE) 93[1] (5f, Dowr, Gd, Jun 21)
Strobe (USA) 93[2] (7f, Kemw, SS, Nov 4)
Super Sox 93[1] (7f, Cork, GF, Aug 16)
Tyson Fury 93[2] (1m 6f, Curr, Gd, Jun 5)
Valiant Force (USA) 93[4] (5f, Dunw, SD, Oct 25)
War Rooms (IRE) 93[3] (1m 2f 56y, York, Gd, May 16)
Alflaila 92[4] (1m 1f 212y, Asco, GF, Jun 19)
Arabian Crown (FR) 92[1] (1m 1f 209y, Sand, GS, Apr 26)
Arrest (IRE) 92[2] (1m 4f, Newj, GS, Jul 11)
Booyea (IRE) 92[1] (1m, Curr, Gd, Jun 30)
Checkandchallenge 92[2] (1m, Sand, Gd, Sep 18)
Deauville Legend (IRE) 92[3] (1m 4f, Newj, GF, Jun 29)
Democracy Dilemma (IRE) 92[4] (5f 34y, Newb, Hvy, Sep 21)
Enthralled (USA) 92[1] (1m 1f 21y, Yarm, GF, Sep 18)
Epic Poet (IRE) 92[5] (1m 2f 56y, York, GS, Jul 13)
Heavenly Power (IRE) 92[1] (5f 205y, Naas, Yld, Oct 12)
Houstonn 92[2] (1m 2f, Newb, GF, Aug 17)
Janoobi (IRE) 92[1] (7f, Naas, Hvy, Mar 24)
Kitty Rose 92[2] (1m, Newj, GS, Jul 11)
La Trinidad 92[1] (7f 218y, Thir, Gd, Aug 3)
Marie's Rock (IRE) 92[2] (1m 6f, Bath, Hvy, Oct 10)
Markoon (IRE) 92[1] (1m, Newj, Gd, Jul 19)
Native American (IRE) 92[2] (7f 3y, Epso, GS, May 31)
Nellie Leylax (IRE) 92[1] (1m 37y, Hayd, Sft, May 25)
Never So Brave (IRE) 92[1] (7f, Thir, Sft, Apr 20)
Point Lynas (IRE) 92[1] (7f 192y, York, Gd, May 16)
Quietness 92[1] (1m 4f 23y, Beve, GF, Aug 31)
Rage Of Bamby 92[2] (5f 110y, Ayr, Gd, Sep 20)
Rohaan (IRE) 92[6] (6f, Good, GF, Aug 3)
Room Service (IRE) 92[1] (6f, Pont, Sft, Jul 9)
Samui 92[3] (1m 6f 87y, Ches, Gd, Aug 31)
Shouldvebeenaring 92[2] (6f, York, Gd, May 15)
Socialite (IRE) 92[4] (1m, Newj, GS, Jul 11)

Spiritual (IRE) 92[4] (1m, Sand, Gd, Aug 31)
Star Of Orion (IRE) 92[3] (7f, Sand, Gd, Aug 31)
Stressfree (FR) 92[7] (1m 3f 197y, Donc, Sft, Nov 9)
Terwada (IRE) 92[2] (1m 2f 23y, Yarm, GS, Aug 25)
The Caltonian 92[3] (6f, Ncsw, SS, Aug 22)
Toimy Son (FR) 92[3] (1m 1f, Newm, Sft, Sep 28)
Topgear (FR) 92[1] (7f, Newm, GS, Oct 11)
Trevaunance (IRE) 92[2] (1m 4f, Cork, Gd, Jun 14)
Vantheman (IRE) 92[1] (5f 3y, Pont, Gd, Jul 19)
Zarabanda (IRE) 92[4] (1m 2f 56y, York, GF, Jul 26)
American Affair 91[2] (5f 3y, Pont, GF, Aug 18)
Beamish (FR) 91 (1m 6f 34y, Asco, GF, Jun 18)
Black Run (FR) 91[3] (1m 1f 212y, Asco, GF, Jun 22)
Blues Emperor (IRE) 91[1] (1m, Dunw, SD, Dec 11)
Breege 91[1] (1m 113y, Epso, GS, Jun 1)
Bucanero Fuerte 91[6] (6f, Hayd, Gd, Sep 7)
Cash (IRE) 91[3] (1m, Sand, Gd, Sep 18)
Dancing Tango (IRE) 91[5] (1m 6f, Good, GF, Aug 3)
Dawn Rising (IRE) 91[5] (2m 170y, Curr, Gd, Sep 29)
Diego Velazquez (IRE) 91[1] (1m 1f, Leop, Gd, Jul 18)
Easy (IRE) 91[1] (6f, Cork, Hvy, Mar 30)
Equilateral 91[2] (6f, Kemw, SS, Oct 2)
Fairbanks 91[4] (1m 6f 87y, Ches, Gd, Aug 31)
Fairy Glen (FR) 91[3] (1m 4f, Newj, GF, Aug 3)
Frost At Dawn (USA) 91[3] (5f 110y, Ayr, Gd, Sep 20)
Holloway Boy 91[1] (1m 37y, Hayd, Gd, Sep 7)
Jumby (IRE) 91[3] (7f, Newj, GF, Aug 10)
Marine Wave (IRE) 91[4] (5f 110y, Ayr, Gd, Sep 20)
Metier (IRE) 91[8] (2m 179y, Galw, Yld, Jul 29)
Miss Cynthia 91[3] (2m 50y, Sand, Gd, Jul 5)
Mondo Man 91[4] (1m 3f 211y, Asco, GF, Jun 21)
Oliver Show (IRE) 91[3] (7f 3y, Yarm, GF, Jul 25)
Ostraka (IRE) 91[1] (5f, Dunw, SD, Oct 25)
Padishakh (FR) 91[2] (1m, Ayr, GF, Sep 21)
Pappano 91[3] (1m 6f 34y, Asco, Sft, Oct 4)
Place Of Safety (IRE) 91[2] (1m 4f, Newj, GF, Aug 3)
Ramatuelle (USA) 91[3] (1m, Newm, Gd, May 5)
Relentless Voyager 91[1] (1m 4f 6y, Epso, GS, Jun 1)
Rogue Lightning (IRE) 91[2] (5f, York, GS, Jul 13)
Spartan Army (IRE) 91[3] (2m 56y, Ncsw, SD, Mar 29)
Spirit Mixer 91[1] (1m 7f 196y, Ches, Sft, Sep 14)
Street Kid (IRE) 91[1] (7f 36y, Wolw, SD, Mar 16)
Toca Madera (IRE) 91[3] (5f, Good, GF, Aug 1)
Tony Montana 91[3] (1m 2f 56y, York, GS, Jul 13)
Vaguely Royal (IRE) 91[3] (1m 7f 169y, Linw, SD, Mar 1)
Village Voice 91[4] (1m 3f 133y, Asco, Sft, Oct 19)
Witch Hunter (FR) 91[3] (1m, Asco, Sft, Oct 19)
Woolhampton (IRE) 91[1] (5f, Asco, Sft, Sep 7)
Yosemite Valley 91[2] (6f, Cork, Hvy, Mar 30)
Allonsy 90[2] (1m 6f 34y, Asco, Sft, Oct 4)
Audience 90[1] (1m, Newb, Gd, May 18)
Battle Cry (IRE) 90[1] (7f 30y, Leop, Hvy, Apr 7)
Bedford Flyer (IRE) 90[3] (5f 6y, Linw, SD, Dec 31)
Bergerac (IRE) 90[3] (6f, Ayr, GF, Sep 21)
Chally Chute (IRE) 90[2] (1m 4f, Galw, Sft, Aug 2)
Chemistry (IRE) 90[2] (1m 5f, Leop, Gd, Sep 14)
Coachella (FR) 90[4] (6f 1y, Linw, SD, Feb 4)
Danielle 90[6] (1m 3f 211y, Asco, GF, Jun 20)
Dream Harder (IRE) 90[2] (1m 3f 211y, Asco, Gd, Aug 10)
Duke Of Oxford 90[3] (2m 56y, Ncsw, SS, Jun 29)
Dunum (IRE) 90[3] (7f, Galw, Hvy, Aug 4)
Earls (IRE) 90[1] (6f 212y, Hayd, Sft, Apr 27)
Ejaabiyah 90[5] (1m 2f 56y, York, GF, Jul 26)
Fivethousandtoone (IRE) 90[2] (6f, Ncsw, SD, Jan 1)
Forest Fairy 90[3] (1m 6f, Bath, Hvy, Oct 10)
Gentleman Joe 90[5] (1m 6f 34y, Asco, GF, Jun 18)
Gleneagle Bay (IRE) 90[2] (7f, Leop, Gd, Sep 14)
Glor Tire (IRE) 90[1] (1m, Leop, Gd, Jun 6)

88

TOPSPEED: LAST SEASON'S TOP PERFORMERS 3YO+

KEY: Horse name, best Topspeed figure, finishing position when earning figure, (details of race where figure was earned)

Going Remote (IRE) 90[7] (1m 5f 188y, York, GF, Aug 24)
Hiya Maite 90[2] (5f 3y, Pont, Gd, Jul 19)
Hurricane Ivor (IRE) 90[1] (7f, Curr, Gd, May 24)
Ice Max 90[1] (1m 2y, Muss, GS, Apr 21)
Jer Batt (IRE) 90[2] (5f, Hayd, Gd, Sep 7)
Kamboo (IRE) 90[1] (1m 4f 98y, Ncsw, SS, Aug 22)
Korker (IRE) 90[3] (6f, Ayr, GF, Sep 21)
La Pasionaria 90[6] (1m 2f, Newm, GS, Oct 5)
Lion's Pride 90[3] (1m 1f 209y, Sand, Gd, Jul 5)
Love De Vega (IRE) 90[2] (1m 3ty, Wind, GF, Aug 15)
Master Milliner (IRE) 90[1] (2m 4f 97y, Good, GF, Aug 2)
Maxux (IRE) 90[2] (1m 2f, Curr, Hvy, Apr 20)
Mega Force (IRE) 90[5] (1m 3f 211y, Asco, GF, Jun 20)
Miaharris 90[4] (5f 10y, Sand, Gd, Apr 26)
Mickley (IRE) 90[1] (1m, Asco, GF, Jun 20)
Nakheel (FR) 90[3] (1m 3f 188y, York, GF, Aug 22)
Native Warrior 90[2] (1m 1f 11y, Good, GF, Aug 3)
Prague (IRE) 90[2] (1m 37y, Hayd, Gd, Sep 7)
Prime Art (IRE) 90[5] (6f, York, GS, Jul 12)
Relief Rally (IRE) 90[2] (5f 34y, Newb, Hvy, Sep 21)
Sakti (IRE) 90[4] (1m 1f, Curr, Gd, Aug 31)
Scarlett O'hara (FR) 90[3] (1m 4f, Cork, Gd, Jun 14)
Serene Seraph (IRE) 90[1] (7f 1y, Linw, SD, Aug 13)
Serious Challenge (IRE) 90[3] (1m 6f, Curr, Gd, Jun 5)
Sir Busker (IRE) 90[3] (1m 2f 42y, Ncsw, SD, Jan 1)
Spirit Genie (IRE) 90[1] (7f 37y, Hayd, Hvy, Sep 27)
Sturlasson (IRE) 90[2] (5f, Epso, GS, Jun 1)
Sunchart 90[1] (1m 2f 98y, Naas, Hvy, Mar 24)
Tempus 90[2] (1m, Newj, GS, Jul 11)
Theoryofeverything 90[1] (1m 1f 35y, Hami, Sft, Aug 13)
Thunder Blue 90[2] (6f, Ncsw, SS, Aug 22)
Too Friendly 90[4] (2m 56y, Ncsw, SS, Jun 29)
Treasure 90[2] (1m 2f, Newm, GS, Oct 5)
Voyage 90[3] (1m 2f, Newb, GF, Aug 17)
Zero Carbon (FR) 90[3] (6f, Kemw, SS, Oct 2)
Accidental Agent 89[3] (7f, Kemw, SS, Nov 6)
Ahlain 89[2] (7f 1y, Linw, SD, Aug 13)
Aragon Castle (IRE) 89[1] (1m, Ayr, GF, Sep 21)
Art Power (IRE) 89[5] (6f, York, Gd, May 15)
Assail (IRE) 89[1] (1m 3f 219y, Kemw, SS, Sep 7)
Bracken's Laugh (IRE) 89[5] (1m 2f, Wind, Sft, Aug 24)
Dark Vintage (IRE) 89[6] (5f, Asco, GF, Jun 21)
Eagle's Way 89[1] (1m 4f, Galw, Sft, Aug 2)
Electric Storm (IRE) 89[3] (5f, Dunw, SD, Oct 25)
Emaraaty Ana 89[8] (5f, Asco, GF, Jun 18)
Estrange (IRE) 89[1] (1m 1f 197y, Good, Sft, Aug 25)
Evaluation 89[2] (2m 56y, Ncsw, SS, Jun 29)
Flying Frontier 89[1] (1m 1f 209y, Sand, Gd, Aug 31)

Galileo Dame (IRE) 89[2] (1m 4f, Curr, Yld, Nov 3)
Grateful (IRE) 89[6] (1m 6f, Good, GF, Aug 3)
Gunzburg (IRE) 89[3] (7f, Curr, Gd, May 25)
Havana Blue 89[4] (7f, Leop, Gd, Sep 14)
Hot Fuss (IRE) 89[2] (1m 1f 197y, Good, Sft, Aug 24)
James Mchenry 89[2] (1m 1f, Newm, Sft, Sep 28)
Jasour 89[3] (6f, Asco, GF, Jun 21)
Key To Cotai (IRE) 89[1] (7f, Newm, Gd, May 4)
Kikkuli 89[2] (7f, Asco, GF, Jun 22)
Leuven Power (IRE) 89[2] (1m, Asco, GS, Jul 12)
Lexington Belle (IRE) 89[3] (7f 37y, Hayd, Hvy, Sep 27)
Long Tradition (IRE) 89[5] (1m 1f 21y, Yarm, GF, Sep 18)
Magical Zoe (IRE) 89[1] (1m 5f 188y, York, GF, Aug 24)
Makanah 89[4] (5f, Newm, Gd, Apr 16)
Matters Most 89[2] (6f 12y, Wind, GF, Jun 3)
Metabolt 89[1] (1m 3ty, Wind, GF, Jun 17)
Metal Merchant (IRE) 89[4] (7f, Asco, GF, Jul 27)
Michaela's Boy (IRE) 89[3] (5f 34y, Newb, GF, Aug 17)
Naqeeb (IRE) 89 (1m 6f 34y, Asco, GF, Jun 18)
Noble Dynasty 89[1] (7f, Newm, Gd, May 3)
Notre Belle Bete 89[1] (1m 113y, Epso, GS, May 31)
Ombudsman (IRE) 89[1] (1m, Newj, GF, Jun 22)
Orazio (IRE) 89[3] (6f, Asco, GF, Jun 22)
Popmaster (IRE) 89[3] (1m, Kemw, SS, Dec 4)
Qirat 89[2] (7f, Asco, Sft, Oct 5)
Rocket Rodney 89[9] (6f, Good, GF, Aug 3)
Salt Bay (GER) 89[4] (1m 5f 188y, York, GS, Jul 13)
Sergeant Wilko (IRE) 89[1] (6f, Good, GS, Aug 25)
Shining Jewel 89[2] (1m 4f, Newj, GF, Jul 20)
Silver Samurai 89[2] (7f, Kemw, SS, Jan 31)
Skysail 89[1] (1m, Good, Gd, Jun 7)
Solomon 89[1] (1m 2f 42y, Hayd, Gd, Aug 4)
Sound Angela 89[5] (1m 2f 56y, York, GF, Aug 23)
Stag Night (IRE) 89[1] (5f, Cork, Hvy, Mar 30)
Strike Red (IRE) 89[6] (6f, Good, GF, Aug 3)
Sweet Memories (IRE) 89[4] (1m 3f 175y, Hayd, Gd, Jul 6)
The Bell Conductor (IRE) 89[1] (4f 214y, Souw, SD, Jan 23)
The Reverend 89[1] (1m 3f 211y, Asco, Sft, Sep 7)
Thunder Moor (IRE) 89[1] (4f 214y, Souw, SD, Aug 29)
Thunder Roll (IRE) 89[5] (1m 3f 133y, Asco, Sft, Oct 19)
True Legend (IRE) 89[5] (2m 56y, Ncsw, SS, Jun 29)
Uxmal (IRE) 89[1] (2m 5f 143y, Asco, GF, Jun 22)
Vafortino (IRE) 89[6] (6f, Asco, GF, Jun 22)
Venture Capital 89[3] (5f, Asco, Sft, Oct 5)
Wiltshire 89[1] (6f, Ncsw, SS, Jun 29)
Adjuvant (IRE) 88[9] (1m 3f 197y, Donc, Sft, Nov 9)
Al Barez 88[1] (6f, Kemw, SS, Apr 1)
Al Riffa (FR) 88[2] (1m 1f 209y, Sand, Sft, Jul 6)
Ambiente Amigo 88[4] (1m 4f, Newj, GF, Aug 3)
Aratus (IRE) 88[3] (7f, Kemw, SS, Jan 31)

THE EXPERTS

VIEW FROM IRELAND DAVID JENNINGS

Can Lion roar and become next Troy?

THE burning question on everyone's lips ahead of the forthcoming Flat season is whether another City Of Troy is lurking in the long grass at Ballydoyle.

This time last year his Triple Crown bid was the main topic of conversation no matter where you went and you weren't getting juicy odds about him achieving the mammoth feat either. He only managed to land one leg of it in the end – the most important one in the Derby – but his topsy-turvy campaign was the main narrative throughout the whole season right up until his almighty flop at Del Mar. Now we want another City Of Troy.

The only real candidate to fill the role is **The Lion In Winter**. He is a strapping son of Sea The Stars and won both his starts handsomely at two, but wasn't seen after a dominant display in the Acomb Stakes at York's Ebor festival. That power-packed performance oozed class and everything about him screamed Derby.

The Lion In Winter had been odds-on to hand Aidan O'Brien a record ninth win in the Dewhurst – a race he won with Rock Of Gibraltar (2001), Beethoven (2009), War Command (2013), Air Force Blue (2015), Churchill (2016), U S Navy Flag (2017), St Mark's Basilica (2020) and City Of Troy (2023) – but a bruised foot on the morning of the race scuppered those hopes and left the door ajar for Godolphin to strike with Shadow Of Light.

The Lion In Winter was devastating in midsummer in a Curragh maiden. Talk about exploding on to the scene. It looked a hot contest beforehand and he was up against a pair of experienced rivals, but he produced a scintillating turn of foot to gun down Currawood and stablemate Ides Of March, now rated 108. In doing so, he defied an in-running high of 28-1 on the Betfair Exchange.

O'Brien had some nice things to say afterwards, too. "He's a lovely horse and had been working lovely. He'll have no problem going up in trip but he has plenty of class."

We certainly saw that class in the Acomb. It was billed as a big showdown between Coolmore and Godolphin as The Lion In Winter took on Ruling Court, but we didn't get the humdinger we expected as the Irish challenger was in a different league. The further he went the better he looked.

Words like uncomplicated and straightforward were the ones O'Brien opted for this time before suggesting he "always thought he'd get further than seven". The master trainer added: "He's not short of pace but you'd imagine he'd get further than a mile and a quarter."

That suggests the Derby is the ultimate aim for The Lion In Winter and he is currently no bigger than 5-1 to provide O'Brien with a third win in a row in the famous Epsom Classic and an 11th win in all. Is it value? Possibly.

Given the way he relaxes and how hard he hit the line over seven furlongs as a juvenile, the trip should pose no problem. His pedigree suggests the same. The dam, What A Home, was a close-up third in the Pinnacle

Stakes at Haydock back in 2018 over 1m4f and her final start was over 1m6f at Goodwood. Staying was her game.

The Lion In Winter appears to have the perfect temperament for Epsom. From the two pieces of evidence we have seen so far, the occasion doesn't look like it will get to him. In fact, he could thrive on the big day.

The 2,000 Guineas has been a tale of woe for the Ballydoyle big guns for the last two seasons. Auguste Rodin and Little Big Bear were both badly beaten in the driving rain back in 2023 and we all know what happened to City Of Troy last year, so it will be fascinating to see whether O'Brien sticks to the same route for The Lion In Winter.

If he does swerve Newmarket with him, who would replace him? Dewhurst runner-up **Expanded**, who got within a neck of Shadow Of Light in the Dewhurst, would be a potential replacement, but he doesn't have the same sort of swagger as The Lion In Winter. Then there is

Twain, a Wootton Bassett colt who is a half-brother to Just Wonderful and seemed to shock everyone when running away with a Leopardstown maiden in the autumn by six lengths under 3lb claimer Mark Crehan. It looked as though it might be a fluke but those of us who thought it was were left with egg on our faces when he came out eight days later and landed the Criterium International at Saint-Cloud fair and square. It was emphatic.

This time he was ridden with more restraint but, once he got clear daylight a furlong and a half out, there was only going to be one winner and he galloped right to the line for a comfortable victory over stablemate Mount Kilimanjaro.

It is those three colts – The Lion In Winter, Expanded and Twain – who look the most likely Ballydoyle representatives to take 2025 by storm, but only one of them has the X factor and that is your Acomb winner of last year.

Aidan's son Joseph will be readying **Scorthy Champ** for a crack at a Classic. The Mehmas colt is two from three and left us with a big impression over the winter having

stormed to victory in the National Stakes on day two of the Irish Champions Festival at the Curragh. He may have been 12-1 on the day but his trainer was not one bit surprised by the performance. Far from it, in fact.

"I thought it was very impressive," urged O'Brien. "Dylan [Browne McMonagle] said he idled in front and that he is a top-notcher."

He looked it and he is priced between 12-1 and 16-1 for the 2,000 Guineas. There must be a chance he stays at home and waits for the Irish equivalent, though.

And, what about the ageless Jessica Harrington? Could 2025 be the year she breaks her Derby duck? Stranger things have happened.

Hotazhell showed an attitude to die for when battling back to beat Delacroix in the Futurity Trophy at the backend of the season at Doncaster, scoring by a nose under Shane Foley, and odds of 33-1 for the Epsom showpiece look a bit of a bargain.

As usual, there are a whole host of potential top-class three-year-old fillies at Ballydoyle. Breeders' Cup heroine **Lake Victoria** sits on top of most people's pecking order but what **Fairy Godmother** did in the Albany Stakes was extraordinary. There is surely no way she should be almost treble the price of her more esteemed stablemate.

Ger Lyons has some fabulous fillies to go to war with this season and **Red Letter** might just be the best of them.

Time and time again, Lyons told us we wouldn't see the best of her until she turned three, but she wasn't half bad at two and was only a length and a half behind Lake Victoria in the Moyglare Stud Stakes at the Curragh in September when everything went wrong.

She's a beautiful specimen and there are far worse 20-1 shots than her for both the 1,000 Guineas and the Oaks. If she makes either of those, she's a proper player.

Babouche and **Chantez** are two other three-year-old fillies from the same stable who could cut the mustard at the top level.

Finally, last word must go to the king. **Kyprios** has won two Gold Cups already and a third one in 2025 should be a mere formality. Is he better than Yeats? Probably. Could he even win an Arc? Possibly. Maybe this is the year O'Brien lets the standout stayer of his generation have a go on the biggest stage of all at Longchamp.

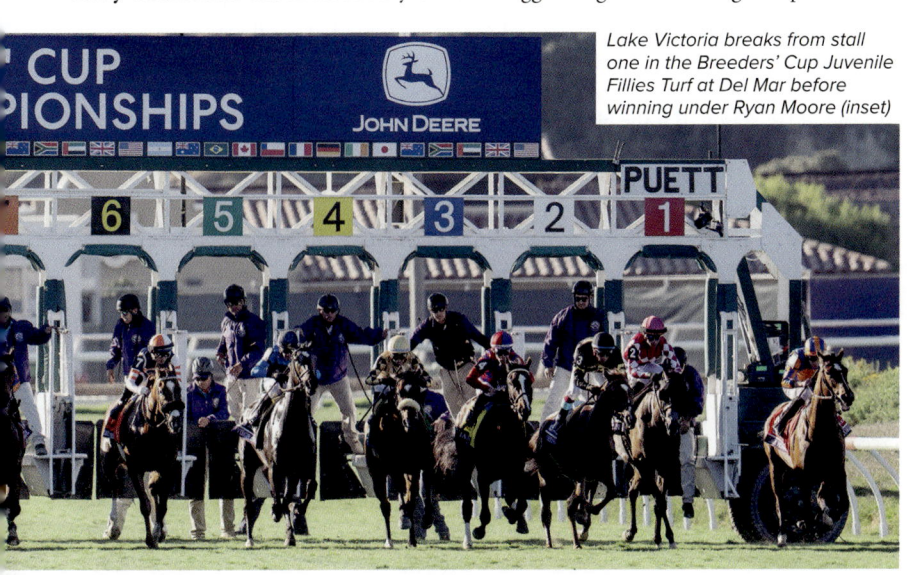

Lake Victoria breaks from stall one in the Breeders' Cup Juvenile Fillies Turf at Del Mar before winning under Ryan Moore (inset)

ANTE-POST ANALYSIS NICK WATTS

50-1 Wimbledon looks big value to serve it up to better fancied rivals

IT makes a nice change going into this year that the first Classic of the season, the 2,000 Guineas, is unusually open, with bookies going 6-1 the field.

The Lion In Winter is favourite, but he hasn't been sighted since landing the Group 3 Acomb Stakes at York in August so there's a fair amount that has to be taken on trust.

Occasionally the Acomb can throw up a good one – Chaldean won it in 2022 before taking the 2,000 Guineas the following year – but it's not normally a race to hang your hat on when you are looking for Classic winners.

Shadow Of Light is next in the betting and his form credentials are more solid as he won the Middle Park and Dewhurst towards the backend of last season. But the big question with him is whether he will stay a mile. Of his five starts last season, four were over 6f, and he had to be supplemented to run in the Dewhurst so it wasn't originally on his radar.

His breeding suggests he might struggle to get the mile so for that reason he is passed over, but who can win?

The one I like is John and Thady Gosden's **Field Of Gold**, who can be backed at 33-1. The son of Kingman was a good rather than exceptional juvenile but he did enough to give hope for the season ahead.

A good third behind Grade 1 winner New Century at Doncaster on his debut in June, he then won his next two starts, at Newmarket, and then the Solario Stakes at Sandown.

On the former occasion he thrashed Group 3 winner Starzintheireyes, with the Group 1-placed Mount Kilimanjaro back in third.

The Solario form didn't work out as well, but Field Of Gold did win easily, and it is a race the Gosdens tend to target with their best.

The reason he is such a big price is because of his apparent failure in the Lagardere at Longchamp on his final start of the campaign. However, he didn't run badly in fourth behind Camille Pissarro, racing keenly before flattening out inside the final furlong.

The soft ground wouldn't have been in his favour, but it has given him more experience and he should be able to kick on this spring. He is exciting, and if he wins his trial he will get popular in the market again very quickly.

The 1,000 Guineas has a stronger favourite in Lake Victoria, and it is hard to pick holes in her chances after a faultless two-year-old campaign which saw her win five times from as many starts.

She took the Cheveley Park in the autumn before going to America and taking the Breeders' Cup Juvenile Fillies Turf. The only thing not to like about her is the price as she is already 3-1 – and there will be plenty coming out of the woodwork this spring.

One of those, I am hoping, is Lake Victoria's Ballydoyle stable companion, **Giselle**.

She had a stop-start juvenile season, making her debut at Leopardstown in June but not returning to the track until four months later, where she won easily at the Curragh.

On the back of that she was made market leader for a Group 3 on her final start of the campaign, but was unable to justify favouritism, finishing third behind Whirl. That was disappointing on the face of it, but Ryan Moore wasn't hard on her and the experience should have done her a lot of good.

Having missed a vast chunk of the season, she had to do a lot in a short space of time, and that third run will stand her in good stead when she reappears this spring.

By Frankel out of Breeders' Cup winner Newspaperofrecord, Giselle has been spoken of very highly by Aidan O'Brien and odds of 25-1 look attractive.

Moving on to Epsom, and we have the familiar name of The Lion In Winter as Derby favourite. He is the only horse quoted in single figures and it is 20-1 bar, so there's some great value out there and one whom I like – his price ranges between 25-1 and 50-1 – is **Wimbledon Hawkeye**, trained by James Owen.

He finished second to The Lion In Winter in the Acomb, beaten a shade under two lengths, and then went on to take the Royal Lodge in comfortable style on his next outing.

Last time out he finished only third in the Futurity at Doncaster behind Hotazhell, quite well beaten at the line, but he was a bit keen that day in soft conditions and he did stay on well to the line.

On better ground he would have been a different horse, and the effort doesn't detract from the generally positive impression he made as a juvenile.

Owen has shown in a short space of time what a capable operator he is, and based on his York form alone there is no way he should be as big as 50-1.

It's 10-1 the field for the Oaks with Lake Victoria the current favourite. The Fillies' Mile winner Desert Flower is next in, available at a best price of 12-1. She ought to stay and is a big danger, but at twice the price I prefer the Aidan O'Brien-trained **Dreamy**.

She was beaten a long way by Desert Flower at Newmarket, but O'Brien was very unsure beforehand as to whether to let her take her chance in that contest, and the main reason he did so was to add to her experience ahead of this season.

It is not a performance to take literally, and before that she had done everything right, winning at Goodwood on her debut before landing a Group 3 at the Curragh on her next outing in good fashion.

She is by American Pharoah out of a Yorkshire Oaks winner in Tapestry, so middle distances will suit her very well, and it is best to remember her first two starts rather than marking her down for that late-season defeat at Newmarket.

Finally, the St Leger, which seems an awfully long way off, has been priced up by Unibet and one who is of some interest is the David Menuisier-trained filly **Janey Mackers**.

The daughter of New Bay started out at Yarmouth in October, finishing a promising third before putting it all together at Doncaster next time, thrashing Rock Camelot by over five lengths.

By New Bay out of a Montjeu mare, she should stay no problem and has been mentioned by her trainer for an Oaks or Prix de Diane bid. She could be very good and her quote of 40-1 could look big.

RACING POST

MY TEN TO FOLLOW RICHARD BIRCH

From American Affair to Wisper – ten to score on the smaller stages

SPRING is in the air, and Flat racing aficionados are counting the days to the Lincoln with growing vigour. Getting into the spirit, I have spent an enjoyable couple of days compiling a list of ten horses to follow for the 2025 turf season . . .

AMERICAN AFFAIR Jim Goldie

This talented sprinter improved with almost every run in 2024, highlighted by a last-gasp success in the Portland at Doncaster.

Poorly placed and short of room under two furlongs out, he had to be switched twice before producing a stunning burst of speed to nail Apollo One.

He was officially rated 92 that day and, judged on the manner of victory, will have no trouble bridging the gap between top handicaps and Listed/Group races this term.

American Affair boasts a very high cruising speed and the family improves with age. The best is yet to come.

BAILEYS KHELSTAR Charlie Johnston

Baileys Khelstar looked a much-improved model from three to four when making an impressive winning seasonal reappearance at Southwell over 1m6f last April.

He beat his six rivals senseless that day, and duly justified 11-10 favouritism when following up under a 5lb penalty at Ascot.

Baileys Khelstar appealed strongly at the

time as a typical, improving Charlie Johnston stayer who would run at many of the big meetings in valuable handicaps at 1m6f or 2m, and bag one or two.

However, things didn't pan out like that, and he was restricted to just two more runs, disappointing on his final start at Yarmouth in July.

If the Baileys Khelstar of early last season returns, he can resume his progress off 83.

ECTOCROSS Simon Dow

Ectocross showed improved form during the second half of the 2023 season, landing a valuable Nottingham final over 1m2f.

He seems to act on any ground, but his ability to sluice through deep mud makes him one to keep firmly onside for the autumn.

Ectocross was gelded at the end of 2023 and only ran four times in 2024, performing well below his best on each occasion.

As a result, he starts 2025 off a mark just 1lb higher than when scoring at Nottingham.

HK FOURTEEN Tony Carroll

This big, backward type was punted from 25-1 to 11-4 when opening his account at the fifth attempt at Bath last October.

Firmly on top at the finish, HK Fourteen also won his next two starts at Newcastle to complete a quick-fire hat-trick.

The five-year-old sprinter is still only rated 64 and, with further improvement almost certain, there will be abundant opportunities at the likes of Bath and Brighton for him in 2025.

LETSBEFRANK Jim Goldie

What's not to like about this lightly raced, highly progressive stayer?

Winner of three of his last five starts, this slow-to-mature five-year-old promises to reach his peak this season, and a mark of 78 is unlikely to prove his ceiling.

The son of Frankel gives the impression he could well develop into a leading contender for the Cesarewitch, and ought to bag at least a couple of 2m handicaps before then.

He is primarily about stamina, but doesn't lack tactical speed.

MIGHTY QUIET Harry Charlton

After three qualifying runs for handicaps,

American Affair (left): winner of the Portland at Doncaster can improve again

RACING POST

Mighty Quiet came alive when opening her account off a mark of 64 at Bath in October.

Equipped with a first-time tongue tie, the daughter of Ulysses made all, maintaining a relentless gallop over 1m2f on soft ground to slam solid yardstick Meet Me In Meraki by two and three-quarter lengths.

Her stable excels in bringing handicappers through the ranks, and Mighty Quiet is emphatically one to follow as she progresses from her low base.

SACRED FALLS Katie Scott

A strike-rate of just two wins from 20 starts might be alarming to some, but I'm adamant Sacred Falls will come good at some point and rack up a sequence.

The way in which this sprinter travels through her races strongly suggests she possesses far more ability than an official mark of 68 suggests.

Katie Scott's sprinter simply bolted up off 66 at Carlisle last May, but failed to build on that and lost her next seven starts.

I have a hunch 2025 will be her year.

SHAW PARK Scott Dixon

When you watch a horse come down the hill at Brighton, it's easy to spot those who love it and those who hate it.

Shaw Park absolutely adores the contours of Race Hill. He never changes his stride pattern; he is a Brighton natural.

Scott Dixon placed him to win three Brighton handicaps over 7f last summer off marks of 62, 65 and 69.

Owing to a stack of defeats away from the Sussex track, Shaw Park goes into the 2025 turf campaign on 64.

It wouldn't surprise me if he manages to repeat last year's feat of three Brighton wins.

UNCLE DICK Eve Johnson Houghton

Uncle Dick is the archetypal Brighton specialist; he is a stone better at that track than anywhere else.

He enjoyed the crowning moment of another splendid summer at the seaside when landing the valuable Brighton Mile, unleashing his trademark finishing burst to catch Lunatick in the last two strides.

All seven of Uncle Dick's Brighton wins have been achieved at a mile, but he does stay 1m2f and that opens up further options.

Oliver Carmichael, one of only two apprentices who properly caught my eye last year as potentially the real deal – Tom Kiely-Marshall being the other – has a great rapport with Uncle Dick.

WISPER Marcus Tregoning

At the end of last year I was asked by the Racing Post news editor to come up with a big-race winner for 2025.

I immediately thought, 'Wisper for the Class 3 fillies' handicap at Brighton on April 29', but the fact there wasn't ante-post betting on the race meant I couldn't choose her.

A five-time Brighton winner, Wisper finished second in that Class 3 in 2024 off a mark of 84. She won the race 12 months earlier off 82.

She is rated 85, and is my bet of the year.

Sacred Falls: appeals as one who could run up a sequence when clicking

Injured Jockeys Fund

We are here
to help you all

Flat Jockeys
(including Apprentices)

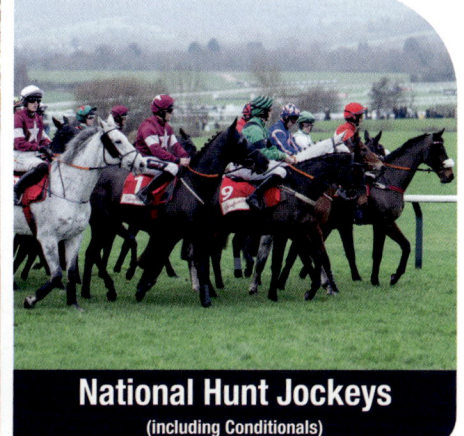

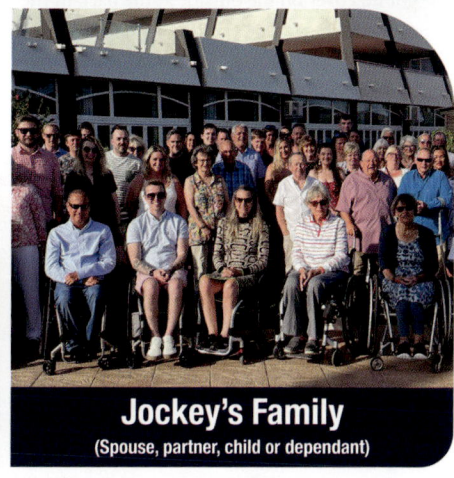

National Hunt Jockeys
(including Conditionals)

Amateur and Point-to-Point Jockeys

Jockey's Family
(Spouse, partner, child or dependant)

www.ijf.org.uk • 01638 662246

Compassion • Care • Support

Injured Jockeys Fund (Registered Charity No. 1107395)

NAMES TO MAKE IT PAY PAUL KEALY

The horses to side with throughout the season

ACAPULCO BAY Aidan O'Brien

There are obviously loads of lightly raced Aidan O'Brien-trained juveniles from last year to pick out, but Acapulco Bay might be one of the less obvious ones as he never ran outside of maiden company.

On his first outing at the Curragh he was clear stable second string to the well-touted Delacroix, who duly won by a length and three quarters, but there was major promise in his second place.

By Dubawi out of a sister to the top-class Magic Wand (won Ribblesdale and a Grade 1 in Australia among others), Acapulco Bay got no cover on the outside at the back in the early stages, but settled well enough, although got caught flat-footed when they first started to quicken. Once he got the message, though, he powered down the outside for second to a horse who finished the season rated 116, having run second in the Futurity Trophy at Doncaster.

Acapulco Bay ran only once more, and had clearly learned plenty as he made all this time and ran out a comfortable winner from stablemate Genealogy. This time he was the one with the advantage of a previous run, but the second has done his bit for the form by winning next time and earning a rating of 95, while the third is rated 99.

Acapulco Bay will definitely get 1m2f this season and, with his dam a winner and Group-placed at 1m6f, there's every chance he'll get 1m4f.

ALMERAQ William Haggas

Another who raced just twice as a juvenile, in this case not starting until the autumn at Newbury. On that debut he was a highly encouraging second to Fast Track Harry, one of three horses who seemed to have the advantage of track position down the middle.

Despite running green just over a furlong out, he edged back out to the middle and closed nicely to get within three-quarters of a length of the winner, who raced widest of all.

While the winner did not cut any ice in Listed company subsequently, the third, who raced on the same side as Almeraq, won next time and was awarded a rating of 87, so there are reasons to be positive about the form.

Almeraq had certainly learned from the experience himself, as just under four weeks later he ran out an impressive winner at Yarmouth, scoring by three and three-quarter lengths.

It's fair to say he didn't beat much, but he was in a class of his own, and jockey Jim Crowley said the feel he gave him was exciting, although he may always want plenty of cut in the ground. His pedigree suggests he's a sprinter through and through, and he might take high rank in that division among his age group.

ASUKA George Boughey

A close relation of Boiling Point, who was beaten a short head in Group 3 company as a juvenile and won the Listed King Charles

Stakes for Roger Varian last season, this one is with George Boughey.

The son of Night Of Thunder has raced only once, and he looked in a class of his own in a 15-runner 6f Newmarket maiden in August, bursting clear just over a furlong out and winning by just over four lengths.

Quite what he achieved given the short-priced favourite Beccali could manage only seventh remains to be seen, but that one has won since and is now rated 82, while fourth-placed Qetaifan has a rating of 85.

Asuka is clearly going to stay at least another furlong and, while it's always a slight worry that a maiden winner in August is not seen again that season, he gave the impression he is going to be at least as good as his sibling.

Cathedral (left) finishes runner-up in the Oh So Sharp Stakes at Newmarket

CATHEDRAL Ralph Beckett

Cathedral cost Amo Racing a punchy €800,000 at the Arqana Breeze-up Sales in May, but that's hardly surprising given her pedigree and she looks well on the way to repaying her owners' faith in her.

By Too Darn Hot out of an unraced Frankel mare who had already produced two decent winners (RPRs 101 and 103), this filly was all the rage for her September debut on the all-weather at Lingfield and, despite showing signs of greenness when losing her position briefly three furlongs out, she powered down the outside, cutting back the deficit on the Godolphin-owned second favourite in a matter of strides and going on to score by just over four lengths.

Her next assignment came in the Group 3 Oh So Sharp Stakes and, while she was a beaten 3-1 favourite in an open race, she again showed bundles of promise in going down by half a length to the Aidan O'Brien-trained Merrily. The winner was a 25-1 outsider, but had miles more experience and had been Group-placed already. In any case, Beckett has always seen her as a filly for this season rather than last, and it won't be a surprise if she leaves that form behind.

EXPANDED Aidan O'Brien

Another Coolmore horse, but this one has already dipped his toe into top company. A son of Wootton Bassett, he didn't make his debut until the first week in October, and he had to work hard enough to beat stablemate First Wave by a neck, recording an RPR of 85, which is respectable but nothing out of the ordinary for an O'Brien debutant.

It was somewhat surprising, then, that Expanded was thrown into the Group 1 Dewhurst Stakes at Newmarket just seven days later as a second string to favourite The Lion In Winter. He became first string when that one was taken out, and almost caused a surprise when splitting the Charlie Appleby-trained pair Shadow Of Light and Ancient Truth, the three of them separated by a neck and the same.

It's true the Dewhurst probably wasn't a vintage running with The Lion In Winter missing, but it was a massive improvement in the space of a week by a horse who showed a good attitude to win the tussle on the near side with Ancient Truth and was just pegged back by Shadow Of Light, who raced in the centre and joined them late.

GUIDE TO THE FLAT **2025**

Expanded goes to post in the Group 1 Dewhurst Stakes at Newmarket, in which he finished second to Shadow Of Light (inset second left)

A Racing Post Rating of 113 for a horse going that close to winning a juvenile Group 1 is not great, but it's actually exceptional for a horse having only his second start so quickly after the first.

Since 2009 just seven other juveniles in Britain have run to a figure of 110 or higher within two weeks of their debuts, and only three of those did so when making their debuts in September or later. One of those was Lyric Of Light, who won the Fillies' Mile on her third start, and the other two were Magna Grecia and Night Of Thunder, who both won the 2,000 Guineas.

Even just slight improvement, which you'd hope for, is going to make him a major contender at Newmarket in May.

GALLANT Andrew Balding

Gallant showed only modest form on his Salisbury debut in August, finishing fifth of 12, but Andrew Balding has never been the type to rush his juveniles and they always tend to improve with experience.

That was very much the case next time on the all-weather at Kempton in early October, as he put up a professional performance in a first-time tongue-tie to see off 5-4 favourite West Acre by a length and three-quarters.

It's hard to rate the bare form of that effort particularly highly (he earned an RPR of 88), especially as West Acre was conceding 7lb, but the form has worked out very well and the son of Hello Youmzain could find himself well treated when going into handicaps. The runner-up finished his juvenile campaign with a six-length win at Southwell, and has since gone to Meydan, finishing second first time out and then running away with a Group 2, while the 50-1 third has won twice since and is now rated 87.

Hello Youmzain has produced a few decent sprinters already, but Gallant should stay at least 7f and may get a mile, and could have a decent future.

KIND OF BLUE James Fanshawe

One of only two older horses in this list, and hardly unexposed given he won the Champions Sprint at Ascot and finished second in the Sprint Cup at Haydock, but there's a fair chance he will carry all before him this season.

He is by Blue Point out of a dam who was a half-sister to Deacon Blues and The Tin Man, both of whom showed their best form at four and above, and Kind Of Blue is certainly keeping it in the family, although he was a good deal better than that pair at three.

James Fanshawe, responsible for training those two, rarely overfaces his horses, so the fact he was prepared to chuck Kind Of Blue into the Commonwealth Cup after just a pair of wins in novice races was a strong indicator that he thought him potentially a bit special, and he rewarded that faith with an excellent fourth to Inisherin at Ascot.

He arguably improved again when third to Elite Status in the Group 3 Hackwood Stakes at Newbury in July, but then failed by a head in the Phoenix Sprint at the same level at the Curragh the following month on the only occasion he has been sent off favourite.

Then came his big runs back in Group 1 company, starting with a head second to Montassib on good ground at Haydock, when he was in front inside the final furlong but was headed at the finish. There are no stamina issues, though, as after that it was on to Ascot, where he again travelled strongly, hit the front just over a furlong out and kept on well to deny the consistent Swingalong by a head. His sire was a superior sprinter (by British standards at least) and this one is well on the way to being his best son yet.

NARDRA William Haggas

It's always hard to know what a horse has achieved when it makes its debut in a small field at a short price and wins by a long way, but there's more than enough encouragement to suggest the well-bred Nardra is going to be a Group performer at the very least.

She made her debut in a four-runner novice contest at Haydock in September and, despite missing the kick and then being keen and green in rear, she quickened up smartly to win eased down by eight and a half lengths from a horse now rated 79.

You really can't put a big number on the bare form as they went a crawl in the early stages, but Nardra certainly has plenty of speed and, while that run came on soft

Red Letter: Classic potential

ground, her action suggests it's not going to be necessary.

Her dam acted on all ground with her best run a place in Group 3 company on good to firm, while sire Night Of Thunder was also thoroughly versatile.

William Haggas has introduced some decent first-time winners at Haydock in recent seasons, with two of his last three being Lake Forest and Desert Hero, and there's every hope Nardra can get up to that sort of level. She should stay a mile.

NEBRAS John & Thady Gosden

Nebras has plenty to live up to as he's a half-brother to the top-class Nashwa. He started well enough by winning a seven-runner maiden at Newmarket in October despite doing almost everything wrong. After missing the break he ran green and had to be niggled along in the early stages, but he seemed to get the message a couple of furlongs out and ended up pulling clear with Godolphin-owned favourite Wild Nature (now rated 90 after winning in handicap company), who had previous experience, and winning by half a length.

John & Thady Gosden saw enough merit in that effort to throw him straight into Group 1 company in the Futurity at Doncaster, but he looked like a duck out of water at that level and finished a well-beaten seventh of eight. I would be perfectly happy to forgive him as it obviously came far too soon in his education, and the chances are we are going to see a much better model as a three-year-old.

His trainers do not often get the level of their horses wrong and Nebras will be making his mark soon enough.

RED LETTER Ger Lyons

Has form that ties in closely with 1,000 Guineas favourite Lake Victoria, but is a much bigger price in the ante-post markets.

Red Letter made her debut in the same 7f

Curragh maiden at the end of June as Lake Victoria and the pair, 5-2 joint-favourites, pulled the best part of four lengths clear of the rest, Ger Lyons' filly just coming off worse by a head.

Sent for another fillies' maiden at the Curragh the following month, she was sent off at 8-11 and this time made no mistake, making all and kicking just over four lengths clear of a 50-1 outsider, with the subsequent Fillies' Mile third Ballet Slippers in third.

A big step up in class was the obvious move next time and Red Letter was kept at the Curragh for the Group 1 Moyglare Stud Stakes, in which she finished fourth of the five runners. However, the bare result tells only half the story as Red Letter was caught in a pocket on the rail and had to wait for favourite and winner Lake Victoria to make her move before she could.

Had she been able to get out earlier she'd have been a fair bit closer as she took her time to hit top gear, but she was beaten only a length and a half at the line, so is clearly very classy.

That was her first run outside of maiden company, so she's fully entitled to improve for the experience. She certainly doesn't have that much to find with a filly who is 3-1 for the 1,000 Guineas, and quotes of 20-1 could look very big in early May.

Treasure Time: could be one for the Hunt Cup

British Champions Fillies And Mares Stakes at Ascot.

Star Of Light obviously has a country mile to go to match her mother, but she did get the job done first time out despite being incredibly green throughout.

She was apparently quite flighty as a two-year-old and had to wear a hood on the way to the start at Wolverhampton, but she didn't settle too badly once they started racing, and did quicken up nicely when they straightened up for home, although there were signs of a high head carriage.

We can put that down to inexperience, though, and Star Of Light looks sure to come into her own over middle distances this summer.

TREASURE TIME William Haggas

This four-year-old started life in handicap company last season with a mark of just 77, and he hardly set the world alight off that rating on his first try at Chester when finishing only fifth of 11.

It was all a learning process for him, however, and he took off afterwards, winning a Class 4 handicap a shade cosily by a head at Newmarket in June, and then being a tad unlucky when beaten a neck in a much better race off a 4lb higher mark back there the following month.

A further 6lb rise ensued for that success, but Treasure Time showed he might be able to deal with that when not getting the run of the race but still finishing fifth of 14 at Glorious Goodwood. He proved as much just three weeks later when sent to York for the Sky Bet Mile, a much better race than he'd been beaten in, and won a shade comfortably by a length from Volterra.

Treasure Time again didn't get the run of the race when fourth in another high-quality handicap at Doncaster, but wasn't disgraced.

He's going to be a threat in all the top mile handicaps this season and, given how well he goes on fast ground, he has Royal Hunt Cup written all over him.

STAR OF LIGHT
John & Thady Gosden

This is a filly who is all about promise rather than proven form as you certainly cannot rate her debut success at Wolverhampton very highly, especially as the form hasn't worked out. However, the Gosdens often introduce a useful performer on the all-weather at the end of the year and Star Of Light's pedigree is impeccable.

She is by Frankel out of Star Catcher, who didn't show very much at all on her December juvenile debut back in 2018, but won five out of her six outings as a three-year-old, including the Irish Oaks, Prix Vermeille and

VIEW FROM FRANCE SCOTT BURTON

Big names from across the Channel – and some progressive lesser lights

THERE are any number of reasons to begin with a reflection on the death in February of the Aga Khan, the pre-eminent owner-breeder of his generation.

It might seem unlikely for someone who celebrated victory in the Derby only weeks after taking ownership of Charlottesville in 1960, but His Highness has left the Aga Khan Studs in a healthier state than the one in which he found the enterprise, and the famous emerald green silks could be in for a rare time of things in 2025 as his family and those trusted lieutenants he worked with over many years chart a course for the future.

Zarigana looked a filly of immense promise in both her maiden victory at Chantilly and a dominant performance in the Group 3 Prix d'Aumale, with her acceleration giving visual confirmation of what her starry pedigree says might be possible for a granddaughter of Zarkava by the Aga Khan's own supersire, Siyouni.

Defeat appeared out of the question in the Prix Marcel Boussac but Zarigana was undone by a combination of a tricky wide draw and the talent and determination of her Francis Graffard-trained stablemate **Vertical Blue** who enjoyed a charmed run around the inside under Alexis Pouchin.

The pair ended the season as the top-rated juveniles in France, with Vertical Blue edging championship honours 114 to 113, and was subsequently bought for 3.2 million gns at Tattersalls to race in the black and blue silks of US investor John Stewart's Resolute Racing.

That sets up an in-house rivalry that is mirrored between Graffard's outstanding older horses.

Whether their trainer will seek to try to keep them apart by exploring the option of sending one to Newmarket remains to be seen, but if they do renew rivalry in the Emirates Poule d'Essai des Pouliches over a mile at Longchamp on May 11, it will be an occasion to savour.

Zarigana remains the horse in France with the most buzz around her and, while both fillies have been given entries in the Prix de Diane Longines, hers is the pedigree which looks best equipped to stretch out to 1m2½f and perhaps, if we allow ourselves to dream, the 1m4f of the Vermeille and the Arc which her celebrated ancestress Zarkava devoured.

The Aga Khan Studs' Classic aspirations don't rest solely with Zarigana, and newly retained rider Mickael Barzalona can look forward to riding a number of promising three-year-olds this spring.

Among the colts, **Azimpour** made a winning start over 1m1f at Longchamp in the Prix de Belleville, a newcomers' race in which the son of Dubawi justified warm favouritism when passing most of his rivals to win cosily.

A brother to top-class Australian performer The Autumn Sun, Azimpour holds the Classic entry over a mile but on what we've

108

GUIDE TO THE FLAT **2025**

Vertical Blue (left) beats stablemate Zarigana in the Prix Marcel Boussac

109

seen to date, he looks like a prime candidate for a Jockey Club campaign.

Diane entry **Cankoura** is a Persian King half-sister to last season's Prix de la Grotte winner Candala and broke her maiden second up on the Chantilly Polytrack in December over 1m1½f, running down Bogota late after being given plenty to do by Clement Lecoeuvre.

Behind Vertical Blue and Zarigana, the best two juvenile colts in France were **Maranoa Charlie** (112) and **Misunderstood** (110).

Both ended the season with defeat in Group 1 company but each is in the care of a young trainer with Classic winner already tattooed on their resumes, and there is no obvious reason for them not to progress at three.

Maranoa Charlie won his first three starts without seeing another horse for Christopher Head and it was undoubtedly a disappointment that he was unable to once again gallop his rivals into the ground in the Criterium International, finishing a leg-weary fourth to Twain.

Head is a man who likes to set out his plan well in advance and the son of Wootton Bassett was only entered in the Poule d'Essai des Poulains among the French Classics, though it would be no surprise to see the 2,000 Guineas added to his list of engagements.

Either way, Head believes he has a miler on his hands in the image of former star inmate Big Rock, and there doesn't seem much intent to change tactics and drop him in.

Misunderstood also showed a liking for getting on with the job when leaving the talented **Nesthorn** in his wake in the Group 3 Prix des Chenes.

It is possible the Prix Jean-Luc Lagardere came a little quickly afterwards – trainer Mario Baratti did not immediately commit to Arc day following his trial success – while attempting to force the issue from a wide draw back over seven furlongs might not have been ideal either.

Like Maranoa Charlie, Misunderstood

Calandagan chases home City Of Troy in the Group 1. Top middle-distance races will be on his agenda, and also that of Goliath (inset)

(who is by a Jubilee Stakes winner in Hello Youmzain) is only entered in the Poulains, and should the pair meet in the Prix de Fontainebleau in April, we'll all know a lot more about the identity of France's leading three-year-old miling colt.

A winner on debut at Deauville, the Graffard-trained Nesthorn was not seen again after the Chenes but Juddmonte's imposing son of Expert Eye remains on the radar, arguably with the Jockey Club more in mind than the Poulains.

This time last year Andre Fabre looked to be stocked with a huge number of potential Classic springers who had run once or twice but, in typical fashion for the yard, had not been tried at Pattern level the previous autumn.

In scanning the Classic entries, what is most striking about the Fabre contingent in 2025 is just how many of them did not race at all at two.

Of those that did see action last year, **Gun Of Brixton** gained more experience than most in three runs over the late spring and early summer.

Not seen since scoring over a mile at Clairefontaine in early July, Haras Voltaire's homebred Frankel colt had to be switched around three rivals before coasting clear of Rosa Salvaje, one of Christopher Head's better two-year-old fillies.

How Gun Of Brixton has progressed physically over the winter will be interesting – he made his debut over 6f in May and still looked to have some growing to do the last time we saw him – and what trip he wants also remains to be seen, as he's in the Poulains, the Jockey Club and the Grand Prix de Paris.

Reine De Medicis wasn't given an overly hard time once Zarigana had taken off when the pair made their debuts on Bastille Day at Chantilly but Edouard de Rothschild's daughter of Romanised – a sister to the same owner/breeder's **Alcantor**, who might rival the Jerome Reynier-trained pair Facteur Cheval and Lazzat as the best older miler in France this season – was a comfortable winner second time up at Deauville over 7f and looks a beautiful long-term project.

More Fabre inmates who caught the eye include **Percival** – a Juddmonte homebred son of Camelot who put four lengths between himself and subsequent Prix Policeman winner Aidan's Phone over 1m2f on soft ground at Chantilly in November – and **Nitoi**, winner of his sole start over nine furlongs for Wertheimer et Frere.

Their blue and white silks were also carried to success on his sole start by **Uther**, a Christophe Ferland-trained Camelot half-brother to last season's Grand Prix de Paris winner Sosie.

Fabre also produced the imposing **Zerket** to land an often-informative newcomers' race at Deauville during sales week in late October, and the son of Zarak is well entered up.

The first two home in the fillies' race on the same card, Fiona Carmichael's **Bonnet** and the Gestut Schlenderhan homebred **Galene** – who received a bump and showed plenty of immaturity in second – should also go in the tracker.

One filly who was campaigned in plenty of black type races was **Daylight**, who hit the board in both the Morny and the Cheveley

111

RACING POST

Park, and hopefully can train on into a Commonwealth Cup prospect for Patrice Cottier and the Chehboub family.

While it can be a dangerous game getting too attached to all-weather form in January and February, Galene's trainer Victoria Head sent out the giant **Tito Mo Cen** to land a colts' maiden at Chantilly in relentless fashion, while the Graffard-trained **Audubon Park** showed a sparkling turn of foot to land the fillies' race on the same card.

If there is a Group-class springer lurking in the provinces in the mould of last season's Prix Jean Prat winner Puchkine, then it could be **Eponine**, who won her first two starts at Pau for Didier Guillemin.

And now that Ace Impact has shown the way, we're allowed at least one *coup de coeur* from the Cagnes-sur-Mer's winter sojourn; step forward **Isneauville**, who earned herself entries in the Pouliches and the Diane when finishing well on top in the very opening race of the meeting for Reynier.

As if Graffard doesn't have one headache in plotting parallel campaigns for Zarigana and Vertical Blue, he has a near identical problem with France's two best older horses, with the Aga Khan Studs' International and Champion Stakes runner-up **Calandagan** a likely candidate for many of the same middle-distance prizes as Stewart's **Goliath**.

Given both are geldings there is probably less pressure to keep the pair apart, and a meeting is likely at some stage given the acknowledgement that Calandagan is probably a better horse at 1m4f, for all his heroics at York and Ascot over two furlongs shorter.

The Dubai Sheema Classic seems a logical jumping off point for the son of Gleneagles, though he may well mix and match if the opportunity comes up to drop back to a mile and a quarter on a stamina-favouring track.

Goliath produced a spellbinding performance in last season's King George and, while he was undoubtedly favoured by the relentless pace set by Coolmore on behalf of Auguste Rodin, the raw ability he showed means he will be dangerous in any truly run race over a mile and a half.

France can boast several more middle-distance horses to watch among the four-year-olds, with the Wertheimers welcoming back Grand Prix de Paris winner **Sosie**, as well as Vermeille and Arc runner-up **Aventure**, who still had considerable scope for physical development at three and should be worth following with the benefit of another winter under her belt.

Wathnan Racing bought several colts last spring and summer, with **First Look** – who denied Sosie the runner-up spot behind the now-retired Look De Vega in the Jockey Club – **Map Of Stars** and the Alex Pantall-trained **Fast Tracker** all in contention for ambitious campaigns.

All three finished behind the progressive Ombudsman in the Prix Prince d'Orange last September, a race from which runner-up **Start Of Day** has now moved across Chantilly to join Christopher Head for owner Masaaki Saito, having rounded off 2024 when fifth in the Prix de l'Opera.

Both of last season's Chantilly Classic winners have departed the scene, with Diane heroine Sparkling Plenty sold to the United States.

Zarakem and Ramadan will continue their careers in Australia and Hong Kong respectively, while Mqse De Sevigne and Big Rock have retired.

Topgear showed he belongs at Group 1 level with a stunning success at Newmarket, while another older horse who might be tailor-made for the newly promoted City of York Stakes is **Lazzat**, who Reynier is convinced will stay an easy mile but who is a proper 'flyer' at 7f.

At the other end of the distance spectrum, **Double Major** reinforced his status as the best stayer in France in the Prix-Royal-Oak last back end, with the Dubai Gold Cup and another Pattern upgrade, the Prix Vicomtesse Vigier, looking obvious early season objectives.

Horseboxes – Uprating and Downplating

Uprating Horseboxes

As you may be aware, the DVSA is paying close attention to the horsebox industry and in particular, to lightweight horseboxes which they suspect may be operating overweight.

We have seen cases of horseboxes being stopped, checked and impounded on the roadside, owing to running overweight. The horses in transit have to be loaded into a different box and taken away, and the resultant fines are ever increasing in size. Yet, there is an alternative.

SvTech is keen to promote its uprating service for lightweight horseboxes (3500kg), whereby the horsebox can gain an extra 200-300kg in payload. This provides vital payload capability when carrying an extra horse and/or tack and offers peace of mind for the owner.

SvTech has carried out extensive work and testing on lightweight models and has covered uprates for most lightweight vehicles.

It is worth noting that some uprates require modifications or changes to the vehicle's braking, tyres and/or suspension, for which SvTech provides a simple purpose-built suspension assister kit. This will take between 1-2 hours for you to fit. Your horsebox will then go for a formal inspection to bring it into the 'Goods' category, and, depending on the vehicle's age, may also require fitment of a speed limiter, for which there are one or two options. Most importantly, vehicles registered after May 2002 must be fitted with manufacturer's ABS, if going above 3500kg.

If you're unsure, or don't believe that you need to uprate your lightweight horsebox, try taking it to a public weighbridge when you're fully loaded with your horse, tack, passenger, hay, etc. and weigh off each axle individually and the vehicle as a whole. There could be a distinct chance that you've overloaded one of the axles, even if you're within the GVW. If there is a problem, we can help. Call us to discuss your options.

Downplating Horseboxes

Do you own a 10 - 12.5 tonnes horsebox and do you want non-HGV licence holder to drive it? Your horsebox could be downplated to 7.5 tonnes so that any driver with a licence issued prior to 1st Jan 1997 could drive it.

- You are paying too much Vehicle Excise Duty.
- You want to escape the need for a tachograph.

The most important aspect when downplating is to leave yourself suitable payload to carry your goods. The Ministry requires that for horseboxes of 7500kg there is a minimum payload of 2000kg. Hence, when downplating to 7500kg, the unladen weight must not exceed 5500kg. For 3500kg horseboxes, you must ensure that you have a payload of at least 1000kg, thus, when empty it cannot weigh more than 2500kg.

Due to recent changes at DVSA, we are no longer required to make a mechanical change to the vehicle and, once downrated, we will be supplying you with a revised set of Ministry plating certificates, or if exempt, plating and testing, a converter's plate and certificate at the lower weight.

Depending upon vehicle usage, it is at the discretion of DVSA as to whether they will require a formal inspection of your vehicle.

TO DISCOVER YOUR OPTIONS, PLEASE DOWNLOAD, FILL IN AND RETURN OUR ENQUIRY FORM – WWW.SVTECH.CO.UK

SvTech
Special Vehicle Technology

T +44 (0)1772 621800
E webenquiries@svtech.co.uk

ON THE UP ROBBIE WILDERS

Unexposed with the ability to make strides

COSMIC YEAR Harry Charlton

Harry Charlton enjoyed a good first season in his own name, and Cosmic Year is expected to be one of the stable's leading lights this year.

This Irish 2,000 Guineas-entered colt could hardly have won any easier on his debut, readily brushing aside an odds-on favourite whose form tied in with unbeaten Champagne Stakes winner Bay City Roller.

The son of Kingman has a persuasive pedigree as a half-brother to the yard's former superstar Time Test and it will be fascinating to see how he fares up in class. A Guineas trial seems an inevitability and he rates an exciting project going forward.

ELSIE'S RUAN Gemma Tutty

Gemma Tutty has made a promising start to her training career and Elsie's Ruan looks capable of flying the flag for the team this season.

Elsie's Ruan sprang a surprise when picking up a competitive York novice at big odds on her debut and coped with a rise in class by keeping on into third behind the exceptional Lake Victoria in the Sweet Solera.

A daughter of Ulysses who is out of a Helmet mare, Elsie's Ruan looks the type to thrive for middle distances once she learns to settle. Her keen-going nature cost her on her final start at Doncaster. Relaxing will be the key if the abundant potential she possesses is to be fulfilled.

POCKLINGTON Geoff Oldroyd

You sense there is a big day or two in Pocklington this season. A breathing issue emerged after his Commonwealth Cup disappointment when he was overfaced at that point of his career. However, he was a big eyecatcher on his handicap debut at York two months later, flashing home after being drawn on the wrong side. He should come into his own this term and is expected to take a handicap off the same mark before rising in class.

POWERFUL GLORY Richard Fahey

Powerful Glory ran out a wildly impressive winner on his debut at Pontefract on fast ground and elevated his form to new levels to double up in the Mill Reef.

The expectation is he makes up into a Commonwealth Cup type for Richard Fahey, who has a proven track record at extracting the most from his speedsters. He looks the heir apparent to connections' crack sprinter Perfect Power if training on at three. There is little reason why he won't stay a bit further as well.

PRAGUE Dylan Cunha

The slow-burning Prague never made the track when trained by Aidan O'Brien and debuted in the summer of his four-year-old career for Dylan Cunha.

He proved a shrewd acquisition with a 40-1 strike at Sandown on his first run and quickly established himself at a higher level, recording an eyecatching second in the Superior Mile at Haydock with a first-time tongue-tie. He was deprived of a clear run at a crucial stage and that made the difference.

A dominant winner of the Joel Stakes next time, Prague can be forgiven for his struggles in the QEII on his final start of the season.

He begins the new campaign as a miler of potential and races like the Lockinge and Queen Anne should be under consideration.

SPARKS FLY David Loughnane

Few horses in training are as ground-dependent as Sparks Fly. The daughter of Muhaarar has form figures of 11116111151 on soft ground or slower. On other surfaces, she is a modest 2-10.

She has little left to prove against her own sex and signed off with a career-best Racing Post Rating of 116 against the girls over a mile on heavy terrain at Saint-Cloud. With her mares' allowance factored in, that sort of level would put her on the cusp of open Group 1s. Follow her wherever she goes when the mud flies.

TYCOON John & Thady Gosden

The Gosdens are no strangers to unleashing their bright prospects at Sandown for their debuts and Tycoon caught the eye on his first run at the Esher track.

Slowly away, Tycoon found himself with a mountain to climb at the two-furlong pole, but passed plenty of well-bred rivals to stay on into third under a hands-and-heels ride.

It takes a good horse to make up that sort of ground at Sandown and he will have no issues capturing a maiden.

The Gosdens have enjoyed plenty of success with progeny of Kingman and Tycoon, who changed hands for 500,000gns,

is expected to thrive in the second half of the season for an operation renowned for its patient approach.

UXMAL Joseph O'Brien

Uxmal has raced only seven times since his debut in October 2021. However, his engine is huge and he created a superb impression when bolting up in the Queen Alexandra at Royal Ascot.

Unseen for the rest of the campaign, Uxmal looks the type to mix it with Kyprios et al if he can remain sound. The staying division is crying out for new blood and he may provide it.

VOLTERRA Kevin Ryan

Handicaps may now be a thing of the past for Volterra, who sauntered home for an eased-down success in the Challenge Cup at Ascot in October. He thrived over that 7f distance on soft ground, registering an excellent Topspeed figure and doing it the hard way from the front.

Given the narrow deficit between top handicapper and Group 1 performer in the sprinting division, it would be little surprise if he made hay in a top race on soft ground.

WALEEFY William Haggas

This son of Night Of Thunder is a half-brother to the William Haggas yard's brilliant miler and Juddmonte International winner Baaeed. That also makes him a close relative to King George hero Hukum.

His siblings thrived with age and Waleefy, who has been campaigned over 6f and 7f on turf, appears to be crying out for a mile.

With standout form on fast ground, Waleefy could make up into a contender for the Royal Hunt Cup. A mark of 88 can be left behind before long.

THIS SEASON'S KEY HORSES

By Dylan Hill

GUIDE TO THE FLAT 2025

Acapulco Bay (Ire)
3 b c Dubawi - Je Ne Regretterien (Galileo)
Aidan O'Brien (Ire)　　　　Westerberg, Magnier, Tabor & Smith
PLACINGS: 21-　　　　　　　　　　　　　　　　　RPR **93+**

Starts	1st	2nd	3rd	4th	Win & Pl
2	1	1	-	-	£13,565

8/24　Curr　1m Mdn 2yo good £10,431

Lightly raced colt who ran only in two Curragh maidens last season but looked a fine prospect for middle distances; strong-finishing second on debut before making all to justify 2-11 favouritism over a mile in workmanlike fashion; should progress over further.

Aesterius (Ire)
3 b c Mehmas - Jane Doe (Hallowed Crown)
Archie Watson　　　　　　　　　　　　　　　Wathnan Racing
PLACINGS: 1512116-　　　　　　　　　　　　　　RPR **108**

Starts	1st	2nd	3rd	4th	Win & Pl
7	4	1	-	-	£170,203

9/24　Donc　5f Cls1 Gp2 2yo good £73,723
9/24　Lonc　5f Gp3 2yo gd-sft £34,783
7/24　Sand　5f Cls1 List good £17,013
5/24　Bath　5f Cls5 2yo good £3,402

Last season's highest-rated two-year-old over 5f; progressed through the ranks and won the Flying Childers Stakes at Doncaster, reversing form with Big Mojo after a narrow defeat in the Molecomb; not quite at his best when sixth at the Breeders' Cup on final run.

Aftermath (Ire)
3 b/br c Justify - Flying (Galileo)
Aidan O'Brien (Ire)　　　　Westerberg, Magnier, Tabor & Smith
PLACINGS: 231-　　　　　　　　　　　　　　　　RPR **100**

Starts	1st	2nd	3rd	4th	Win & Pl
3	1	1	1	-	£36,713

9/24　Curr　7f Mdn 2yo good £10,431

Big, imposing colt who got better and better last season and hacked up when getting off the mark in a Curragh maiden on final run; had been thrown in at the deep end when third in the Champagne Stakes on second run (second string in the market but ridden by Ryan Moore).

Al Aasy (Ire)
8 b g Sea The Stars - Kitcara (Shamardal)
William Haggas　　　　　　　　Shadwell Estate Company Ltd
PLACINGS: 12248/1/51125/21123-　　　　　　　RPR **118**

Starts	1st	2nd	3rd	4th	Win & Pl
22	9	5	2	1	£472,709

8/24　Newb　1m5½f Cls1 Gp3 gd-fm £51,039
8/24　Gdwd　1m4f Cls1 Gp3 gd-fm £56,710
8/23　Hayd　1m2½f Cls1 Gp3 gd-sft £42,533
7/23　Newb　1m2f Cls1 Good £22,684
5/22　Asct　1m4f Cls1 List good £29,489
5/21　Newb　1m4f Cls1 Gp3 gd-sft £56,710
4/21　Newb　1m4f Cls1 Gp3 good £25,520
7/20　NmkJ　1m5f Cls1 Gp3 3yo gd-sft £23,081
6/20　NmkR　1m4f Cls5 2yo soft £3,493

Veteran middle-distance performer who

won Group 3 races at Goodwood and Newbury last season to take tally to six at that level; once looked likely to prove even better than that (neck second in 2021 Coronation Cup) but kept to Group 3/Listed races in last two seasons.

Al Nayyir
7 b g Dubawi - Bright Beacon (Manduro)
Tom Clover　　　　　　　　　　Elbashir Salem Ab Elhrari
PLACINGS: 1/143061214/2425215-　　　　　　　RPR **116**

Starts	1st	2nd	3rd	4th	Win & Pl
22	6	4	2	4	£535,912

9/24　NmkR　2m Cls1 List soft £28,355
9/23　StCl　1m6f List soft £23,009
7/23　Deau　1m7f List soft £23,009
1/23　Meyd　1m2f 76-97 Hcap good £12,867
12/22　Meyd　1m4f 77-90 Hcap good £11,469
11/22　Meyd　1m2f 62-80 Hcap fast £10,563

Globetrotting stayer who flourished following switch to Britain last season; finished a short-head second to Vauban in the Lonsdale Cup on first run for Tom Clover before a brilliant eight-length win in a Listed race at Newmarket; fifth in the Long Distance Cup on final run.

Al Qareem (Ire)
6 b g Awtaad - Moqla (Teofilo)
Karl Burke　　　　　　Nick Bradley Racing, Burke & Partner
PLACINGS: 715/00112/245252114-　　　　　　　RPR **116**

Starts	1st	2nd	3rd	4th	Win & Pl
26	8	8	-	4	£467,463

10/24　Asct　1m4f Cls1 Gp3 soft £48,204
9/24　Ches　1m4½f Cls1 List good £33,612
10/23　Asct　1m4f Cls1 Gp3 good £45,368
9/23　Ches　1m4½f Cls1 List gd-sft £33,612
10/22　Lonc　1m7f Gp2 3yo v sft £95,798
89　5/22　York　1m4f Cls3 76-89 3yo Hcap good £12,885
81　4/22　Nott　1m2f Cls4 73-82 3yo Hcap gd-sft £5,616
12/21　Newc　7f Cls5 2yo std-slw £3,780

Very useful middle-distance performer who has pulled off the same autumn double in the last two seasons, following a Listed win at Chester with victory in the Cumberland Lodge Stakes at Ascot; finished second in four Group 3 races in between; best with cut in the ground.

Al Riffa (Fr)
5 b h Wootton Bassett - Love On My Mind (Galileo)
Joseph O'Brien (Ire)　　Masaaki Matsushima & Al Riffa Syndicate
PLACINGS: 211/22/46210-　　　　　　　　　　RPR **121+**

Starts	1st	2nd	3rd	4th	Win & Pl
10	3	4	-	1	£575,359

8/24　Hopp　1m4f Gp1 good £86,967
9/22　Curr　7f Gp1 2yo soft £198,319
8/22　Curr　7f Mdn 2yo good £8,181

Dual Group 1 winner, adding last season's Grosser Preis von Berlin to the 2022 National Stakes having been lightly raced due to injury in between; also went close at the top level in the Prix Ganay and Eclipse (length second to City Of Troy) but well beaten in the Arc.

117

RACING POST

Alcantor (Fr)
4 b c New Bay - Bianca De Medici (Medicean)
Andre Fabre (Fr) — Baron Edouard De Rothschild

PLACINGS: 13112/63631- — RPR **118+**

Starts	1st	2nd	3rd	4th	Win & Pl
10	4	1	3	-	£237,600

10/24	StCl	1m Gp3 heavy	£34,783
9/23	StCl	1m Gp3 2yo soft	£35,398
8/23	Deau	7½f 2yo gd-sft	£15,044
6/23	StCl	7f 2yo gd-sft	£13,274

Smart miler who benefited from a drop in grade when running away with a Group 3 at Saint-Cloud on final run last season; has twice been placed in Group 1 races, including when a half-length third in the Poule d'Essai des Poulains, and worth another crack at that level.

Alflaila
6 b h Dark Angel - Adhwaa (Oasis Dream)
Owen Burrows — Shadwell Estate Company Ltd

PLACINGS: 246/102111/15/4104-5 — RPR **120**

Starts	1st	2nd	3rd	4th	Win & Pl
19	7	3	-	4	£558,038

7/24	York	1m2½f Cls1 Gp2 gd-fm	£76,559
7/23	York	1m2½f Cls1 Gp2 good	£70,888
10/22	NmkR	1m1f Cls1 Gp3 good	£45,368
8/22	York	1m1f Cls1 Gp3 gd-fm	£85,065
7/22	Pont	1m Cls1 List good	£28,010
102	5/22	Asct	7f Cls2 83-102 3yo Hcap good	£15,462
	6/21	Sals	6f Cls4 2yo gd-fm	£3,726

Smart middle-distance performer who has been lightly raced in recent seasons, running just twice in between back-to-back wins in the York Stakes; has won his last five races below Group

118

GUIDE TO THE FLAT **2025**

Alflaila working on the track at Al Rayyan racecourse in Doha during February

l level in Europe but managed no better than fourth in three runs in the top grade.

Almaqam
4 b c Lope De Vega - Talmada (Cape Cross)
Ed Walker   Sheikh Ahmed Al Maktoum

PLACINGS: 4/11632-   RPR **116**

Starts	1st	2nd	3rd	4th	Win & Pl
6	2	1	1	1	£115,476
5/24	Sand		1m Cls1 List 3yo soft		£25,520
4/24	Yarm		1m Cls5 Mdn good		£4,320

Lightly raced colt who finished last season with a head second in the Prix Dollar at Longchamp; had first hinted at that ability when running away with a Listed race at Sandown on just his third

run; relished soft ground both times and twice disappointed in between on quicker.

Alobayyah
3 b f Ghaiyyath - Aquatinta (Samum)
William Haggas   Sheikh Mana Bin Mohammed Al Maktoum

PLACINGS: 1-   RPR **91+**

Starts	1st	2nd	3rd	4th	Win & Pl
1	1	-	-	-	£5,372
10/24	Yarm		1m Cls4 2yo soft		£5,373

Once-raced filly who made a hugely eyecatching start on sole run at Yarmouth last autumn, barely coming off the bridle to beat a strong favourite (pair clear); bred to stay middle distances and could be an Oaks filly.

119

RACING POST

Alsakib
5 gr g Kingman - America Nova (Verglas)
Andrew Balding   Al Wasmiyah Stud

PLACINGS: 2113117/634178-   RPR **113**

Starts	1st	2nd	3rd	4th	Win & Pl
13	5	1	2	1	£224,953

96	7/24	York	1m6f Cls1 Gp3 gd-sft................................	£48,204
87	10/23	NmkR	1m4f Cls2 88-102 3yo Hcap soft..................	£61,848
	9/23	Asct	1m4f Cls2 81-102 3yo Hcap gd-fm................	£51,540
	7/23	Wind	1m Cls2 gd-fm..	£21,600
	5/23	Ches	7½f Cls4 good...	£5,154

Finished 2023 by winning valuable three-year-old handicaps over 1m4f at Ascot and Newmarket and gradually got to grips with higher grades last season, breaking his Group duck when winning over 1m6f at York; below par twice subsequently and has since been gelded.

Alyanaabi (Ire)
4 b g Too Darn Hot - Alyamaama (Kitten's Joy)
Owen Burrows   Shadwell Estate Company Ltd

PLACINGS: 1412/5549-   RPR **112**

Starts	1st	2nd	3rd	4th	Win & Pl
8	2	1	-	2	£190,957

9/23	NmkR	7f Cls1 Gp3 2yo gd-fm..............................	£34,026
6/23	Sals	6f Cls4 2yo gd-fm...................................	£5,400

Group 3 winner and Dewhurst runner-up as

GUIDE TO THE FLAT 2025

a two-year-old in 2023 but just came up short at the top level last season, finishing fifth in the 2,000 Guineas and St James's Palace Stakes; well below par on final two runs and has since been gelded.

Ambiente Friendly (Ire)
4 b c Gleneagles - Roxity (Fastnet Rock)
James Owen — The Gredley Family
PLACINGS: 13/412305- — RPR **120+**

Starts	1st	2nd	3rd	4th	Win & Pl
8	2	1	3	1	£488,314

5/24	Ling	1m3½f Cls1 List 3yo good	£34,488
9/23	Leic	7f Cls3 Mdn 2yo gd-sft	£8,100

Fine second in last season's Derby behind City Of Troy having proved a revelation up in trip when winning the Lingfield trial; failed to build on that when third in the Irish Derby and lost his way in two further runs; has since left James Fanshawe.

Ancient Truth (Ire)
3 b c Dubawi - Beyond Reason (Australia)
Charlie Appleby — Godolphin
PLACINGS: 1113- — RPR **112**

Starts	1st	2nd	3rd	4th	Win & Pl
4	3	-	1	-	£129,580

7/24	NmkJ	7f Cls1 Gp2 2yo good	£56,710
6/24	NmkJ	7f Cls4 2yo gd-fm	£5,154
5/24	NmkR	6f Cls4 2yo gd-fm	£10,823

Smart colt who won three out of four races last season; completed a hat-trick in the Superlative Stakes and went down fighting when losing his unbeaten record in the Dewhurst, finishing a half-length third having raced keenly; could still be a leading 2,000 Guineas contender.

Ancient Wisdom (Fr)
4 b c Dubawi - Golden Valentine (Dalakhani)
Charlie Appleby — Godolphin
PLACINGS: 11311/2813- — RPR **114**

Starts	1st	2nd	3rd	4th	Win & Pl
9	5	1	2	-	£351,662

7/24	NmkJ	1m5f Cls1 Gp3 3yo gd-sft	£113,420
10/23	Donc	1m Cls1 Gp1 2yo heavy	£127,576
10/23	NmkR	1m Cls1 Gp3 2yo soft	£34,026
6/23	NmkJ	7f Cls4 2yo good	£4,320
6/23	Hayd	7f Cls4 2yo gd-fm	£5,400

Began last season as a Derby horse after winning the Futurity Trophy in 2023 but was no match for Economics in the Dante and only eighth at Epsom; won the Bahrain Trophy but finished

third on only subsequent run in Germany having missed bigger targets owing to quick ground.

Anmaat (Ire)
7 b g Awtaad - African Moonlight (Halling)
Owen Burrows — Shadwell Estate Company Ltd
PLACINGS: 2/132112/111/21/151- — RPR **124+**

Starts	1st	2nd	3rd	4th	Win & Pl
15	9	4	1	-	£1,230,730

10/24	Asct	1m2f Cls1 Gp1 soft	£737,230
8/24	Hayd	1m2¼f Cls1 Gp3 gd-fm	£48,204
5/23	Lonc	1m1f Gp1 gd-sft	£126,416
10/22	Lonc	1m2f Gp2 v soft	£95,798
8/22	Hayd	1m2¼f Cls1 Gp3 good	£45,368
103	7/22	York	1m2½f Cls2 89-107 Hcap gd-fm	£103,080
94	9/21	Donc	1m2f Cls2 83-98 Hcap gd-fm	£16,200
86	8/21	Bath	1m2f Cls3 74-92 Hcap good	£6,281
	5/21	Ling	1m Cls5 3yo stand	£3,024

Remarkable winner of last season's Champion Stakes, overcoming major traffic issues to beat Calandagan; came in under the radar as a 40-1 shot but had won the Prix d'Ispahan in 2023 and run just twice since due to injury; still very lightly raced for his age.

Aomori City (Fr)
3 b c Oasis Dream - Setsuko (Shamardal)
Charlie Appleby — Godolphin
PLACINGS: 13143- — RPR **112+**

Starts	1st	2nd	3rd	4th	Win & Pl
5	2	-	2	1	£198,507

7/24	Gdwd	7f Cls1 Gp2 2yo good	£99,243
6/24	Nott	6f Cls5 2yo good	£3,725

Highly tried last season and won the Vintage Stakes at Glorious Goodwood on second crack at Group 2 level; below par when a never-dangerous fourth in the National Stakes but bounced back with a strong-finishing third behind Henri Matisse in the Breeders' Cup Juvenile Turf.

Apollo One
7 ch g Equiano - Boonga Roogeta (Tobougg)
Peter Charalambous & James Clutterbuck — Pcracing.Co.Uk
PLACINGS: 7321/322230/2362821- — RPR **114**

Starts	1st	2nd	3rd	4th	Win & Pl
33	5	9	5	4	£425,973

	10/24	Asct	6f Cls1 Gp3 soft	£48,204
94	11/22	Kemp	6f Cls2 80-102 Hcap std-slw	£41,232
	3/21	Ling	7f Cls1 List 3yo stand	£17,013
	10/20	Sals	6f Cls2 2yo soft	£9,057
	8/20	NmkJ	7f Cls5 Auct 2yo gd-fm	£3,493

Remarkably consistent in top sprint handicaps before going up in grade to win a Group 3 at Ascot on final run last season; had been beaten

Alsakib and PJ McDonald in the winner's enclosure after their victory at York last summer

121

no more than a length when second in back-to-back Stewards' Cups, a Wokingham and a Portland since previous win in 2022.

Arabian Crown (Fr)
4 b c Dubawi - Dubai Rose (Dubai Destination)
Charlie Appleby   Godolphin
PLACINGS: 3111/1-   RPR **113+**

Starts	1st	2nd	3rd	4th	Win & Pl
5	4	-	1	-	£112,127

4/24	Sand	1m2f Cls1 Gp3 3yo gd-sft	£48,204
10/23	NmkR	1m2f Cls1 Gp3 2yo soft	£34,026
8/23	Sals	1m Cls1 List 2yo good	£22,684
7/23	Sand	7f Cls4 Mdn 2yo soft	£5,400

Exciting colt who looked a leading contender for last year's Derby until suffering a season-ending injury; had signed off for 2023 with a runaway win in the Zetland Stakes and was similarly impressive when landing the Classic Trial last April; should stay 1m4f.

Arabian Dusk
3 b f Havana Grey - Lady Macduff (Iffraaj)
Simon & Ed Crisford   Shaikh Duaij Al Khalifa
PLACINGS: 23173-   RPR **103**

Starts	1st	2nd	3rd	4th	Win & Pl
5	1	1	2	-	£94,111

7/24	NmkJ	6f Cls1 Gp2 2yo good	£56,710

525,000gns breeze-up purchase who proved a smart sprinting filly last season; soon tackled Pattern company as a maiden and gained a valuable win in the Duchess of Cambridge Stakes; flopped in the Prix Morny but put that behind her with a fine third in the Cheveley Park.

Arabie
3 ch c Dandy Man - Mamma Morton (Elnadim)
Karl Burke   Mohamed Saeed Al Shahi
PLACINGS: 21114-   RPR **102**

Starts	1st	2nd	3rd	4th	Win & Pl
5	3	1	-	1	£129,423

7/24	Chan	6f Gp2 2yo gd-sft	£64,435
6/24	Chan	6f Gp3 2yo gd-sft	£34,783
5/24	York	6f Cls3 2yo gd-sft	£10,800

Sharp two-year-old last season, flourishing in the first half of the year and completing a hat-trick when winning the Prix Robert Papin at Chantilly; ran just once more when far from disgraced in fourth in the Prix Morny.

Arizona Blaze
3 b c Sergei Prokofiev - Liberisque (Equiano)
Adrian Murray (Ire)   Amo Racing Limited & Giselle De Aguiar
PLACINGS: 121333242-   RPR **111**

Starts	1st	2nd	3rd	4th	Win & Pl
9	2	3	3	1	£359,372

5/24	Curr	6f Gp3 2yo good	£30,783
3/24	Curr	5f Mdn 2yo heavy	£10,261

Remarkably tough and durable two-year-old last season, finishing second in the Breeders' Cup Juvenile Turf Sprint eight runs and more than seven months after a winning debut; scored just once more in that time but was third in the Norfolk and Phoenix Stakes among many fine runs.

Art Power (Ire)
8 gr g Dark Angel - Evening Time (Keltos)
Tim Easterby   King Power Racing Co Ltd
PLACINGS: 810415601/054042500-   RPR **115**

Starts	1st	2nd	3rd	4th	Win & Pl
40	9	1	3	8	£858,873

10/23	Asct	6f Cls1 Gp1 soft	£283,550
7/23	Curr	5f Gp2 soft	£62,655
5/23	Curr	6f Gp2 good	£62,655
9/22	Curr	6f Gp3 yld-sft	£27,269
9/21	Curr	6f Gp3 good	£26,339
7/20	Naas	6f Gp3 3yo yld-sft	£25,000
97	6/20	Asct	5f Cls2 83-104 3yo Hcap gd-sft	£22,642
6/20	Newc	6f Cls5 std-slw	£3,493
10/19	York	5f Cls3 2yo soft	£9,704

Veteran sprinter who broke his Group 1 duck at the 15th attempt when winning the Champions Sprint at Ascot in 2023; has also won five times at lesser Group level but rarely threatened last year, though still a fair fourth in the July Cup.

Audience
6 b g Iffraaj - Ladyship (Oasis Dream)
John & Thady Gosden   Cheveley Park Stud
PLACINGS: /220331/16223/15140-   RPR **123**

Starts	1st	2nd	3rd	4th	Win & Pl
17	5	4	3	1	£601,832

7/24	Gdwd	7f Cls1 Gp2 good	£102,029
5/24	Newb	1m Cls1 Gp1 good	£226,840
7/23	NmkJ	7f Cls1 Gp3 good	£45,368
99	10/22	Leic	7f Cls2 87-99 Hcap gd-fm	£10,468
10/21	NmkR	7f Cls4 2yo good	£5,400

One of last season's big surprise packages; won the Lockinge Stakes as an apparent pacemaker and went some way to backing that up by adding the Lennox Stakes; didn't get home when fifth in the Queen Anne but found 6f too sharp in the Champions Sprint.

Aventure (Ire)
4 b f Sea The Stars - Balladeuse (Singspiel)
Christophe Ferland (Fr)   Wertheimer & Frere
PLACINGS: 12/214122-   RPR **119**

Starts	1st	2nd	3rd	4th	Win & Pl
8	3	4	-	1	£1,307,900

8/24	Deau	1m4½f Gp2 good	£64,435
6/24	Chan	1m4f Gp3 3yo heavy	£34,783
9/23	Chan	1m 2yo gd-sft	£22,124

High-class French filly who was unlucky to bump into Bluestocking last season, finishing second behind that rival in the Prix Vermeille and the Arc; had won 1m4f Group races at Deauville and Chantilly either side of a length fourth when favourite for the Prix de Diane.

GUIDE TO THE FLAT **2025**

Art Power (grey) scores at Group 1 level in the 2023 Champions Sprint at Ascot

Babouche
3 b f Kodiac - Pavlosk (Arch)
Ger Lyons (Ire) — Juddmonte

PLACINGS: 1114- — RPR **111+**

Starts	1st	2nd	3rd	4th	Win & Pl
4	3	-	-	1	£232,646

	8/24	Curr	6f Gp1 2yo gd-fm	£179,565
	7/24	Curr	6½f Gp3 2yo good	£28,217
	6/24	Cork	6f Mdn 2yo gd-yld	£9,235

High-class filly who won three out of four races last season, even against the colts at Group 1 level when beating Whistlejacket into second in the Phoenix Stakes; lost unbeaten record when a below-par fourth in the Cheveley Park, failing to settle on much softer ground.

Ballet Slippers (Ire)
3 ch f Dubawi - Magical (Galileo)
Aidan O'Brien (Ire) — Tabor, Smith & Magnier

PLACINGS: 3213- — RPR **101**

Starts	1st	2nd	3rd	4th	Win & Pl
4	1	1	2	-	£68,752

| | 9/24 | Asct | 1m Cls4 2yo soft | £8,100 |

Beautifully bred filly (first foal out of multiple Group 1 winner Magical) who made a promising start last season; twice placed in Curragh maidens before winning a novice at Ascot; solid third when stepped up sharply in class for the Fillies' Mile; should improve with time.

RACING POST

Bay City Roller (Ire)
3 b c New Bay - Bloomfield (Teofilo)
George Scott Victorious Racing

PLACINGS: 111- RPR **107+**

Starts	1st	2nd	3rd	4th	Win & Pl
3	3	-	-	-	£99,434

9/24	Donc	7f Cls1 Gp2 2yo good £88,800
8/24	Chmf	7f Cls4 2yo stand £5,234
7/24	Sand	7f Cls4 2yo gd-fm £5,400

Unbeaten colt who coped with a sharp rise in class when adding his third win last season in the Champagne Stakes at Doncaster; had landed two novices before making the most of a soft opening at Group level (favourite withdrawn); proven on quick ground but should act on soft.

Beautiful Diamond
4 gr f Twilight Son - Babylon Lane (Lethal Force)
Karl Burke Sheikh Rashid Dalmook Al Maktoum

PLACINGS: 1351/351282- RPR **107**

Starts	1st	2nd	3rd	4th	Win & Pl
10	3	2	2	-	£107,112

6/24	Ayr	5f Cls1 List gd-fm £19,553
9/23	Ayr	5f Cls1 List 2yo gd-sft £20,132
6/23	Nott	5f Cls5 Mdn 2yo gd-fm £3,699

Very useful sprinter who has won Listed races at Ayr in each of the last two seasons, albeit in a dead-heat last year; also finished second in the Sapphire Stakes and third in the Palace House; kept to 5f since disappointing in the Lowther in 2023.

Bay City Roller (right) makes it three from three with victory at Doncaster

HORSERAIL FENCING

- Limited manufacturers warranty of 30 years

- Safety is an important factor with Horses. Horserail provides an injury free, maintenance free, stylish and affordable fencing system

- Can be electrified along the top of the rail Highly Conductive Carbon Compound strip

- Available in black, brown, and white

- Each rail has a 2-tonne breaking strain

CONTACT

Ruth Todd
Sales Manager
Bicester, Oxfordshire,
OX27 8RH

T: 07785 986645
E: info@horserail.co.uk
W: www.horserail.co.uk

FOR MORE INFORMATION

SCAN

HOTCOTE®
Electrifiable Coated Wire

Hotcote is a much needed and far superior alternative to electrified tape or rope often seen on equestrian establishments where the cost of post and rail fencing cannot be justified. It combines the versatility of an electric tape or rope with the safety of a much more substantial fence and will still be looking great after years of use.

Technical Specifications

High Tensile 2.5mm galvanized fencing wire encased in high quality medium density polyethylene to create a safe 10mm thick highly visible wire, electrified through strands.

4 Points of Electrification carried through the Carbon Compound. Each Hotcote wire has a breaking strain of 600 kilograms.

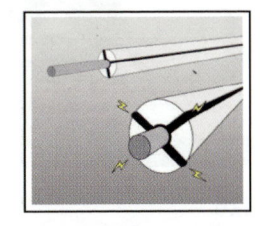

RACING POST

Beauvatier (Fr)
4 b/br c Lope De Vega - Enchanting Skies (Sea The Stars)
Yann Barberot (Fr) — Philippe Allaire/Haras D'Etreham

PLACINGS: 11113/2033334- — RPR **117**

Starts	1st	2nd	3rd	4th	Win & Pl
12	4	1	5	1	£303,035

9/23	Lonc	7f Gp3 2yo gd-sft	£35,398
7/23	Deau	7f List 2yo soft	£26,549
5/23	StCl	6f 2yo gd-sft	£15,044
5/23	Chan	5f 2yo heavy	£22,124

Developed into a smart colt last season despite failing to win; made the frame four times at Group 1 level and improved all year, with best run on final start when a length fourth in the Champions Sprint at Ascot; has also shown useful form up to a mile.

Bedtime Story (Ire)
3 gb f Frankel - Mecca's Angel (Dark Angel)
Aidan O'Brien (Ire) — Smith, Magnier & Tabor

PLACINGS: 111155- — RPR **108+**

Starts	1st	2nd	3rd	4th	Win & Pl
6	4	-	-	-	£175,737

8/24	Curr	7f Gp2 2yo good	£61,565
7/24	Leop	7½f Gp3 2yo gd-yld	£25,652
6/24	Asct	7f Cls1 List 2yo gd-fm	£62,381
6/24	Leop	7½f Mdn 2yo good	£9,235

Looked a potential superstar for much of last season but lost her way in the autumn; won her first four races, including a nine-and-a-half-length demolition job in the Chesham at Royal Ascot; only fifth when odds-on for the Moyglare and filled the same spot at the Breeders' Cup.

GUIDE TO THE FLAT 2025

Believing (Ire)
5 b m Mehmas - Misfortunate (Kodiac)
George Boughey   Magnier, Smith & Tabor
PLACINGS: 3/5110130/914413223-   RPR **118**

Starts	1st	2nd	3rd	4th	Win & Pl
24	6	5	4	3	£625,638

7/24	Curr	5f Gp2 good	£61,565
6/24	Hayd	5f Cls1 List good	£31,191
8/23	Pont	6f Cls1 List gd-fm	£33,612
5/23	Chan	6f Gp3 3yo soft	£35,398
4/23	Chmf	6f Cls1 List 3yo stand	£45,368
5/22	Wolv	6f Cls5 2yo stand	£3,942

Brilliant mare who has been remarkably consistent in top sprints; has made the frame in six out of eight Group 1 runs and finished second to Bradsell in the Nunthorpe and Flying Five last season; ran below the top level three times, winning a Group 2 and a Listed race.

Bellum Justum (Ire)
4 b c Sea The Stars - Natural Beauty (Oasis Dream)
Andrew Balding   King Power Racing Co Ltd
PLACINGS: 5241/17321-   RPR **112**

Starts	1st	2nd	3rd	4th	Win & Pl
9	3	2	1	1	£928,108

8/24	KenD	1m2½f Gd3 3yo firm	£830,165
4/24	Epsm	1m2f Cls1 List 3yo good	£28,355
9/23	NmkR	1m Cls4 Mdn 2yo gd-fm	£5,400

Fair seventh in last season's Derby after winning the trial at Epsom and continued to progress subsequently; did best when a half-length second in the Gordon Stakes at Glorious Goodwood, relishing quick ground, and was well placed to win a Grade 3 in the US.

Big Mojo (Ire)
3 b c Mohaather - Jm Jackson (No Nay Never)
Michael Appleby   RP Racing Ltd
PLACINGS: 21424-   RPR **109**

Starts	1st	2nd	3rd	4th	Win & Pl
5	1	2	-	2	£139,331

7/24	Gdwd	5f Cls1 Gp3 2yo gd-fm	£56,710

Tough and consistent performer in top two-year-old sprints last season; beat Flying Childers winner Aesterius in the Molecomb at Glorious Goodwood but couldn't quite confirm that form at Doncaster; didn't quite stay 6f in the Gimcrack and filled the same spot at the Breeders' Cup.

Bolster
5 b h Invincible Spirit - Quilting (King's Best)
Karl Burke   Sheikh Mohammed Obaid Al Maktoum
PLACINGS: 1/100/1147211-   RPR **115**

Starts	1st	2nd	3rd	4th	Win & Pl
11	6	1	-	1	£144,374

11/24	NmkR	1m2f Cls1 List soft	£25,520
10/24	York	1m2½f Cls2 86-105 Hcap gd-sft	£23,193
5/24	Epsm	1m2f Cls2 82-106 Hcap gd-sft	£50,960
4/24	Pont	1m2f Cls2 78-97 Hcap soft	£13,916
6/23	Wind	1m2f Cls5 good	£4,320
10/22	Leic	1m Cls4 2yo good	£4,860

Progressive middle-distance performer who won four times last season; gained most valuable win in a handicap at Epsom's Derby meeting; twice struggled in Group company but struck again in a handicap at York and a Listed race at Newmarket; best with cut in the ground.

Bedtime Story wins the Chesham Stakes at Royal Ascot on his second start

127

RACING POST

Botanical (Ire)
5 b g Lope De Vega - Bloomfield (Teofilo)
George BougheySheikh Mohammed Obaid Al Maktoum

PLACINGS: 21231/1022-RPR **117**

Starts	1st	2nd	3rd	4th	Win & Pl
9	3	4	1	-	£109,497

97	5/24	York	1m2½f Cls2 79-98 Hcap good	£25,770
87	10/23	Haml	1m1f Cls3 71-92 Hcap soft	£10,308
	7/23	Haml	1m½f Cls5 gd-sft	£4,320

Progressive middle-distance performer who ran away with a handicap at York's Dante meeting last season and improved in defeat subsequently; fine second under a big weight in the John Smith's Cup and beaten just a short-head when stepped up to Listed level on final run.

Bright Times Ahead (Ire)
3 b f Lope De Vega - Xaarienne (Xaar)
Ralph BeckettMrs Doreen Tabor

PLACINGS: 1-RPR **93+**

Starts	1st	2nd	3rd	4th	Win & Pl
1	1	-	-	-	£4,380

	11/24	NmkR	7f Cls4 2yo gd-sft	£4,381

€460,000 yearling who made an excellent start on her sole run last season in a 7f novice at Newmarket, travelling notably well and pulling clear late on; had been strong in the market and could progress into a smart filly at a mile and possibly further.

Bubbling (Ire)
3 b f No Nay Never - Lumiere Noire (Dashing Blade)
Aidan O'Brien (Ire)Tabor, Smith & Magnier

PLACINGS: 4131-RPR **104+**

Starts	1st	2nd	3rd	4th	Win & Pl
4	2	-	1	1	£75,423

	9/24	NmkR	7f Cls1 Gp2 2yo soft	£56,710
	7/24	Gway	7f Mdn 2yo yield	£10,261

Progressive two-year-old last season who might well have won her last three but for an unlucky run when a length third in a Listed race at Leopardstown; made amends when justifying favouritism in a modest running of the Rockfel Stakes at Newmarket.

Caius Chorister (Fr)
6 b m Golden Horn - Corpus Chorister (Soldier Of Fortune)
David MenuisierClive Washbourn

PLACINGS: 0/22056231/2264204-8RPR **114**

Starts	1st	2nd	3rd	4th	Win & Pl
28	6	7	1	2	£269,541

	10/23	StCl	1m6f Gp3 v soft	£35,398
85	7/22	Gdwd	1m3f Cls3 77-89 3yo Hcap gd-fm	£15,462
68	7/22	Epsm	1m4f Cls5 68-80 Hcap gd-fm	£4,536
62	7/22	Epsm	1m4f Cls6 47-67 3yo Hcap gd-fm	£3,456
57	6/22	Sals	1m4f Cls6 56-65 3yo Hcap gd-fm	£3,186
53	5/22	Yarm	1m3½f Cls6 46-56 3yo Hcap good	£2,970

Very useful stayer who hasn't won since a Group 3 at Saint-Cloud in 2023 but was unlucky not to

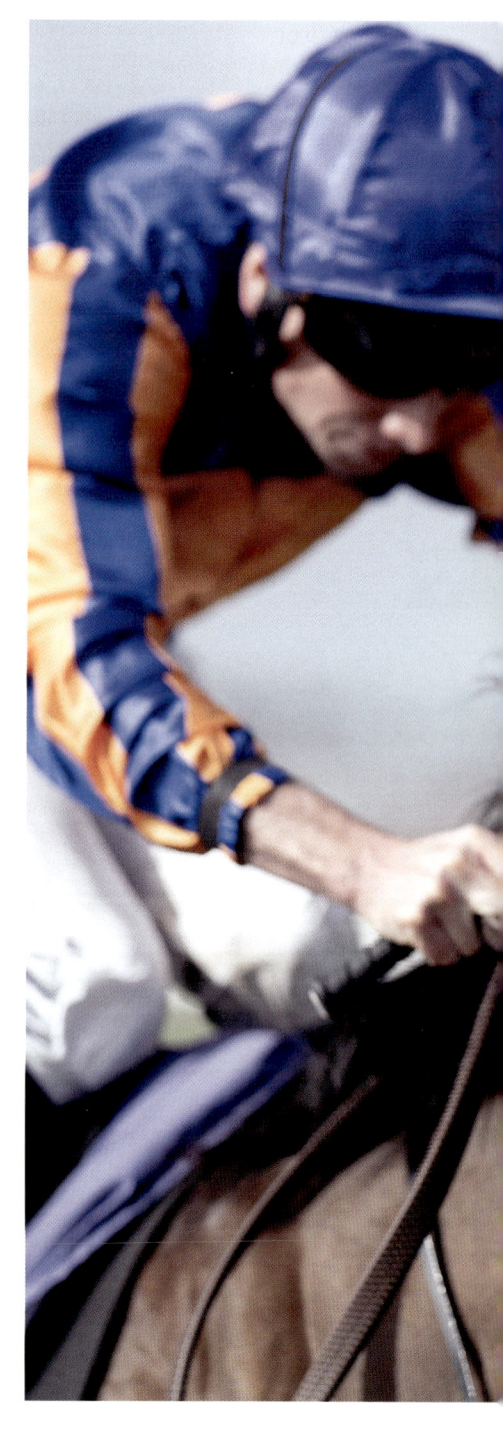

GUIDE TO THE FLAT **2025**

Bubbling powers to victory in the Group 2 Rockfel Stakes at Newmarket

RACING POST

score in the same grade last season; beaten a head in the Sagaro Stakes at Ascot and Henry II at Sandown; highly tried subsequently and ran best race when fourth in the Long Distance Cup.

Calandagan (Ire)
4 b g Gleneagles - Calayana (Sinndar)
Francis Graffard (Fr)   H H Aga Khan
PLACINGS: 31/211122-   RPR **127+**

Starts	1st	2nd	3rd	4th	Win & Pl
8	4	3	1	-	£799,455
6/24	Asct	1m4f Cls1 Gp2 3yo gd-fm			£154,818
5/24	Lonc	1m3f Gp3 3yo heavy			£34,783
4/24	Lonc	1m2½f Gp3 3yo v soft			£34,783
10/23	Chan	1m1½f 2yo stand			£13,274

Top-class three-year-old last season whose prowess led to a debate around the exclusion of geldings from the Arc; instead dropped back to 1m2f after a fine win in the King Edward VII Stakes, finishing second in the Juddmonte International and Champion Stakes.

Calif (Ger)
6 b/br g Areion - Cherry Danon (Rock Of Gibraltar)
Carlos & Yann Lerner (Fr)   Victorious Racing
PLACINGS: 643/231661dis/3711436-   RPR **120**

Starts	1st	2nd	3rd	4th	Win & Pl
25	5	3	5	3	£594,062
7/24	Muni	1m2f Gp1 soft			£86,957
6/24	Lonc	1m2f Gp3 good			£34,783
9/23	Badn	1m Gp2 good			£35,398
5/23	Badn	1m Gp3 good			£28,319
7/22	Kref	1m½f 3yo good			£3,025

Much-travelled gelding who found career-best form for a fourth trainer last season, landing his first Group 1 in Germany after an impressive Group 3 win at Longchamp; not quite at that

GUIDE TO THE FLAT 2025

level in the autumn, finishing third in Bahrain and sixth in Hong Kong.

Camille Pissarro (Ire)
3 br c Wootton Bassett - Entreat (Pivotal)
Aidan O'Brien (Ire)   Tabor, Smith, Magnier & P M Brant

PLACINGS: 1202621-   **RPR 113**

Starts	1st	2nd	3rd	4th	Win & Pl
7	2	3	-	-	£307,446

| 10/24 | Lonc | 7f Gp1 2yo soft........................£198,748 |
| 4/24 | Navn | 6f Mdn 2yo gd-yld......................£9,235 |

Frustrating for much of last season (beaten favourite four times) but got things right when showing much-improved form to win the Prix Jean-Luc Lagardere on final run; appreciated step up to 7f that day and should stay a mile, though seems prone to inconsistency.

Carrytheone
8 b g Lope De Vega - Song Of Passion (Orpen)
Michael Bell   Stuart Mizon

PLACINGS: 4733266/90134513461-   **RPR 115**

Starts	1st	2nd	3rd	4th	Win & Pl
31	6	3	4	4	£289,039

104	10/24	Asct	1m Cls2 95-110 Hcap soft............£103,080
101	8/24	Chep	7f Cls2 78-102 Hcap gd-sft...........£38,655
99	5/24	NmkR	7f Cls2 81-105 Hcap good............£51,540
	9/21	Gowr	7f yield.......................................£7,112
97	9/20	Curr	1m 79-97 Hcap good....................£7,750
	7/20	Curr	1m Mdn yield..............................£7,500

Did well in top handicaps last season; finished off with a clearcut victory in the Balmoral at Ascot on Champions Day, having won another valuable prize at Newmarket early in the year and caught the eye several times in between; might find life tougher after 6lb rise.

Carrytheone (yellow and green): three times a winner during 2024

131

RACING POST

Cathedral
3 b f Too Darn Hot - War And Peace (Frankel)
Ralph Beckett — Amo Racing Limited
PLACINGS: 12- — RPR **104**

Starts	1st	2nd	3rd	4th	Win & Pl
2	1	1	-	-	£17,377

9/24 Ling 6f Cls5 Mdn 2yo stand.................................£3,402

Very lightly raced filly who made a big impression when winning easily on debut at Lingfield last season; sent off favourite for the Oh So Sharp Stakes on her only subsequent run and ran well when a half-length second behind Merrily; should make a smart miler.

Celandine
3 b f Kingman - Pepita (Sir Prancealot)
Ed Walker — Rockcliffe Stud
PLACINGS: 7113415- — RPR **100+**

Starts	1st	2nd	3rd	4th	Win & Pl
7	3	-	-	1	£194,905

8/24 York 6f Cls1 Gp2 2yo gd-fm.........................£141,775
6/24 NmkJ 6f Cls1 List 2yo gd-fm.........................£22,684
6/24 Wind 6f Cls4 2yo gd-fm.................................£5,373

Tough two-year-old last season and won the Lowther Stakes at York, adding to a Listed victory over the same 6f trip at York; achieved both those victories on good to firm ground and

not quite as effective on softer, including when fifth in the Cheveley Park; not certain to train on.

Celestial Orbit
3 b f No Nay Never - Rose Bonheur (Danehill Dancer)
Ollie Sangster — Magnier, Shanahan & Maclennan
PLACINGS: 711- — RPR **96+**

Starts	1st	2nd	3rd	4th	Win & Pl
3	2	-	-	-	£28,084

7/24 Sand 7f Cls1 List 2yo good.............................£22,684
7/24 Hayd 7f Cls3 2yo good....................................£5,400

Missed the second half of last season but had been making rapid strides, winning her last two races; got off the mark at the second attempt in a modest Haydock novice and left that form behind when comfortably landing a Listed race over 7f at Sandown.

Centigrade (Ire)
3 b c Too Darn Hot - Turko Beach (Hard Spun)
Ralph Beckett — Highclere Thoroughbred Racing - Buzzard
PLACINGS: 21- — RPR **99+**

Starts	1st	2nd	3rd	4th	Win & Pl
2	1	-	-	-	£9,015

10/24 Newb 1m Cls4 2yo heavy.............................£6,480

Lightly raced colt who made a big impression

Chantez and Colin Keane (left) secure Listed success at Leopardstown

when winning on his final run last season in a mile novice at Newbury; beaten a short-head on debut at Sandown but made no mistake next time, storming home by five and a half lengths on heavy ground; could be a smart miler.

Certain Lad
9 b g Clodovil - Chelsey Jayne (Galileo)
Jack Channon   C R Hirst

PLACINGS: 03/730062511/421221-   RPR **115+**

Starts	1st	2nd	3rd	4th	Win & Pl
45	11	8	5	5	£445,744

	9/24	Lonc	1m2f Gp3 soft..	£34,783
	6/24	Comp	1m2f List v soft..	£26,087
105	10/23	Donc	1m2f Cls2 86-105 Hcap heavy	£15,702
100	10/23	York	1m2½f Cls2 85-103 Hcap soft	£15,462
	8/20	York	1m1f Cls1 Gp3 gd-sft.......................................	£28,355
100	1/20	Meyd	1m2f List 97-112 Hcap good.........................	£78,947
98	9/19	Ayr	1m2f Cls2 84-98 Hcap good	£15,563
96	7/19	Hayd	1m Cls3 76-96 Hcap gd-fm	£10,350
	9/18	Pari	1m List 2yo gd-sft...	£26,549
	6/18	Hayd	7f Cls4 2yo gd-fm	£6,469
	5/18	Rdcr	6f Cls5 Auct 2yo gd-fm..................................	£4,464

Veteran middle-distance performer who was better than ever last season and managed his first wins at Group 3 and Listed level since 2020; finally achieved Group 3 victory at Longchamp having finished second in that grade at Sandown, Haydock and Windsor earlier in the year.

Chancellor
3 b c Kingman - Queen's Trust (Dansili)
John & Thady Gosden   Cheveley Park Stud

PLACINGS: 131-   RPR **97+**

Starts	1st	2nd	3rd	4th	Win & Pl
3	1	1	-	-	£22,552

	8/24	Donc	7f Cls3 2yo gd-fm	£13,500
	7/24	Donc	6f Cls5 Mdn 2yo gd-sft..................................	£3,672

Dual winner last season in maiden/novice company either side of an odds-on third in a Listed race at Ascot; evidently thought capable of better as was set to start favourite for the Champagne Stakes until declared a non-runner (broke out of stalls).

Chantez (Ire)
3 b f Wootton Bassett - Lady Lara (Excellent Art)
Ger Lyons (Ire)   Newtown Anner Stud Farm Ltd

PLACINGS: 211-   RPR **93+**

Starts	1st	2nd	3rd	4th	Win & Pl
3	2	1	-	-	£63,513

	9/24	Leop	7f List 2yo good...	£51,304
	8/24	Leop	7f Mdn 2yo good...	£9,235

Won two out of three races as a two-year-old last season, most notably a 7f Listed race at Leopardstown; had also run over that course and distance in two maidens, building on a narrow defeat to win second time out, and stepped forward again to justify favouritism on final run.

Cicero's Gift
5 b g Muhaarar - Terentia (Diktat)
Charlie Hills   Rosehill Racing
PLACINGS: 1/117/17487-   RPR **114**

Starts	1st	2nd	3rd	4th	Win & Pl
9	4	-	-	1	£86,121
107	7/24 Sand	1m Cls2 83-107 Hcap soft			£50,960
	5/23 Gdwd	1m Cls2 3yo gd-sft			£15,702
	3/23 Wolv	1m¹/₂f Cls3 3yo stand			£9,504
	10/22 Newb	1m Cls4 2yo soft			£5,399

Hinted at big potential as a three-year-old (sent off 12-1 for the St James's Palace Stakes after winning first three races) and did so again first time out last year, landing a good handicap at Sandown; badly lost his way subsequently and has since been gelded.

Coltrane (Ire)
8 b g Mastercraftsman - Promise Me (Montjeu)
Andrew Balding   Mick & Janice Mariscotti
PLACINGS: 14212/123155/015643-   RPR **116**

Starts	1st	2nd	3rd	4th	Win & Pl
29	8	7	2	4	£930,271
	5/24 Asct	2m Cls1 Gp3 gd-sft			£45,368
	8/23 York	2m¹/₂f Cls1 Gp2 gd-fm			£141,775
	5/23 Asct	2m Cls1 Gp3 gd-sft			£45,368
	9/22 Donc	2m2f Cls1 Gp2 gd-sft			£73,723
	7/22 Sand	2m Cls1 List good			£29,489
98	6/22 Asct	2m4f Cls2 90-100 Hcap gd-fm			£51,540
86	8/20 York	1m6f Cls2 79-99 3yo Hcap gd-sft			£40,463
	7/20 Chep	1m4f Cls5 Mdn gd-fm			£3,493

Veteran stayer who landed his second successive Sagaro Stakes last season and fourth Group win in total; had gone on to finish second in the 2023 Gold Cup but was only fifth this time and largely struggled subsequently, though still a good third in the Prix du Cadran.

Continuous (Jpn)
5 b h Heart's Cry - Fluff (Galileo)
Aidan O'Brien (Ire)   Smith, Magnier, Tabor & Westerberg
PLACINGS: 11/382115/513009-   RPR **115+**

Starts	1st	2nd	3rd	4th	Win & Pl
14	5	1	2	-	£847,530
	8/24 Curr	1m2f Gp3 good			£28,217
	9/23 Donc	1m6¹/₂f Cls1 Gp1 3yo soft			£421,355
	8/23 York	1m4f Cls1 Gp2 3yo gd-fm			£141,775
	9/22 StCl	1m Gp3 2yo v soft			£33,613
	8/22 Curr	7f Mdn 2yo good			£8,181

Seen as a leading Group 1 contender last season but proved bitterly disappointing, winning only a Group 3 and regularly down the field; had won the St Leger and Great Voltigeur before finishing fifth in the Arc as a three-year-old and interesting that connections persist with him.

Cool Hoof Luke
3 b c Advertise - Dutch Monument (Dutch Art)
Andrew Balding   John Wallinger & Partner
PLACINGS: 1431-   RPR **108**

Starts	1st	2nd	3rd	4th	Win & Pl
4	2	-	1	1	£174,172
	8/24 York	6f Cls1 Gp2 2yo good			£141,775
	6/24 Chmf	6f Cls5 Mdn 2yo stand			£4,187

Only horse to beat Shadow Of Light last season when leaving previous form behind to run out a convincing winner of the Gimcrack Stakes at York; bred to be a sprinter and seemed to appreciate return to 6f that day having been a well-beaten third in the Vintage Stakes.

Cosmic Year
3 br c Kingman - Passage Of Time (Dansili)
Harry Charlton   Juddmonte
PLACINGS: 1-   RPR **99+**

Starts	1st	2nd	3rd	4th	Win & Pl
1	1	-	-	-	£5,400
	9/24 Sand	7f Cls4 2yo good			£5,400

Once-raced colt who won sole start by six and a half lengths at Sandown last season, storming clear on good ground and achieving a remarkable first-time-out RPR of 99; bred to be smart (half-brother to Group 1 winner Time Test) and should be ideally suited by a mile.

Coto De Caza (Ire)
3 b f Sioux Nation - Coto (Fast Company)
Simon & Ed Crisford   Mohammed Sultan
PLACINGS: 31131-   RPR **107**

Starts	1st	2nd	3rd	4th	Win & Pl
5	3	-	2	-	£84,060
	10/24 NmkR	5f Cls1 Gp3 2yo gd-sft			£36,862
	7/24 Gdwd	5f Cls2 2yo gd-fm			£38,655
	7/24 Bevl	5f Cls5 2yo soft			£3,926

Smart and progressive sprinter last season, winning three of her last four races; slightly disappointing when third in a Listed race at Ayr but left that form behind when winning the Cornwallis Stakes on final run; looks all speed and likely to prove best at 5f.

Courage Mon Ami
6 b g Frankel - Crimson Ribbon (Lemon Drop Kid)
John & Thady Gosden   Wathnan Racing
PLACINGS: 11/1162/

Starts	1st	2nd	3rd	4th	Win & Pl
6	4	1	-	-	£426,128
	6/23 Asct	2m4f Cls1 Gp1 gd-fm			£340,260
98	5/23 Gdwd	1m6f Cls2 86-104 Hcap gd-fm			£15,702
	10/22 Newc	1m4¹/₂f Cls5 std-slw			£4,324
	9/22 Kemp	1m4f Cls4 std-slw			£5,346

Won the Gold Cup at Ascot on just his fourth

IRISH INJURED JOCKEYS

Irish Injured Jockeys would like to Thank all our supporters within the industry and from the public whose generosity enables us to provide our services

**CURRAGH HOUSE, RACE,
DUBLIN RD, KILDARE, CO
KILDARE, R51AT80**

045 533011

E : INFO@IRISHINJUREDJOCKEYS.COM

W : WWW.IRISHINJUREDJOCKEYS.COM

DESPITE WHAT OUR NAME SUGGESTS WE DEAL WITH MUCH MORE THAN INJURED JOCKEYS.

WE ARE HERE TO HELP RIDERS WITH PERSONAL CRISES WHETHER MEDICAL, FINANCIAL OR PSYCHOLOGICAL.
WE HAVE A SUPPORT TEAM WHO PROVIDE A PROMPT PROFESSIONAL RESPONSE TO POTENTIAL BENEFICIARIES.
WE HAVE EMPLOYED A PHYSIOTHERAPIST AND NUTRITIONIST TO PROVIDE SERVICES TO JOCKEYS BOTH AT THE IIJ FACILITY IN RACE AND ALSO AT THE RACECOURSES.
IN CONJUNCTION WITH HRI/EQUUIP WE HAVE IMPLEMENTED A FINANCIAL LITERACY COURSE FOR RIDERS.
WE ALSO HAVE SCHEMES FOR PAYMENT OF BURSARIES TO ASSIST JOCKEYS UPSKILL/STUDY FOR ALTERNATIVE CAREERS WHEN RIDERS FINISH RACING.

ALL OUR FUNDING COMES FROM FUNDRAISING AND DONATIONS.
OUR AIM IS TO MAKE A DIFFERENCE TO THE LIVES AND WELFARE OF JOCKEYS PAST AND PRESENT, AND THEIR FAMILIES BY EFFECTIVE USE OF THESE FUNDS.

run, maintaining an unbeaten record at the time in Kyprios's absence; disappointed in the Goodwood Cup (only run on ground softer than good) but bounced back when a good second under a penalty in the Lonsdale Cup; missed all of last year.

Crystal Black (Ire)
7 b g Teofilo - She's Our Mark (Ishiguru)
Gerard Keane (Ire)   Wear A Pink Ribbon Syndicate

PLACINGS: 63/6600/990131/1111-   RPR **116+**

Starts	1st	2nd	3rd	4th	Win & Pl
19	7	-	2	-	£238,274

	8/24	Leop	1m4f Gp3 good	£26,935
103	6/24	Asct	1m4f Cls2 93-105 Hcap gd-fm	£56,694
98	5/24	Curr	1m2f 81-101 Hcap good	£25,652
94	4/24	Curr	1m 73-94 Hcap heavy	£15,391
85	9/23	Curr	1m2f 79-103 Hcap gd-yld	£78,319
77	8/23	Curr	1m 77-96 Hcap gd-yld	£11,487
	7/21	Baln	1m1½f Mdn good	£6,321

Rapidly progressive gelding who has won his last five races, including all four last season; showed remarkable versatility by winning over a mile on heavy ground and the Duke of Edinburgh at Royal Ascot over 1m4f on good to firm; finished with a Group 3 win at Leopardstown.

Damysus
3 ch c Frankel - Legerete (Rahy)
John & Thady Gosden   Wathnan Racing

PLACINGS: 1-   RPR **91+**aw

Starts	1st	2nd	3rd	4th	Win & Pl
1	1	-	-	-	£3,402

	12/24	Sthl	7f Cls5 2yo stand	£3,402

460,000gns son of Frankel who had two-year-old season delayed by a setback when declared for July debut but made up for lost time with an impressive start six months later, winning sole run at Southwell in good fashion; should come into his own over middle distances.

Dance Sequence
4 b f Dubawi - Tearless (Street Cry)
Charlie Appleby   Godolphin

PLACINGS: 11/29207-   RPR **110**

Starts	1st	2nd	3rd	4th	Win & Pl
7	2	2	-	-	£175,951

	10/23	NmkR	7f Cls1 Gp3 2yo soft	£34,026
	7/23	NmkJ	7f Cls4 Mdn 2yo good	£5,400

Fine second in last year's Oaks but otherwise disappointing in a winless campaign last season; just outstayed by Ezeliya at Epsom having found a mile too sharp in the 1,000 Guineas; dropped back to 1m2f but finished weakly again when seventh in a Group 3 on final run.

Dancing Gemini (Ire)
4 b c Camelot - Lady Adelaide (Australia)
Roger Teal   Fishdance Limited

PLACINGS: 25115/26654-   RPR **113+**

Starts	1st	2nd	3rd	4th	Win & Pl
10	2	2	-	1	£278,372

	9/23	Donc	7f Cls1 List 2yo soft	£34,026
	8/23	Newb	7f Cls2 Mdn 2yo gd-sft	£15,462

Ran a huge race first time out last season when a half-length second in the Poule d'Essai des Poulains but didn't quite build on that, albeit in good company; fair sixth in the Derby (weakened late) and fourth in the Queen Elizabeth II Stakes; seems best with cut in the ground.

GUIDE TO THE FLAT **2025**

Jubilant scenes in the Royal Ascot top spot after Crystal Black's victory in the Duke of Edinburgh

Danielle
4 ch f Cracksman - Crimson Ribbon (Lemon Drop Kid)
John & Thady Gosden   A E Oppenheimer
PLACINGS: 3/2136922-   RPR **108**

Starts	1st	2nd	3rd	4th	Win & Pl
8	1	3	2	-	£48,631
	4/24	Weth	1m2f Cls5 soft		£4,320

Big springer in the Oaks market last spring after a 12-length novice win at Wetherby but only third when favourite for the Lingfield trial and lost her way subsequently; bounced back with two good efforts in defeat at Group 3/Listed level after a break and open to further improvement.

Daylight (Fr)
3 b f Earthlight - Latita (Silver Frost)
Patrice Cottier (Fr)   Gousserie Racing & Mme Sandrine Gavrois
PLACINGS: 131322-   RPR **105**

Starts	1st	2nd	3rd	4th	Win & Pl
6	2	2	2	-	£192,085
	7/24	Deau	6f Gp3 2yo gd-sft		£34,783
	5/24	Chan	6f 2yo v soft		£13,043

Smart French filly who won a Group 3 at Deauville on her third run last season and was knocking on the door at a higher level subsequently; produced her best run when second behind Lake Victoria in the Cheveley Park; looks a Commonwealth Cup type.

137

RACING POST

Deira Mile (Ire)
4 b c Camelot - Fastnet Mist (Fastnet Rock)
Owen Burrows   Green Team Racing
PLACINGS: 3324/1423d-   RPR **117**

Starts	1st	2nd	3rd	4th	Win & Pl
8	1	2	2	3	£161,265

4/24 Wind 1m2f Cls5 3-5yo good................£4,320

Has won only once in his career but has run several big races in defeat, finishing fourth in the Derby and St Leger last season; won a novice and finished a close second in a Listed race on only other two runs last year; should benefit from stiffer tests of stamina.

Desert Flower: capped perfect season by winning the Group 1 Fillies' Mile

138

GUIDE TO THE FLAT 2025

Delacroix (Ire)
3 b c Dubawi - Tepin (Bernstein)
Aidan O'Brien (Ire)　　　　　　　　Smith, Magnier & Tabor
PLACINGS: 21212-　　　　　　　　　　　　　　RPR **116**

Starts	1st	2nd	3rd	4th	Win & Pl
5	1	3			£123,129

10/24　NmkR　1m Cls1 Gp3 2yo gd-sft £36,862
8/24　Curr　7f Mdn 2yo gd-fm £10,261

Smart and progressive two-year-old last season despite winning just two out of five races; gained biggest win in the Autumn Stakes at Newmarket; twice narrowly beaten either side of that, notably when a nose second in the Futurity Trophy; should appreciate at least 1m2f.

Desert Flower (Ire)
3 ch f Night Of Thunder - Promising Run (Hard Spun)
Charlie Appleby　　　　　　　　　　　　　　　　　　　Godolphin
PLACINGS: 1111-　　　　　　　　　　　　　　RPR **115+**

Starts	1st	2nd	3rd	4th	Win & Pl
4	4				£366,806

10/24　NmkR　1m Cls1 Gp1 2yo gd-sft £283,550
9/24　Donc　1m Cls1 Gp2 2yo good £68,052
8/24　NmkJ　7f Cls4 2yo gd-fm £4,381
7/24　NmkJ　7f Cls5 Mdn 2yo good £10,823

Top-class filly who won all four races as a two-year-old last season; particularly impressive when a wide-margin winner of the Fillies' Mile at Newmarket, looking a relentless galloper on good to soft ground; set to return a strong fancy for the 1,000 Guineas and should get further.

Desert Hero
5 ch g Sea The Stars - Desert Breeze (Dubawi)
William Haggas　　　　　　　　　　HM The King & HM The Queen
PLACINGS: 131/8113/258-　　　　　　　　　　　RPR **116+**

Starts	1st	2nd	3rd	4th	Win & Pl
10	4				£282,047

94　8/23　Gdwd　1m4f Cls1 Gp3 3yo soft £113,420
　6/23　Asct　1m4f Cls2 87-104 3yo Hcap good £51,540
　10/22　Rdcr　1m1f Cls5 2yo heavy £4,320
　6/22　Hayd　7f Cls4 2yo soft £5,400

Looked an exciting prospect in 2023, winning at Royal Ascot and Glorious Goodwood before a fine third in the St Leger; began last season with a close second behind Okeechobee but surprisingly regressed in two further runs and missed the second half of the year.

Detain (Ire)
3 b c Wootton Bassett - Nisriyna (Intikhab)
John & Thady Gosden　　　　　　　　　　　　　　　Juddmonte
PLACINGS: 116-　　　　　　　　　　　　　　RPR **103+aw**

Starts	1st	2nd	3rd	4th	Win & Pl
3	2				£9,018

10/24　Kemp　7f Cls5 2yo std-slw £3,672
8/24　Kemp　7f Cls4 2yo std-slw £5,346

Dual winner on the all-weather at Kempton last season and particularly impressive when defying a penalty by seven lengths in October; only sixth when thrown in at the deep end on turf debut in the Futurity Trophy, though travelled strongly until fading late on soft ground.

Diego Velazquez (Ire)
4 b c Frankel - Sweepstake (Acclamation)
Aidan O'Brien (Ire)　　　Smith, Magnier, Tabor, Westerberg & Brant
PLACINGS: 116/48011-　　　　　　　　　　　　RPR **118+**

Starts	1st	2nd	3rd	4th	Win & Pl
8	4	-	-	1	£249,295

9/24　Leop　1m Gp2 good £102,609
7/24　Leop　1m1f Gp3 good £25,652
9/23　Leop　1m Gp2 2yo good £78,319
8/23　Curr　7f Mdn 2yo good £10,442

Took a long time to build on promising fourth in the Poule d'Essai des Poulains but finished last season on a high; twice disappointed over middle distances but benefited from drop in class and trip to win last two races; could yet make the grade at Group 1 level over 1m-1m2f.

Docklands
5 b h Massaat - Icky Woo (Mark Of Esteem)
Harry Eustace　　　　　　　　　　　OTI Racing, PJ Bartholomew Et Al
PLACINGS: 2/211163/2227560-　　　　　　　　　RPR **118**

Starts	1st	2nd	3rd	4th	Win & Pl
14	3	5	-		£428,576

94　6/23　Asct　1m Cls2 89-101 3yo Hcap gd-fm £61,848
80　5/23　Asct　1m Cls4 74-82 3yo Hcap soft £8,191
　4/23　Kemp　7f Cls5 Mdn 3-5yo std-slw £3,780

Ascot specialist who ran the race of his life when second in last season's Queen Anne Stakes; won the Britannia at Royal Ascot in 2023 and ran several other good races in handicap/Listed company at the track; below par on ambitious tour of Australia and Hong Kong late last year.

Double Major (Ire)
5 b g Daiwa Major - Dancequest (Dansili)
Christophe Ferland (Fr)　　　　　　　　　　　Wertheimer & Frere
PLACINGS: 214122211/331151-　　　　　　　　RPR **116**

Starts	1st	2nd	3rd	4th	Win & Pl
15	7	4	2	1	£673,857

10/24　StCl　1m7½f Gp1 heavy £173,904
8/24　Deau　1m7f Gp2 gd-sft £64,435
7/24　Lonc　1m6f Gp2 soft £64,435
10/23　Lonc　1m7½f Gp1 heavy £176,982
9/23　Lonc　1m7f Gp2 3yo gd-sft £100,885
5/23　Ange　1m3½f 3yo good £13,274
4/23　Toul　1m2½f 3yo v soft £9,292

Smart French stayer who won a second successive Prix Royal-Oak on final run last season in a much stronger edition of the race; has also won three Group 2 races, including at Longchamp and Deauville last summer, all just short of 2m; didn't stay when fifth in the Prix du Cadran.

139

RACING POST

Dreamy (Ire)
3 b f American Pharoah - Tapestry (Galileo)
Aidan O'Brien (Ire) Flaxman Stables, Magnier, Tabor & Smith
PLACINGS: 114- RPR **100+**

Starts	1st	2nd	3rd	4th	Win & Pl
3	2	-	-	1	£91,071

8/24	Curr	1m Gp3 2yo good	£33,348
8/24	Gdwd	7f Cls2 Mdn 2yo gd-fm	£30,924

Fine middle-distance prospect who won first two races last season, building on Goodwood maiden win with a decisive Group 3 victory when stepped up to a mile at the Curragh; well beaten on final run when fourth in the Fillies' Mile; big, rangy filly who should do better at three.

Dubai Honour (Ire)
7 b g Pride Of Dubai - Mondelice (Montjeu)
William Haggas Mohamed Obaida
PLACINGS: 2426/11346/17317222- RPR **119**

Starts	1st	2nd	3rd	4th	Win & Pl
28	8	7	2	6	£4,109,301

6/24	StCl	1m4f Gp1 gd-sft	£198,748
4/24	Kemp	1m2f Cls1 List std-slw	£28,355
4/23	Rand	1m2f Gp1 soft	£1,731,356
3/23	Rose	1m2f Gp1 good	£331,638
10/21	Lonc	1m2f Gp2 v soft	£101,786
8/21	Deau	1m2f Gp2 3yo gd-sft	£203,571
93	7/21	NmkJ	1m2f Cls2 85-102 3yo Hcap gd-fm	£38,655
	9/20	Hayd	1m Cls4 2yo good	£5,175

High-class middle-distance performer who won last season's Grand Prix de Saint-Cloud to add to Group 1 double in Australia in 2023; hasn't threatened at the top level in Britain since coming second in the 2021 Champion Stakes, winning only a Listed race at Kempton on home soil.

Economics
4 ch c Night Of Thunder - La Pomme D'Amour (Peintre Celebre)
William Haggas Isa Salman Al Khalifa
PLACINGS: 4/11116- RPR **124+**

Starts	1st	2nd	3rd	4th	Win & Pl
6	4	-	-	1	£955,679

9/24	Leop	1m2f Gp1 good	£619,565
8/24	Deau	1m2f Gp2 2yo good	£198,261
5/24	York	1m2$^{1}/_{2}$f Cls2 Gp2 3yo good	£108,997
4/24	Newb	1m Cls4 Mdn 3yo gd-sft	£10,800

Breathtaking winner of last season's Dante Stakes and lived up to that promise by landing the Irish Champion Stakes in the autumn; bled from the nose when only sixth in the Champion Stakes on final run; patiently handled last season with the aim of peaking at four.

Elite Status
4 b c Havana Grey - Dotted Swiss (Swiss Spirit)
Karl Burke Sheikh Mohammed Obaid Al Maktoum
PLACINGS: 113178/1180- RPR **119+**

Starts	1st	2nd	3rd	4th	Win & Pl
10	5	-	1	-	£158,655

7/24	Newb	6f Cls1 Gp3 gd-fm	£48,204
5/24	Newb	6f Cls1 List 3yo good	£36,862
7/23	Deau	6f Gp3 2yo soft	£35,398
5/23	Sand	5f Cls1 List 2yo good	£22,684
5/23	Donc	5f Cls5 Mdn 2yo soft	£3,672

Very smart sprinter on his day and impressed when winning Group 3 and Listed races over 6f at Newbury on first two starts last season; twice well beaten at Group 1 level subsequently, having similarly lost his way at the end of an otherwise strong two-year-old campaign in 2023.

140

GUIDE TO THE FLAT 2025

Elmalka
4 b f Kingman - Nahrain (Selkirk)
Roger Varian — Sheikh Ahmed Al Maktoum
PLACINGS: 1/31444- — RPR **113**

Starts	1st	2nd	3rd	4th	Win & Pl
6	2	-	1	3	£394,952
	5/24	NmkR	1m Cls1 Gp1 3yo good		£297,019
	11/23	Sthl	7f Cls5 2yo stand		£3,564

Narrow winner of last season's 1,000 Guineas, scoring at 28-1 on just her third run; ideally suited by that strongly run mile and failed to confirm the form in different circumstances, proving less effective off steadier gallops and not quite seeing out 1m2f in the Nassau Stakes.

Elmonjed (Ire)
4 b g Blue Point - Naafer (Oasis Dream)
William Haggas — Shadwell Estate Company Ltd
PLACINGS: 11/63311- — RPR **105+**

Starts	1st	2nd	3rd	4th	Win & Pl
7	4	2	-	-	£115,768
91	8/24	York	6f Cls2 83-107 Hcap gd-fm		£51,540
89	8/24	Wind	6f Cls2 79-101 Hcap gd-fm		£38,655
	9/23	Hayd	6f Cls4 2yo good		£5,400
	8/23	Ling	6f Cls4 Mdn 2yo gd-fm		£5,373

Progressive sprinter who won his last two races last season in valuable 6f handicaps; followed up victory in a series final at Windsor by winning at York's Ebor meeting (both on preferred good to firm ground); looks a future Group horse but likely type for more handicap success first.

Enfjaar (Ire)
5 b g Lope De Vega - Tesoro (Galileo)
Roger Varian — Shadwell Estate Company Ltd
PLACINGS: 1/1006/11252- — RPR **117+**

Starts	1st	2nd	3rd	4th	Win & Pl
10	4	2	-	-	£165,926
99	7/24	York	1m2½f Cls2 92-111 Hcap gd-sft		£103,080
94	6/24	Chmf	1m2f Cls3 78-94 Hcap stand		£13,085
	5/23	Chmf	1m Cls4 stand		£5,940
	10/22	NmkR	7f Cls4 Mdn 2yo gd-sft		£5,400

Progressive middle-distance performer who landed a big payday in last season's John Smith's Cup and continued to improve in defeat subsequently; good second under a big weight at Glorious Goodwood and finished a half-length second in a Listed race at Ayr on final run.

English Oak
5 b g Wootton Bassett - Forest Crown (Royal Applause)
Ed Walker — Wathnan Racing
PLACINGS: 71382/2114629- — RPR **114**

Starts	1st	2nd	3rd	4th	Win & Pl
12	3	3	1	1	£123,529
99	6/24	Asct	7f Cls2 91-103 Hcap gd-fm		£56,694
90	5/24	Hayd	7f Cls3 87-91 Hcap soft		£16,200
	7/23	Thsk	1m Cls5 gd-fm		£4,320

Hugely impressive when justifying favouritism in the Buckingham Palace Stakes at Royal Ascot last season; well capable of scoring in a higher grade on that evidence but came up well short last year, running close to that level just once when second in a Listed race at Newbury.

Economics (right): claims the Irish Champion Stakes to make it four wins last season

141

RACING POST

Estrange (Ire)
4 gr f Night Of Thunder - Alienate (Oasis Dream)
David O'Meara — Cheveley Park Stud

PLACINGS: 171-   RPR **104+**

Starts	1st	2nd	3rd	4th	Win & Pl
3	2	-	-	-	£61,658

11/24 Donc 1m2f Cls1 List soft £35,520
8/24 Gdwd 1m2f Cls2 Mdn 3yo soft £25,770

Very lightly raced filly who won two out of three races last season over 1m2f; sent straight into Listed company after a runaway debut win at Goodwood and delivered at the second attempt when beating the promising Danielle at Doncaster, perhaps appreciating return to soft.

Exactly (Ire)
3 ch f Frankel - Heartache (Kyllachy)
Aidan O'Brien (Ire) — Smith, Magnier & Tabor

PLACINGS: 9122331-   RPR **109+**

Starts	1st	2nd	3rd	4th	Win & Pl
7	2	2	2	-	£134,034

10/24 Leop 7f Gp3 2yo soft £25,652
7/24 Leop 7f Mdn 2yo good £9,235

Tough and consistent two-year-old last season; deservedly landed a Group 3 at Leopardstown on her final run having run well in stronger company several times; twice chased home smart stablemate Bedtime Story and finished a half-length third in the Prix Marcel Boussac.

Expanded (Ire)
3 b c Wootton Bassett - Jigsaw (Galileo)
Aidan O'Brien (Ire) — Coolmore, Westerberg & Mrs A M O'Brien

PLACINGS: 12-   RPR **113**

Starts	1st	2nd	3rd	4th	Win & Pl
2	1	1	-	-	£123,942

10/24 Curr 7f Mdn 2yo good £10,261

Lightly raced colt who ran a massive race on just his second start when a neck second to Shadow Of Light in last season's Dewhurst; had made his debut just a week earlier, winning a Curragh maiden, and seems sure to improve again; could prove best over a mile.

Facteur Cheval (Ire)
6 b g Ribchester - Jawlaat (Shamardal)
Jerome Reynier (Fr) — Team Valor International & Gary Barber

PLACINGS: 111241/323232/1632-3   RPR **122**

Starts	1st	2nd	3rd	4th	Win & Pl
18	6	5	5	1	£3,415,237

3/24 Meyd 1m1f Gp1 good £2,283,465
10/22 StCl 1m Gp3 heavy £33,613
7/22 Chan 1m List 3yo good £23,109
6/22 Pari 1m 3yo soft £12,605
5/22 Pari 1m 3yo gd-sft £9,244
4/22 StCl 1m 3yo soft £11,345

High-class miler who has been a standing dish in top mile races in the last two seasons and made his Group 1 breakthrough in last year's Dubai Turf; later finished second in the Queen Elizabeth II Stakes for second successive year and third in the Sussex.

GUIDE TO THE FLAT **2025**

Fairy Godmother (Ire)
3 ch f Night Of Thunder - Scintilating (Siyouni)
Aidan O'Brien (Ire)   Tabor, Smith & Magnier

PLACINGS: 211-   RPR **109+**

Starts	1st	2nd	3rd	4th	Win & Pl
3	2	1	-	-	£109,774
	6/24	Asct	6f Cls1 Gp3 2yo gd-fm		£70,888
	5/24	Naas	6f Gp3 2yo good		£35,913

Breathtaking winner of last season's Albany Stakes at Royal Ascot, storming home to get up by half a length having been repeatedly denied a run when attempting to improve from the rear; missed the rest of the season but has her trainer excited ahead of a likely Classic campaign.

Falakeyah
3 b f New Bay - Alaflaak (War Front)
Owen Burrows   Shadwell Estate Company Ltd

PLACINGS: 1-   RPR **93+** aw

Starts	1st	2nd	3rd	4th	Win & Pl
1	1	-	-	-	£3,402
	11/24	Wolv	1m½f Cls5 Mdn 2yo stand		£3,402

Once-raced filly who made a bright start on the all-weather at Wolverhampton last autumn, hacking up by five and a half lengths over a mile; had been well backed and could well develop into a smart filly.

Fairy Godmother powers to victory in the Albany Stakes at Royal Ascot

Fallen Angel
4 gr f Too Darn Hot - Agnes Stewart (Lawman)
Karl Burke   Wathnan Racing

PLACINGS: 1211/8124-   RPR **116+**

Starts	1st	2nd	3rd	4th	Win & Pl
8	4	2	-	1	£595,614
	5/24	Curr	1m Gp1 3yo gd-yld		£247,826
	9/23	Curr	7f Gp1 2yo gd-yld		£208,850
	8/23	Nmkj	7f Cls1 Gp3 2yo good		£34,026
	5/23	Hayd	7f Cls4 2yo gd-fm		£5,399

Very smart filly who has won two Group 1 races at the Curragh, adding last season's Irish 1,000 Guineas to the 2023 Moyglare; missed nearly four months and not quite at her best in the autumn when second in the Matron and just outstayed in fourth over 1m2f in the Prix de l'Opera.

Falling Snow (Ire)
3 gr f Justify - Winter (Galileo)
Donnacha O'Brien (Ire)   Smith, Magnier & Tabor

PLACINGS: 1-   RPR **90+**

Starts	1st	2nd	3rd	4th	Win & Pl
1	1	-	-	-	£16,417
	8/24	Curr	7f 2yo gd-fm		£16,417

Beautifully bred filly who won sole start last season in a 7f Curragh maiden in August, beating subsequent Fillies' Mile third Ballet Slippers; big, rangy filly who was purposely given a light two-year-old campaign with much better expected at three.

143

RACING POST

Field Of Gold (Ire)
3 gr c Kingman - Princess De Lune (Shamardal)
John & Thady Gosden Juddmonte
PLACINGS: 3114- RPR **107**

Starts	1st	2nd	3rd	4th	Win & Pl
4	2	-	1	1	£68,807

8/24 Sand 7f Cls1 Gp3 2yo good £36,862
7/24 NmkJ 7f Cls3 Mdn 2yo good £10,823

Imposing colt who made a bright start last season, winning twice including the Solario Stakes at Sandown; given a shot at Group 1 level in the Prix Jean-Luc Lagardere and far from disgraced in fourth; looks the type to do better as a three-year-old.

Flora Of Bermuda (Ire)
4 b f Dark Angel - Dubai Power (Cadeaux Genereux)
Andrew Balding Bermuda Racing Limited
PLACINGS: 4261824/921453- RPR **116**

Starts	1st	2nd	3rd	4th	Win & Pl
13	2	3	1	3	£222,269

7/24 York 6f Cls1 Gp3 gd-sft £48,204
8/23 Gdwd 5f Cls2 2yo soft £38,655

Progressive filly who developed into a smart sprinter last season; pulled off a 14-1 upset when winning a Group 3 at York last summer on step up to 6f; continued to improve through three solid runs at Group 1 level, doing best when a half-length third in the Champions Sprint.

Field Of Gold: has potential to excel as a three-year-old

FINEST VINTAGE SILK TOP HATS

We have a full range of vintage silk top hats prepared for Ascot, and available to view at our Cotswold workshop or at the events we will be attending, see web site for details.

...or have your current hat refurbished

Before... ...After

Frogmarsh Mill, South Woodchester,
Stroud, Gloucestershire, GL5 5ET
Tel: 01453 873595
www.honrihats.co.uk

Honri HATS

Formal
3 b f Dubawi - Veracious (Frankel)
Andrew Balding   Cheveley Park Stud

PLACINGS: 114-   RPR **84+**

Starts	1st	2nd	3rd	4th	Win & Pl
3	2	-	-	1	£16,700

9/24 Leic 7f Cls4 2yo soft £4,860
7/24 Newb 7f Cls4 Mdn 2yo gd-fm £6,480

Won two out of three races last season and looked a smart prospect when winning on debut at Newbury; didn't need to step forward when following up on soft ground at Leicester and seemed unsuited by similar conditions when fourth in the Rockfel Stakes; should do better back on quicker ground.

Friendly Soul
4 b f Kingman - In Clover (Inchinor)
John & Thady Gosden   George Strawbridge

PLACINGS: 1/17111-   RPR **118**

Starts	1st	2nd	3rd	4th	Win & Pl
6	5	-	-	-	£398,771

10/24 Lonc 1m2f Gp1 v soft £248,435
8/24   Deau 1m2f Gp2 3yo gd-sft £64,435
7/24   Asct 1m Cls1 Gp3 gd-fm £48,204
5/24   NmkR 1m2f Cls1 List 3yo good £34,026
12/23 Kemp 1m Cls5 Mdn 2yo std-slw £3,672

Top-class filly who has won five out of six races, culminating in the Prix de l'Opera last season; bounced back from sole blip in the Musidora to win well over a mile at Ascot before going back up in trip to win twice more; could have more to come, especially on quicker ground.

Ghostwriter (Ire)
4 b c Invincible Spirit - Moorside (Champs Elysees)
Clive Cox   J C Smith

PLACINGS: 111/44335-   RPR **120**

Starts	1st	2nd	3rd	4th	Win & Pl
8	3	-	2	2	£429,624

9/23 NmkR 1m Cls1 Gp2 2yo gd-fm £70,888
9/23 Asct 7f Cls2 2yo gd-fm £16,200
8/23 NmkJ 7f Cls4 Mdn 2yo good £4,320

Hasn't won since the 2023 Royal Lodge Stakes but was very highly tried last season, running only in Group 1 company, and progressed throughout; fine third at 33-1 in the Juddmonte International and beaten just two lengths when third in the Eclipse and fifth in the Irish Champion.

Giavellotto (Ire)
6 ch h Mastercraftsman - Gerika (Galileo)
Marco Botti   Scuderia La Tesa Limited & Vaibhav Shah

PLACINGS: 1432132/9153/351131-   RPR **123**

Starts	1st	2nd	3rd	4th	Win & Pl
18	7	2	5	1	£2,095,478

12/24 ShTn 1m4f Gp1 good £1,352,113
7/24   NmkJ 1m4f Cls1 Gp2 gd-sft £70,888
5/24   York 1m6f Cls1 Gp2 good £102,078
5/23   York 1m6f Cls1 Gp2 gd-fm £102,078
8/22   NmkJ 1m6f Cls2 86-100 Hcap gd-fm £13,500
3/22   Newc 1m2f Cls4 3yo std-slw £5,832
12/21 Kemp 1m3f Cls5 2yo std-slw £3,780

Developed into a high-class middle-distance horse last season and won the Hong Kong Vase; has spent nearly his whole career as a stayer (dual Yorkshire Cup winner) but stepped up when dropped back to 1m4f, landing the Princess of Wales's Stakes before Sha Tin heroics.

Giselle (Ire)
3 b f Frankel - Newspaperofrecord (Lope De Vega)
Aidan O'Brien (Ire)   Brant, Magnier, Smith, Tabor & Westerberg

PLACINGS: 213-   RPR **92+**

Starts	1st	2nd	3rd	4th	Win & Pl
3	1	1	1	-	£17,539

10/24 Curr 7f Mdn 2yo good £10,261

Held in very high regard and sent off odds-on for all three races last season but didn't quite live up to expectations, winning just once; had a setback after debut second and returned in October to win a maiden before finishing third at Group 3 level; could be a big improver.

Goliath (Ger)
5 b g Adlerflug - Gouache (Shamardal)
Francis Graffard (Fr)   Resolute Bloodstock & Philip Baron Von Ullmann

PLACINGS: 1114/2142116-   RPR **127+**

Starts	1st	2nd	3rd	4th	Win & Pl
11	6	2	-	2	£934,551

10/24 Lonc 1m3f Gp2 heavy £64,435
7/24   Asct 1m4f Cls1 Gp1 gd-fm £708,875
5/24   Lonc 1m4f Gp3 v soft £34,783
7/23   Claf 1m4f List 3yo soft £24,336
6/23   Claf 1m4f 3yo gd-sft £12,389
5/23   StCl 1m4f 3yo gd-sft £11,947

Brilliant winner of last season's King George, relishing an end-to-end gallop and drawing clear of subsequent Arc heroine Bluestocking; had been lightly raced for his age and has run in only

Friendly Soul gets 2024 off to a winning start by scoring in Listed company at Newmarket

GUIDE TO THE FLAT **2025**

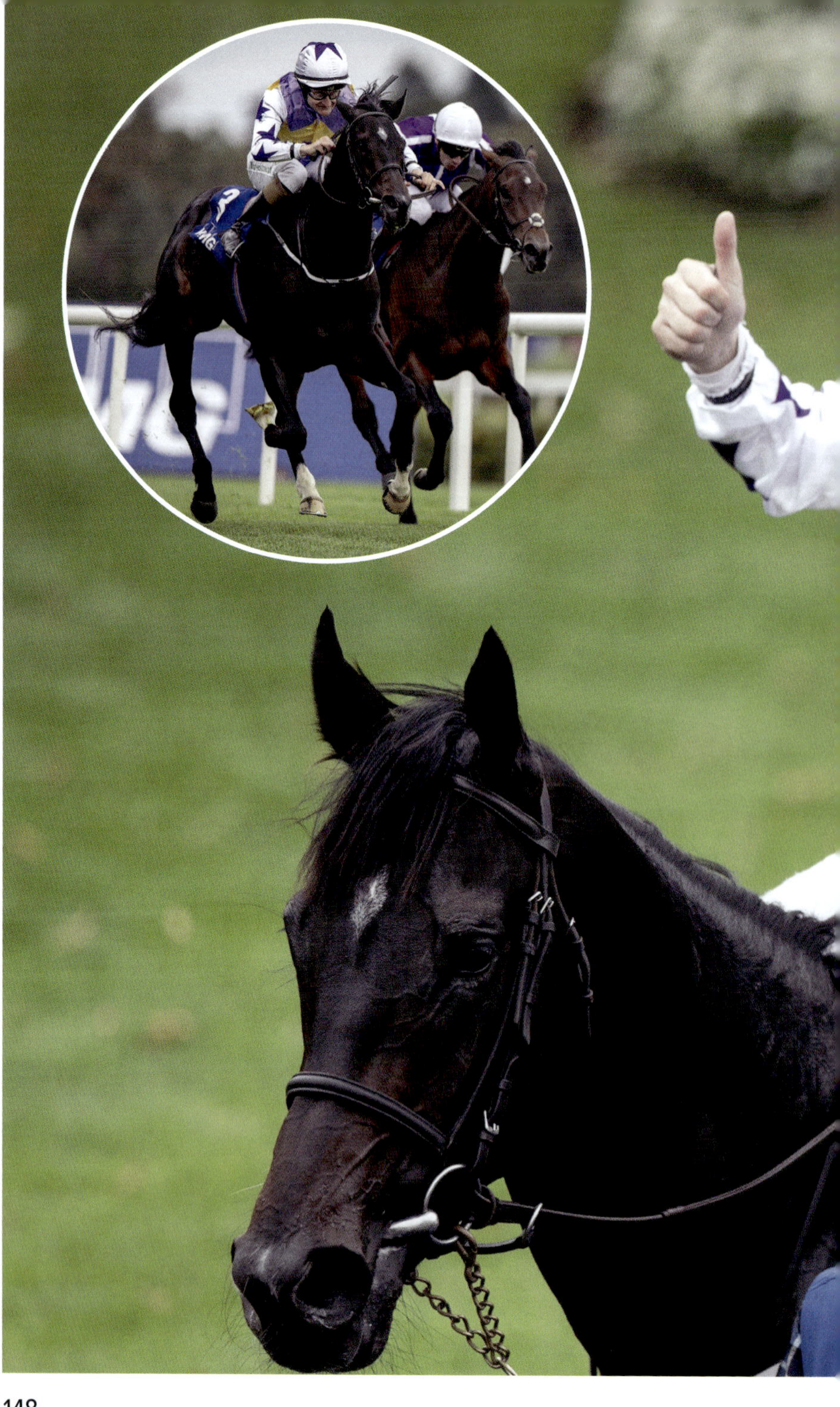

GUIDE TO THE FLAT 2025

one other Group 1, finishing sixth in last season's Japan Cup (unsuited by steady pace).

Green Impact (Ire)
3 b c Wootton Bassett - Emerald Green (Galileo)
Jessica Harrington (Ire)   Marc Chan

PLACINGS: 211-   RPR **104+**

Starts	1st	2nd	3rd	4th	Win & Pl
3	2	1	-	-	£89,495

9/24 Leop 1m Gp2 2yo good £76,957
7/24 Leop 1m Mdn 2yo gd-yld £9,235

Flourished during a light two-year-old campaign last season; twice took the scalp of subsequent Futurity Trophy runner-up Delacroix, most notably in a mile Group 2 at Leopardstown; big horse who should progress as a three-year-old, perhaps over middle distances.

Gregory
5 b g Golden Horn - Gretchen (Galileo)
John & Thady Gosden   Wathnan Racing

PLACINGS: 11135/37315-   RPR **116**

Starts	1st	2nd	3rd	4th	Win & Pl
10	3	-	4	-	£360,798

6/23 Asct 1m6f Cls1 Gp2 3yo good £150,282
5/23 Gdwd 1m3f Cls1 List 3yo good £34,026
4/23 Hayd 1m3¹/₂f Cls2 3yo good £25,770

Looked a future star when winning the Queen's Vase in 2023 (odds-on for the Great Voltigeur next time) but hasn't gone on from there; far from disgraced in five runs in top staying races, doing best when third behind Kyprios in the Goodwood Cup; has since been gelded.

Grey's Monument
5 b g Territories - Matron Of Honour (Teofilo)
Ralph Beckett   Miss Tracey Ashbee

PLACINGS: 4337112/8231/303116-   RPR **116**

Starts	1st	2nd	3rd	4th	Win & Pl
17	5	2	5	1	£158,855

10/24 Rdcr 7f Cls1 List soft £26,654
105 9/24 Asct 7f Cls2 86-105 Hcap soft £41,232
12/23 Kemp 1m Cls1 List std-slw £28,355
86 10/23 York 7f Cls2 74-88 2yo Hcap gd-sft £15,462
76 9/22 Hayd 7f Cls4 66-81 2yo Hcap gd-sft £6,133

Very useful 7f-1m performer who was better than ever last autumn; has won Listed races in each of the last two seasons, most recently at Redcar, and had produced an even better effort on his previous run to defy top weight in a fiercely competitive handicap at Ascot.

Green Impact gets the thumbs-up as one to follow during 2025

149

RACING POST

Haatem (Ire)
4 b c Phoenix Of Spain - Hard Walnut (Cape Cross)
Richard Hannon   Wathnan Racing
PLACINGS: 313521955/1321-   RPR **117**

Starts	1st	2nd	3rd	4th	Win & Pl
13	4	2	3	-	£429,166

6/24	Asct	7f Cls1 Gp3 3yo gd-fm	£85,065
4/24	NmkR	1m Cls1 Gp3 3yo good	£48,204
8/23	Gdwd	7f Cls1 Gp2 2yo gd-sft	£99,243
5/23	Bath	5½f Cls4 Mdn 2yo good	£5,373

Proved himself a very smart colt before missing the second half of last season; had stepped up on solid two-year-old form to win the Craven Stakes and backed that up when third in the 2,000 Guineas and second in the Irish version; dropped in trip and class to win the Jersey Stakes.

Hand Of God
4 ch g Churchill - Barter (Daylami)
Harry Charlton   Mohammed Jaber
PLACINGS: 451/11-   RPR **106+**

Starts	1st	2nd	3rd	4th	Win & Pl
5	3	-	-	1	£85,705

91	6/24	Asct	1m2f Cls2 87-100 3yo Hcap gd-fm	£56,694
88	4/24	Sand	1m Cls2 86-99 3yo Hcap gd-sft	£23,193
	10/23	NmkR	1m Cls4 Mdn 2yo gd-fm	£5,400

Raced just twice last season but made a big impression in claiming two big three-year-old handicaps; returned with victory in the Esher Cup and successfully stepped up to 1m2f when landing the Golden Gates at Royal Ascot; has been gelded during subsequent absence.

Harper's Ferry
4 ch g Lope De Vega - Talent (New Approach)
Ed Walker   M H Dixon & J L Rowsell
PLACINGS: 2/21861-   RPR **107**

Starts	1st	2nd	3rd	4th	Win & Pl
6	2	2	-	-	£25,147

93	10/24	Donc	1m Cls3 78-96 Hcap soft	£9,631
	4/24	Wind	1m2f Cls5 3yo good	£4,320

Lightly raced gelding who took time to live up to initial expectations last season but finished on a high with victory in a mile handicap at Doncaster; benefited from more forceful tactics down in trip having had lofty targets over middle distances previously; likely type for bigger handicaps.

Hazdann (Ire)
3 ch c Night Of Thunder - Hazmiyra (Pivotal)
Dermot Weld (Ire)   Aga Khan
PLACINGS: 91-   RPR **93+**

Starts	1st	2nd	3rd	4th	Win & Pl
2	1	-	-	-	£10,260

	6/24	Curr	7f Mdn 2yo good	£10,261

Missed second half of last season but saw form of Curragh maiden win in June franked in his absence; picked up well to hold off subsequent Group 2 winner Green Impact, looking a smart prospect; looks a miler on pedigree.

Henri Matisse (third from right): Breeders' Cup Juvenile Turf winner

Henri Matisse (Ire)
3 b c Wootton Bassett - Immortal Verse (Pivotal)
Aidan O'Brien (Ire)   Magnier, Tabor, Smith & Merriebelle Irish Fa

PLACINGS: 111251-   RPR **114+**

Starts	1st	2nd	3rd	4th	Win & Pl
6	4	1	-	-	£621,440
11/24	Delm	1m Gd1 2yo firm			£409,449
8/24	Curr	7f Gp2 2yo good			£61,565
6/24	Curr	6f Gp2 2yo yield			£61,565
5/24	Curr	6f Mdn 2yo good			£12,426

Very smart colt on his day and finished his two-year-old season on a high note by landing the Breeders' Cup Juvenile Turf; had won first three races impressively but looked awkward when second in the National Stakes and fitted with blinkers when fifth in the Prix Jean-Luc Lagardere.

Higher Leaves (Ire)
4 b f Golden Horn - Dettoria (Declaration Of War)
Henry de Bromhead (Ire)   James Wigan

PLACINGS: 43/158131-   RPR **114**

Starts	1st	2nd	3rd	4th	Win & Pl
8	3	-	2	1	£77,482
11/24	Toul	1m2½f Gp3 v soft			£34,783
9/24	Lonc	1m2½f List 3yo gd-sft			£23,913
4/24	Dund	1m2½f Mdn 3yo stand			£6,670

Progressive filly who went from strength to strength after a mid-season break last term; particularly impressive when running away with a Group 3 at Toulouse on final run; had also won

GUIDE TO THE FLAT **2025**

a Listed race in France before a creditable third in the Pride Stakes at Newmarket.

Hopewell Rock (Ire)
3 b c New Bay - Tidewalker (Lawman)
George Boughey   Sheikh Mohammed Obaid Al Maktoum

PLACINGS: 11-   RPR **99+**

Starts	1st	2nd	3rd	4th	Win & Pl
2	2	-	-	-	£17,280
10/24	Bath	1m Cls4 2yo heavy			£10,800
8/24	Newb	1m Cls4 Mdn 2yo good			£6,480

Highly promising colt who was unbeaten in two runs last season; not tried above novice company but did well to defy a penalty against a subsequent ten-length winner (pair clear) when winning on final run at Bath; won twice over a mile and should stay further.

Horizon Dore (Fr)
5 b g Dabirsim - Sweet Alabama (Enrique)
Patrice Cottier (Fr)   Gousserie Racing, EC Gribomont & F Delaunay

PLACINGS: 11/52111130/42523-   RPR **120**

Starts	1st	2nd	3rd	4th	Win & Pl
15	6	3	2	1	£613,129
9/23	Lonc	1m2f Gp2 gd-sft			£100,885
9/23	Lonc	1m2f Gp3 3yo gd-sft			£35,398
7/23	StCl	1m2f Gp2 3yo gd-sft			£65,575
6/23	Lonc	1m2f List 3yo gd-sft			£24,336
10/22	Mars	1m½f List 2yo good			£25,210
9/22	Saln	1m1f 2yo heavy			£7,563

High-class middle-distance performer who was

151

knocking on the door in Group 1 races last season; finished a short-head second in the Prix d'Ispahan and a good third in the Prince of Wales's Stakes; dual Group 2 winner and top-level breakthrough might not be far away.

Hotazhell
3 b c Too Darn Hot - Azenzar (Danehill Dancer)
Jessica Harrington (Ire)   Silverton Hill Partnership

PLACINGS: 411211-				RPR **116**
Starts	1st	2nd	3rd	4th	Win & Pl
6	4	1	-	1	£245,506

10/24	Donc	1m Cls1 Gp1 2yo soft	£127,576
9/24	Curr	1m Gp2 2yo gd-yld	£61,565
7/24	Leop	7f Gp3 2yo gd-yld	£25,652
6/24	Curr	7f Mdn 2yo good	£10,261

Tough and classy colt who capped a fine two-year-old season with a narrow win in the Futurity Trophy at Doncaster last year; won four out of six races in all, doing particularly well when stepped up to a mile; should stay at least 1m2f.

Iberian (Ire)
4 b c Lope De Vega - Bella Estrella (High Chaparral)
Charlie Hills   Teme Valley & Ballylinch Stud

PLACINGS: 1216/001-				RPR **103**aw
Starts	1st	2nd	3rd	4th	Win & Pl
7	3	1	-	-	£134,703

12/24	Sthl	6f Cls2 stand	£13,500
9/23	Donc	7f Cls1 Gp2 2yo soft	£71,040
6/23	Newb	6½f Cls4 2yo good	£5,400

Has had little go right since looking a potential star as a two-year-old but took a small step back in the right direction when winning at Southwell in December; won the Champagne Stakes in 2023 and very lightly raced since, disappointing in the 2,000 Guineas and Prix Jean Prat last year.

Ice Max
4 gr g Dark Angel - Cool Kitten (One Cool Cat)
Karl Burke   Sheikh Mohammed Obaid Al Maktoum

PLACINGS: 41715/1145149-				RPR **114**
Starts	1st	2nd	3rd	4th	Win & Pl
12	5	-	-	3	£142,139

8/24	Gdwd	1m Cls1 Gp2 soft	£89,885
97	4/24	Muss	1m Cls3 76-97 3yo Hcap gd-sft	£15,462
89	4/24	Bath	1m Cls3 76-93 3yo Hcap heavy	£14,174
80	10/23	Catt	7f Cls4 73-86 2yo Hcap gd-sft	£5,669
	8/23	Catt	7f Cls5 Mdn 2yo gd-sft	£3,725

Won last season's Celebration Mile at Goodwood, albeit perhaps flattered by Group 2 victory in a modest race for the grade; had won two handicaps early in the year but progress stalled otherwise, with disappointing efforts on final two runs; needs soft ground.

Hotazhell (4): ended last season on a high with success in the Group 1 Futurity Trophy at Doncaster

GUIDE TO THE FLAT **2025**

RACING POST

Ides Of March (Ire)
3 b c Wootton Bassett - Nickname (Scat Daddy)
Aidan O'Brien (Ire) Magnier, Tabor, Smith & Brookdale Racing
PLACINGS: 43117- RPR **107+**

Starts	1st	2nd	3rd	4th	Win & Pl
5	2	-	1	1	£48,613

8/24 Curr 6f Gp3 2yo good.................................£28,217
8/24 Curr 6f Mdn 2yo gd-fm............................£10,261

Promising sprinter who won twice by wide margins over 6f at the Curragh last season, adding a Group 3 to his maiden win; skipped the Middle Park Stakes because of soft ground before finding the Breeders' Cup Juvenile Turf Sprint too sharp, managing only seventh.

Illinois (Ire)
4 b c Galileo - Danedrop (Danehill)
Aidan O'Brien (Ire) Smith, Magnier & Tabor
PLACINGS: 13/3212221- RPR **119**

Starts	1st	2nd	3rd	4th	Win & Pl
9	3	4	2	-	£636,840

10/24 Lonc 1m7f Gp2 3yo soft.................................£99,130
6/24 Asct 1m6f Cls1 Gp2 3yo gd-fm.......................£150,282
10/23 Curr 1m1f Mdn 2yo soft.................................£8,615

Ran consistently well in top middle-distance and staying races last season; beaten a neck in the Great Voltigeur and St Leger having earlier won the Queen's Vase at Royal Ascot; won well when stepped up in trip again for the Prix Chaudenay and looks a smart stayer in the making.

Inisherin
4 b c Shamardal - Ajman Princess (Teofilo)
Kevin Ryan Sheikh Mohammed Obaid Al Maktoum
PLACINGS: 2/161150- RPR **120+**

Starts	1st	2nd	3rd	4th	Win & Pl
7	3	1	-	-	£514,041

6/24 Asct 6f Cls1 Gp1 3yo gd-fm.......................£411,573
5/24 Hayd 6f Cls1 Gp2 3yo soft........................£70,888
3/24 Newc 1m Cls4 3yo stand.................................£6,156

Brilliant winner of last season's Commonwealth Cup at Royal Ascot on quick ground (form strongly franked by second and fourth) but disappointed subsequently; had excuses when fifth in the July Cup but ran worse in the Sprint Cup at Haydock (favourite both times).

Isle Of Jura
5 b g New Approach - Falls Of Lora (Street Cry)
George Scott Victorious Racing
PLACINGS: 5/7411612/11111- RPR **120**

Starts	1st	2nd	3rd	4th	Win & Pl
13	8	1	-	1	£468,511

6/24 Asct 1m4f Cls1 Gp2 gd-fm.......................£141,775
5/24 Gdwd 1m2f Cls1 List good.........................£34,026
3/24 Bhrn 1m4f List gd-fm..............................£94,488
2/24 Bhrn 1m3f gd-fm...................................£63,780
2/24 Bhrn 1m2f List gd-fm..............................£70,866
0 12/23 Bhrn 1m2f Hcap good..........................£40,000
83 7/23 NmkJ 1m Cls5 63-83 Hcap good................£5,234
71 7/23 Newb 1m Cls5 51-72 3yo Hcap good.............£4,527

Massive improver in the first half of last year and looked a proper Group 1 horse when completing

Isle Of Jura: prolific scorer last season, notching five wins from as many starts

154

Don't put your horse at *risk*!

Always use a Registered Farrier

It is illegal in Great Britain to practise farriery if unregistered. Check the Register at
www.farrier-reg.gov.uk

frc@farrier-reg.gov.uk
01733 319911
Farriers Registration Council

a five-timer in the Hardwicke Stakes at Royal Ascot; easily beat subsequent King George winner Goliath but picked up an injury when on course for that race.

Jabaara (Ire)
4 b f Exceed And Excel - Baheeja (Dubawi)
Roger Varian   Sheikh Ahmed Al Maktoum

PLACINGS: 10426/31121d-   RPR **109**

Starts	1st	2nd	3rd	4th	Win & Pl
10	3	3	1	1	£166,278

6/24	Carl	7f Cls1 List 3yo gd-fm	£26,654
6/24	Muss	7f Cls1 List good	£22,684
5/23	NmkR	6f Cls2 2yo good	£15,462

Smart and progressive filly last season; won back-to-back Listed races over 7f before stepping up in class and trip to finish second behind Porta Fortuna in the Falmouth Stakes at Newmarket; first past the post but placed second in a Group 3 at Goodwood on final run.

James's Delight (Ire)
4 b g Invincible Army - Heavens Peak (Pivotal)
Clive Cox   Paul & Clare Rooney

PLACINGS: 1435/19101128-   RPR **116+**

Starts	1st	2nd	3rd	4th	Win & Pl
12	5	1	1	1	£140,673

	7/24	Deau	6f List 3yo soft	£23,913
102	6/24	York	6f Cls2 81-102 3yo Hcap gd-sft	£51,540
97	5/24	NmkR	6f Cls2 77-97 3yo Hcap good	£25,770
88	4/24	Pont	6f Cls3 77-88 3yo Hcap heavy	£10,308
	7/23	Newb	6f Cls4 2yo gd-sft	£6,480

Won four times last season, all over 6f, during a hugely progressive campaign; landed three handicaps, including valuable contests at Newmarket and York, before a Listed strike at Deauville; went close back there on Pattern debut but well beaten in the Champions Sprint.

Jan Brueghel (Ire)
4 b c Galileo - Devoted To You (Danehill Dancer)
Aidan O'Brien (Ire)   Westerberg, Magnier, Tabor & Smith

PLACINGS: 1111-   RPR **120+**

Starts	1st	2nd	3rd	4th	Win & Pl
4	4	-	-	-	£596,340

9/24	Donc	1m6½f Cls1 Gp1 3yo good	£421,355
8/24	Gdwd	1m4f Cls1 Gp3 3yo gd-fm	£113,420
6/24	Curr	1m2f Gp3 yld-sft	£51,304
5/24	Curr	1m2f Mdn 3yo good	£10,261

Exciting unbeaten colt who completed a four-timer when winning last season's St Leger just four months after his debut, also landing a pair of Group 3 races; controversially denied a run when sent to Australia for the Melbourne Cup; likely to go down the staying route.

Jan Brueghel: four wins from four starts at three

GUIDE TO THE FLAT **2025**

RACING POST

Jancis (Ire)
4 ch f Tamayuz - Blame The Ruler (Ruler Of The World)
Willie McCreery (Ire) Arturo Cousino
PLACINGS: 118- RPR **108**

Starts	1st	2nd	3rd	4th	Win & Pl
3	2	-	-	-	£41,043
7/24	Leop	7f Gp3 good			£33,348
6/24	Leop	7f Mdn gd-yld			£7,696

Very lightly raced filly who won two out of three races last season, with sole defeat when below par in the Matron Stakes; had been sent off just 9-1 that day after building on maiden win with a Group 3 victory at Leopardstown; should have lots more to offer.

January (Ire)
3 b f Kingman - I Can Fly (Fastnet Rock)
Aidan O'Brien (Ire) Smith, Magnier & Tabor
PLACINGS: 213122- RPR **102+**

Starts	1st	2nd	3rd	4th	Win & Pl
6	2	3	1	-	£177,604
8/24	Tipp	7½f List 2yo gd-fm			£23,087
6/24	Gowr	7f Mdn 2yo good			£7,696

Unlucky to bump into Desert Flower last season, finishing second behind that rival in the May Hill Stakes and Fillies' Mile; improved as she went up in trip, hacking up in a 7½f Listed race at Tipperary before good efforts over a mile; big filly who should do better as a three-year-old.

GUIDE TO THE FLAT 2025

Jarraaf
4 b c Zoustar - Arabda (Elnadim)
Owen Burrows   Sheikh Ahmed Al Maktoum
PLACINGS: 1/34112-   RPR **113+**

Starts	1st	2nd	3rd	4th	Win & Pl
6	3	1	1	1	£76,796

95	8/24	Asct	6f Cls2 83-96 3yo Hcap gd-fm	£39,344
87	7/24	Asct	6f Cls3 84-95 Hcap good	£10,800
	10/23	Kemp	6f Cls4 2yo std-slw	£5,346

Lightly raced and progressive sprinter who flourished in three runs over 6f at Ascot in the second half of last season; won back-to-back handicaps by wide margins and nearly defied a sharp rise in class when second in a Group 3 in October; should have more to come.

Jasour
4 gr c Havana Grey - Twilight Thyme (Bahamian Bounty)
Clive Cox   Al Mohamediya Racing
PLACINGS: 21189/13600-   RPR **114+**

Starts	1st	2nd	3rd	4th	Win & Pl
10	3	1	1	-	£194,502

5/24	Asct	6f Cls1 Gp3 3yo gd-sft	£45,368
7/23	NmkJ	6f Cls1 Gp2 2yo gd-fm	£56,710
6/23	Nott	5f Cls5 Mdn 2yo gd-fm	£3,699

Looked a smart sprint prospect early last season and finished third in the Commonwealth Cup at Royal Ascot having won the course-and-distance trial; fair sixth in the July Cup (raced keenly) but well below par in final two runs, albeit getting upset in the stalls in the Flying Five.

Kalpana
4 b f Study Of Man - Zero Gravity (Dansili)
Andrew Balding   Juddmonte
PLACINGS: 12123111-   RPR **118+**

Starts	1st	2nd	3rd	4th	Win & Pl
8	5	2	1	-	£424,677

	10/24	Asct	1m3½f Cls1 Gp1 soft	£283,550
	9/24	Kemp	1m4f Cls1 Gp3 std-slw	£48,204
	7/24	Haml	1m3f Cls1 List 3yo good	£28,355
78	4/24	NmkR	1m2f Cls3 78-90 3yo Hcap good	£15,462
	1/24	Wolv	1m½f Cls5 3-4yo stand	£3,942

Developed into a top-class filly last season, ending with a Group 1 win at Ascot; didn't race at two and went handicapping off just 78 but soon climbed through the ranks, following easy Group 3 and Listed wins with another impressive strike over 1m4f on Champions Day.

Kerdos (Ire)
5 b h Profitable - The Mums (Holy Roman Emperor)
Clive Cox   John Connolly & A D Spence
PLACINGS: 11/28326518/8515546-   RPR **117+**

Starts	1st	2nd	3rd	4th	Win & Pl
17	4	2	1	1	£192,170

5/24	Hayd	5f Cls1 Gp2 soft	£70,888
9/23	Bevl	5f Cls1 List good	£28,355
10/22	Wind	6f Cls5 2yo good	£3,672
9/22	Hayd	6f Cls4 Mdn 2yo gd-sft	£5,399

Smart sprinter who won last season's Temple Stakes at Haydock and continued to run well in defeat in top 5f races; came closest when a two-length fifth in the King George Stakes, having filled the same spot in the King Charles III at Royal Ascot; goes on any ground.

Khaadem (Ire)
9 br g Dark Angel - White Daffodil (Footstepsinthesand)
Charlie Hills   Mrs Fitri Hay
PLACINGS: 1149/06031501/01002-   RPR **119**

Starts	1st	2nd	3rd	4th	Win & Pl
38	9	3	4	4	£1,865,572

	6/24	Asct	6f Cls1 Gp1 gd-fm	£567,100
	6/23	Asct	6f Cls1 Gp1 gd-fm	£567,100
	7/22	Gdwd	5f Cls1 Gp2 gd-fm	£170,130
	4/22	NmkR	5f Cls1 Gp3 good	£45,368
	9/21	Donc	5f Cls1 List good	£25,520
107	8/19	Gdwd	6f Cls2 91-107 Hcap gd-fm	£155,625
	5/19	Newb	6f Cls1 List 3yo good	£39,697
	9/18	Donc	5f Cls2 2yo gd-sft	£11,205
	8/18	NmkJ	6f Cls4 2yo good	£5,175

Veteran sprinter who has remarkably won the last two runnings of the Jubilee Stakes at Royal Ascot despite finishing no better than fourth in 13 other runs at Group 1 level; twice well beaten in Europe after latest win but appreciated return to quick ground when second in the US.

Kikkuli
4 b c Kingman - Kind (Danehill)
Harry Charlton   Juddmonte
PLACINGS: 2/122646-   RPR **113**

Starts	1st	2nd	3rd	4th	Win & Pl
7	1	3	-	1	£65,649

4/24	NmkR	7f Cls4 Mdn 3yo good	£5,154

Half-brother to Frankel who has been unlucky not to win more than a maiden; finished a short-head second behind Haatem in last season's Jersey Stakes; unsuited by soft ground either

---

Kalpana: thoroughly likeable filly who went from strength to strength last year after a belated start on the track

159

side of that before a half-length fourth in the Hungerford; likely improver.

Kind Of Blue
4 b c Blue Point - Blues Sister (Compton Place)
James Fanshawe   Wathnan Racing
PLACINGS: 1143221-   RPR **121+**

Starts	1st	2nd	3rd	4th	Win & Pl
7	3	2	1	1	£437,685
	10/24	Asct	6f Cls1 Gp1 soft		£283,550
	5/24	Donc	6f Cls5 gd-fm		£4,320
	4/24	Kemp	6f Cls5 std-slw		£3,780

Lightly raced sprinter who won the Champions Sprint at Ascot by a head on final run last season; had been beaten four times since last win but progressed all year, losing out in similarly tight finishes in previous two races, notably in the Sprint Cup at Haydock.

King's Gambit (Ire)
4 ch c Saxon Warrior - Pure Symmetry (Storm Cat)
Harry Charlton   Wathnan Racing
PLACINGS: 812/12237-4   RPR **119**

Starts	1st	2nd	3rd	4th	Win & Pl
9	2	3	1	1	£275,683
93	5/24	Newb	1m2f Cls2 78-99 3yo Hcap good		£51,540
	8/23	Newb	1m Cls4 Mdn 2yo gd-sft		£6,480

Did well to back up a runaway win in the London Gold Cup first time out last season despite not winning again; beaten less than a length in three Group races, just finding 1m4f too far in the Great Voltigeur after his best run in the York Stakes; below par in the Champion Stakes.

King's Gamble (Ire)
4 b c Kingman - Zondaq (Bernardini)
Ralph Beckett   Clipper Logistics
PLACINGS: 13/252-   RPR **111**

Starts	1st	2nd	3rd	4th	Win & Pl
5	1	2	1	-	£68,367
	8/23	NmkJ	6f Cls4 2yo good		£4,320

Very lightly raced colt who progressed well in three runs despite not winning; beaten at odds-on first time out in a novice before a good fifth in the Britannia at Royal Ascot; took a big step forward when second in a Group 3 at Goodwood on final run behind Lead Artist.

Kinross
8 b g Kingman - Ceilidh House (Selkirk)
Ralph Beckett   Marc Chan
PLACINGS: 11113/731122/283127-   RPR **121+**

Starts	1st	2nd	3rd	4th	Win & Pl
34	11	5	4	2	£1,954,114
	9/24	Donc	7f Cls1 Gp2 good		£79,394
	8/23	York	7f Cls1 Gp2 gd-fm		£283,550
	8/23	Gdwd	7f Cls1 Gp2 gd-sft		£102,078
	10/22	Asct	6f Cls1 Gp1 gd-sft		£283,550
	10/22	Lonc	7f Gp1 v soft		£168,059
	9/22	Donc	7f Cls1 Gp2 soft		£68,052
	8/22	York	7f Cls1 Gp2 gd-fm		£226,840
	7/21	Gdwd	7f Cls1 Gp2 soft		£102,078
	5/21	Hayd	7f Cls1 Gp3 gd-sft		£34,026
	11/20	Kemp	1m Cls1 List std-slw		£22,684
	10/19	NmkR	7f Cls4 2yo gd-sft		£5,175

Standing dish in top 6f-7f races over several seasons, claiming a Group 1 double in the Prix de la Foret and Champions Sprint in 2022 plus six Group 2 races over 7f; generally just below his best last season but still won the Park Stakes at Doncaster and was second in the Foret.

Kind Of Blue (red cap) leads before winning the Group 1 Champions Sprint

GUIDE TO THE FLAT 2025

Kyprios (Ire)
7 ch h Galileo - Polished Gem (Danehill)
Aidan O'Brien (Ire)   Moyglare, Magnier, Tabor, Smith & Westerberg
PLACINGS: 16/14/111111/22-1111111-   RPR **122+**

Starts	1st	2nd	3rd	4th	Win & Pl
19	15	2	-	1	£2,635,558

10/24	Asct	1m7½f Cls1 Gp2 soft	£255,195
10/24	Lonc	2m4f Gp1 soft	£149,061
9/24	Curr	1m6f Gp1 good	£297,391
7/24	Gdwd	2m Cls1 Gp1 good	£283,550
6/24	Asct	2m4f Cls1 Gp1 gd-fm	£368,615
5/24	Leop	1m6f Gp3 good	£26,935
4/24	Navn	1m6f List gd-yld	£26,935
10/22	Lonc	2m4f Gp1 v soft	£144,050
9/22	Curr	1m6f Gp1 yield	£239,496
7/22	Gdwd	2m Cls1 Gp1 good	£283,550
6/22	Asct	2m4f Cls1 Gp1 gd-fm	£283,550
5/22	Leop	1m6f Gp3 good	£24,790
4/22	Navn	1m6f List good	£24,790
4/21	Cork	1m2f 3yo good	£7,112
9/20	Gway	1m½f Mdn 2yo heavy	£8,450

Outstanding stayer who regained his Gold Cup crown and took Group 1 tally to eight during a sensational seven-race unbeaten run last year; had also gone unbeaten in 2022, with only defeats since stepping up to staying trips coming after a long injury layoff the following year.

Lake Forest
4 ch c No Nay Never - Lady Aquitaine (El Prado)
William Haggas   Tony Bloom & Ian McAleavy
PLACINGS: 12417/221-   RPR **122+**

Starts	1st	2nd	3rd	4th	Win & Pl
8	3	3	-	1	£3,160,903

11/24	Rose	7½f 4yo good	£2,807,487
8/23	York	6f Cls1 Gp2 2yo gd-fm	£151,699
6/23	Hayd	6f Cls4 2yo gd-fm	£5,399

Crowned a fine 2024 with a richly deserved win in the £2.8 million Golden Eagle in Australia in November over 7½f; had finished second in the Commonwealth Cup and a strong Group 3 at Newbury, both over 6f, but proved stamina for further in Australia; needs quick ground.

Lake Victoria (Ire)
3 b f Frankel - Quiet Reflection (Showcasing)
Aidan O'Brien (Ire)   Tabor, Smith & Magnier
PLACINGS: 11111-   RPR **116+**

Starts	1st	2nd	3rd	4th	Win & Pl
5	5	-	-	-	£824,308

11/24	Delm	1m Gd1 2yo firm	£409,449
9/24	NmkR	6f Cls1 Gp1 2yo soft	£165,355
9/24	Curr	7f Gp1 2yo good	£205,217
8/24	NmkJ	7f Cls1 Gp3 2yo gd-fm	£34,026
6/24	Curr	7f Mdn 2yo good	£10,261

Last season's champion two-year-old filly after a sensational unbeaten campaign; won five times in all, most impressively when dropped back to 6f for the Cheveley Park Stakes having also landed the Moyglare; followed up at the Breeders' Cup over a mile.

Lazio (Ger)
3 b c Make Believe - La Caldera (Hernando)
Waldemar Hickst (Ger)   Stall Lucky Owner
PLACINGS: 11-   RPR **109**

Starts	1st	2nd	3rd	4th	Win & Pl
2	2	-	-	-	£110,869

10/24	Siro	1m Gp2 2yo heavy	£97,826
9/24	Hanv	1m List 2yo gd-sft	£13,043

Unbeaten German colt who was a sensational eight-length winner of Italy's most prestigious two-year-old race, the Premio Gran Criterium, last season; had won his first two races in

RACING POST

Germany, including a Listed race at Hanover; looks Classic material.

Lazzat (Fr)
4 b g Territories - Lastochka (Australia)
Jerome Reynier (Fr)   Nurlan Bizakov

PLACINGS: 11111129-   RPR **124+**

Starts	1st	2nd	3rd	4th	Win & Pl
8	6	1	-	-	£1,374,850

8/24	Deau	6½f Gp1 gd-sft	£188,810
6/24	Lonc	7f Gp3 3yo good	£34,783
4/24	Deau	7f Gp3 3yo heavy	£34,783
2/24	Cagn	7½f List 3yo heavy	£23,913
2/24	Cagn	7½f 3yo v soft	£13,043
1/24	Cagn	7½f 3yo v soft	£10,000

Unraced as a two-year-old but made rapid strides last season, completing a six-timer with a runaway victory in the Prix Maurice de Gheest; had done all his other racing over further and stepped back up in trip when second in Australia and below par in Hong Kong.

Lead Artist
4 b c Dubawi - Obligate (Frankel)
John & Thady Gosden   Juddmonte

PLACINGS: 2131212-   RPR **122+**

Starts	1st	2nd	3rd	4th	Win & Pl
7	3	3	1	-	£323,861

10/24	NmkR	1m1f Cls1 Gp3 gd-sft	£48,204
8/24	Gdwd	1m Cls1 Gp3 3yo gd-fm	£56,710
5/24	York	1m Cls2 good	£20,616

Dual Group 3 winner at 1m-1m1f last season, impressing in a steadily run Darley Stakes at Newmarket; didn't quite stay 1m2f when denied in Bahrain on final run, having been tapped for toe when second over 7f in another Group 2 at Doncaster; capable of winning at that level.

Lethal Levi
6 b g Lethal Force - Dartrix (Dutch Art)
Karl Burke   Made In Thailand

PLACINGS: 0203557494/80142011-   RPR **115**

Starts	1st	2nd	3rd	4th	Win & Pl
36	9	7	4	5	£342,839

102	9/24	Ayr	6f Cls2 93-107 Hcap gd-fm	£92,772
98	8/24	Newb	7f Cls2 81-102 Hcap gd-fm	£25,770
91	5/24	Newb	6f Cls2 84-105 Hcap gd-fm	£38,655
92	7/22	NmkJ	6f Cls2 82-100 3yo Hcap gd-fm	£25,770
85	7/22	NmkJ	6f Cls2 84-105 3yo Hcap gd-fm	£51,540
81	5/22	Hayd	6f Cls2 80-87 3yo Hcap gd-sft	£6,426
78	4/22	Yarm	6f Cls4 74-82 3yo Hcap gd-fm	£4,995
	8/21	Rdcr	6f Cls5 2yo gd-fm	£3,888
	6/21	Haml	6f Cls4 Mdn 2yo good	£4,266

Battle-hardened sprinter who has a fine record in big handicaps and landed his biggest prize in last season's Ayr Gold Cup; has done most of his racing over 6f but also did well over 7f last year, gaining a first win over the trip at Newbury having come second in the Bunbury Cup.

Lead Artist works under Kieran Shoemark at Sakir Racecourse in Bahrain

GUIDE TO THE FLAT 2025

Liberty Lane (Ire)
5 b g Teofilo - Cape Liberty (Cape Cross)
Karl Burke   Sheikh Mohammed Obaid Al Maktoum
PLACINGS: 1/270410/0170212-   RPR **117**

Starts	1st	2nd	3rd	4th	Win & Pl
14	4	3	-	1	£217,877
105	9/24	NmkR	1m1f Cls2 86-105 Hcap soft............................£90,195
101	5/24	NmkR	1m1f Cls2 90-106 Hcap good........................£51,540
97	9/23	Donc	1m Cls2 84-104 Hcap soft.................................£25,770
	10/22	Nott	1m¹/₂f Cls2 2yo soft..£10,308

Runaway winner of last season's Cambridgeshire, finally realising potential that had also seen him fancied for the race on unsuitably quick ground in 2023; produced mixed form in between but suggested he might be up to Group level when second in the Darley Stakes on final run.

Los Angeles (Ire)
4 b c Camelot - Frequential (Dansili)
Aidan O'Brien (Ire)   Westerberg, Magnier, Tabor & Smith
PLACINGS: 11/1311439-   RPR **121**

Starts	1st	2nd	3rd	4th	Win & Pl
9	5	-	2	1	£1,654,416
	8/24	York	1m4f Cls1 Gp2 3yo gd-fm....................£151,699
	6/24	Curr	1m4f Gp1 3yo good...................................£619,565
	5/24	Leop	1m2f Gp3 3yo good.....................................£41,043
	10/23	StCl	1m2f Gp1 2yo v soft...............................£126,416
	9/23	Tipp	1m1f Mdn 2yo yield..£7,832

High-class middle-distance performer who won last season's Irish Derby as well as finishing third in the Derby and the Arc; also proved effective at 1m2f when a close fourth in the Irish Champion Stakes but might have found the Champion Stakes coming too soon after the Arc.

Magical Zoe (Ire)
7 b m Shantou - Fedaia (Anabaa)
Henry de Bromhead (Ire)   Patrick & Scott Bryceland
PLACINGS: 5131-   RPR **112**

Starts	1st	2nd	3rd	4th	Win & Pl
4	2	-	1	-	£311,991
102	8/24	York	1m6f Cls2 86-108 Hcap gd-fm................£300,000
	6/24	DRoy	1m5f Mdn good...£5,643

One-time jumps horse who made hay when switched to the Flat last season and landed a huge payday when justifying favouritism in the Ebor; had made her Flat debut in April and was having just her fourth run at York after a maiden win and Group 3 third; could be capable of better.

Magnum Force (Ire)
3 b c Mehmas - Tropical Rock (Fastnet Rock)
Ger Lyons (Ire)   Abdulla Al Khalifa
PLACINGS: 21231-   RPR **113**

Starts	1st	2nd	3rd	4th	Win & Pl
5	2	2	1	-	£456,362
	11/24	Delm	5f Gd1 2yo firm...£409,449
	8/24	Cork	5f Mdn 2yo gd-fm...£9,235

Led home a strong European party when winning the Breeders' Cup Juvenile Turf Sprint last season; had been unlucky not to do better in Britain, notably when a neck second in a Listed race at York and again when third in the Flying Childers; should stay 6f.

Maljoom (Ire)
6 b h Caravaggio - Nictate (Teofilo)
William Haggas   Sheikh Ahmed Al Maktoum
PLACINGS: 1114/5/33286-2   RPR **121**

Starts	1st	2nd	3rd	4th	Win & Pl
11	3	2	2	1	£445,668
	5/22	Colo	1m Gp2 3yo good..£84,034
	4/22	Kemp	1m Cls2 3yo std-slw...................................£12,885
	3/22	Donc	7f Cls5 3yo good...£3,942

Perhaps still best known for a desperately unlucky defeat in the 2022 St James's Palace Stakes but confirmed himself a Group 1 miler last season; put long-standing injury issues behind him when third in the Queen Anne and second in the Sussex, though still not the most consistent.

Maranoa Charlie (Fr)
3 b c Wootton Bassett - Koubalibre (Galileo)
Christopher Head (Fr)   Peter Maher, Carl Fitzgerald & John Baxter
PLACINGS: 1114-   RPR **106+**

Starts	1st	2nd	3rd	4th	Win & Pl
4	3	-	-	1	£131,543
	10/24	StCl	1m Gp3 2yo v soft..£34,783
	9/24	Chan	1m 2yo v soft..£14,783
	8/24	Deau	7f 2yo good..£69,565

Remarkable eight-length winner of a Group 3 at Saint-Cloud last season, quickly opening up a big advantage and completing a hat-trick after two similar wins in lesser company; couldn't pull off the same tactics when odds-on for the Criterium International, managing only fourth.

Marshman
5 b g Harry Angel - White Rosa (Galileo)
Karl Burke   Nick Bradley Racing 2 & Mrs E Burke
PLACINGS: 1125/15378/2007-112   RPR **115aw**

Starts	1st	2nd	3rd	4th	Win & Pl
15	5	2	1	-	£185,343
	2/25	Ling	6f Cls1 List stand..£28,355
102	1/25	Newc	6f Cls2 89-108 Hcap stand.....................£23,193
	4/23	Chan	5¹/₂f Gp3 3yo soft..£35,398
	8/22	Thsk	6f Cls4 2yo gd-fm...£4,860
	7/22	Ayr	6f Cls5 Mdn 2yo good...................................£3,510

Smart sprinter who achieved career-high figures on the all-weather early this year, seemingly rejuvenated by gelding and wind operations; hadn't won since a Group 3 victory at Chantilly in 2023 and had regressed after reappearance efforts in each of the last two years.

163

RACING POST

Masai Moon
3 b c Siyouni - Mairwen (Dubawi)
Charlie Appleby   Godolphin
PLACINGS: 1-   RPR **84+**aw

Starts	1st	2nd	3rd	4th	Win & Pl
1	1	-	-	-	£3,780
10/24	Kemp	1m Cls5 2yo std-slw			£3,780

Once-raced colt who made a bright start at Kempton on sole start last season, showing a smart turn of foot to justify 2-5 favouritism in a mile novice; looks the type to improve as a three-year-old over middle distances.

Merrily (USA)
3 b f No Nay Never - Caponata (Selkirk)
Aidan O'Brien (Ire)   Smith, Magnier & Tabor
PLACINGS: 414351-   RPR **105**

Starts	1st	2nd	3rd	4th	Win & Pl
6	2	-	1	2	£58,026
10/24	NmkR	7f Cls1 Gp3 2yo gd-sft			£36,862
6/24	Naas	5f Mdn 2yo good			£9,235

Big filly who got better with experience last season and sprang a 25-1 surprise when winning the Oh So Sharp Stakes at Newmarket on her final run; well held on three previous runs at Group/Listed level but seemed to benefit from hold-up tactics and cut in the ground.

Military Academy
4 b g Fastnet Rock - Sovereign Parade (Galileo)
John & Thady Gosden   Isa Salman & Abdulla Al Khalifa
PLACINGS: 1121-   RPR **115+**aw

Starts	1st	2nd	3rd	4th	Win & Pl
4	3	1	-	-	£62,820
11/24	Kemp	1m4f Cls1 List std-slw			£25,520
9/24	Sals	1m2f Cls4 gd-sft			£4,860
8/24	Haml	1m3f Cls2 heavy			£20,616

Hugely promising gelding who won three out of four races last season; well beaten by Burdett Road when second in a Listed race at Newmarket on big rise in class but romped home in the same grade at Kempton on final run; has lots of size and scope to keep improving.

Misunderstood (Fr)
3 b c Hello Youmzain - Waldjagd (Observatory)
Mario Baratti (Fr)   Haras D'Etreham & Mustapha Bekhti
PLACINGS: 113-   RPR **108**

Starts	1st	2nd	3rd	4th	Win & Pl
3	2	-	1	-	£96,278
9/24	Lonc	1m Gp3 2yo soft			£34,783
7¹/₂f	Deau	7¹/₂f 2yo gd-sft			£21,739

Smart French colt who was far from disgraced when surrendering his unbeaten record in last season's Prix Jean-Luc Lagardère, finishing third; had won twice previously, including a mile Group 3 at Longchamp in impressive fashion; should appreciate returning to that trip.

Mitbaahy (Ire)
6 b g Profitable - Wrood (Invasor)
Charlie Hills   Mrs Fitri Hay
PLACINGS: 2112018/5881/47170-2   RPR **114+**

Starts	1st	2nd	3rd	4th	Win & Pl
23	6	4	1	1	£238,525
5/24	Curr	6f Gp2 good			£61,565
8/23	Ches	6f Cls1 List soft			£28,010
9/22	Newb	5f Cls1 Gp3 good			£39,697
6/22	Sand	5f Cls1 List 3yo good			£29,489
5/22	Haml	5f Cls2 3yo gd-sft			£18,039
8/21	Thsk	5f Cls4 Mdn 2yo good			£5,454

Very useful sprinter who achieved his biggest win in a Group 2 at the Curragh last year, supplementing a Group 3 victory and pair of Listed successes in previous seasons; has finished no better than eighth in four runs at Group 1 level.

Montassib
7 ch g Exceed And Excel - Felwah (Aqlaam)
William Haggas   The Montassib Partnership
PLACINGS: 5442/04100851/16215-   RPR **119**

Starts	1st	2nd	3rd	4th	Win & Pl
20	8	1	-	3	£466,073
9/24	Hayd	6f Cls1 Gp1 good			£234,496
6/24	Newc	6f Cls1 Gp3 std-slw			£51,039
3/24	Donc	6f Cls1 List soft			£34,026
101	10/23	York	6f Cls2 88-104 Hcap soft		£51,540
98	5/23	NmkR	7f Cls2 79-103 Hcap good		£25,770
87	5/22	Gdwd	7f Cls2 81-99 Hcap soft		£13,500
4/22	Weth	7f Cls5 gd-fm			£4,968
9/20	Newc	6f Cls5 2yo stand			£4,075

High-class and progressive sprinter who won on his Group 1 debut last season, pipping Kind Of Blue in the Sprint Cup at Haydock; had risen through the ranks with Group 3 and Listed wins last year following handicap success in 2023; fifth in the Champions Sprint on final run.

Mount Atlas
4 b g Masar - Highland Pass (Passing Glance)
Andrew Balding   Kingsclere Racing Club
PLACINGS: U81312-   RPR **104+**

Starts	1st	2nd	3rd	4th	Win & Pl
6	2	1	1	-	£55,979
87	7/24	Asct	1m4f Cls2 87-101 Hcap good		£23,193
5/24	Rdcr	1m2f Cls5 Mdn 3-5yo good			£3,780

Lightly raced and progressive middle-distance performer; won twice last season, most notably in a 1m4f handicap at Ascot on King George day; sent off favourite for the Old Rowley Cup at Newmarket on return from a break when second behind handicap blot Sun God.

164

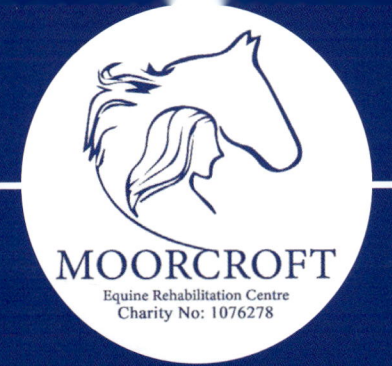

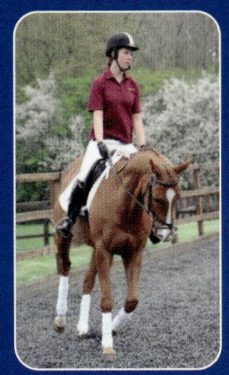

MOORCROFT
Equine Rehabilitation Centre
Charity No: 1076278

Here at the centre in West Sussex, we have over 20 years' experience at retraining ex-racehorses, and we have difference schemes available depending on your needs or your horse's needs. We would love to help, and we do a very thorough caring job with great results. Please come and visit us or call Mary on 0792 666408 for more information and/or to discuss how we can help

www.moorcroftracehorse.org.uk

Huntingrove Stud, Slinfold, West Sussex RH13 0RB Tel:07929 666408

RACING POST

Mutasarref and Colin Keane score in Group 3 company at Leopardstown

Mount Kilimanjaro (Fr)
3 b c Siyouni - Decorating (Galileo)
Aidan O'Brien (Ire) — Magnier, Tabor & Smith
PLACINGS: 5312- — RPR **107**

Starts	1st	2nd	3rd	4th	Win & Pl
4	1	1	1	-	£165,591
	10/24	Lonc	1m 2yo soft		£113,043

Took time to find his feet last season but was a big improver on his final two runs; won a sales race at Longchamp on Arc weekend when stepped up to a mile and progressed again when second to Twain in the Criterium International; should stay further.

Mutasarref
7 b g Dark Angel - Mulkeyya (Mawatheeq)
Ger Lyons (Ire) — Eleanora Kennedy
PLACINGS: 6111/545381/3113121- — RPR **116**

Starts	1st	2nd	3rd	4th	Win & Pl
22	10	2	3	1	£225,308

10/24	Cork	1m List yield	£20,522
8/24	Leop	1m Gp3 good	£26,935
6/24	Leop	7f Gp3 gd-yld	£26,935
5/24	Naas	7f List good	£20,522
10/23	Leop	1m List heavy	£20,885
8/22	Cork	7f List good	£19,832
7/22	Naas	7f good	£8,429
90 6/22	Curr	7f 68-90 Hcap good	£9,916
80 4/22	Leop	7f 70-80 Hcap good	£5,702
9/21	List	7f Mdn yld-sft	£6,321

Consistent gelding who won four times during a terrific campaign last season; has won Listed races in each of the last three seasons and added two Group 3 prizes last term, doing particularly well when stepped back up to a mile.

GUIDE TO THE FLAT **2025**

My Mate Alfie (Ire)
4 b g Dark Angel - Bear Cheek (Kodiac)
Ger Lyons (Ire)   A K Whelan
PLACINGS: 231235/4333163111-   RPR **114+**

Starts	1st	2nd	3rd	4th	Win & Pl
16	5	2	6	1	£319,346

	10/24	Naas	6f List yield..£20,522
	9/24	Curr	6f Gp3 good...£28,217
107	9/24	Curr	6f 84-107 Hcap good...................................£76,957
	6/24	Curr	6f List yield..£51,304
	7/23	DRoy	7f Mdn 2yo good..£7,832

Rapidly improving sprinter who flourished last autumn when winning his last three races, all over 6f; defied 10st to win a valuable handicap on Irish Champions Weekend and followed up to score in Group 3 and Listed company; could try his luck abroad according to connections.

Nakheel (Fr)
4 ch f Dubawi - Into The Mystic (Galileo)
Owen Burrows   Sheikh Ahmed Al Maktoum
PLACINGS: 6/13431-   RPR **110**

Starts	1st	2nd	3rd	4th	Win & Pl
6	2	-	2	1	£113,869

	9/24	Donc	1m6½f Cls1 Gp2 gd-sft............................£85,065
	5/24	Asct	1m2f Cls4 Mdn 3yo gd-sft..........................£8,100

Sharply progressive filly who got better and better as she went up in trip last season, winning the Park Hill Stakes on final run; had improved her rating through three good efforts in Listed races and appreciated return to good to soft ground when winning at Doncaster.

New Century
3 b c Kameko - Potent Embrace (Street Cry)
Andrew Balding   Qatar Racing Limited
PLACINGS: 412114-   RPR **109**

Starts	1st	2nd	3rd	4th	Win & Pl
6	3	1	-	2	£256,091

	9/24	Wood	1m Gd1 2yo firm...................................£177,515
	8/24	Sals	1m Cls1 List 2yo gd-fm.............................£22,684
	6/24	Donc	7f Cls4 2yo gd-fm......................................£5,373

Well placed to win a Grade 1 in Canada last autumn, setting up an even more ambitious raid abroad when fourth at the Breeders' Cup; had been progressive at home, albeit at a lower level, winning a Listed race at Salisbury when stepped up to a mile for the first time.

Night Raider (Ire)
4 br c Dark Angel - Dorraar (Shamardal)
Karl Burke   Clipper Logistics
PLACINGS: 1/100511-   RPR **120+aw**

Starts	1st	2nd	3rd	4th	Win & Pl
7	4	-	-	-	£52,170

	11/24	Newc	6f Cls1 List stand..................................£28,355
	10/24	Kemp	6f Cls2 2yo std-slw..................................£12,885
	3/24	Sthl	7f Cls5 stand..£6,156
	12/23	Sthl	7f Cls5 2yo stand......................................£3,546

Has looked a superstar on the all-weather but miles off that form on turf last year; made it four out of four on artificial surfaces when running away with a 6f Listed race at Newcastle on final run last year; had been well down the field in the 2,000 Guineas and did little better down in grade.

No Half Measures
4 b f Cable Bay - Fascinator (Helmet)
Richard Hughes   R P Gallagher
PLACINGS: 21115311615-   RPR **112**

Starts	1st	2nd	3rd	4th	Win & Pl
11	6	1	1	-	£139,321

		9/24	Newb	5f Cls1 Gp3 heavy..................................£48,204
		8/24	Deau	6f List 3yo gd-sft....................................£23,913
91		7/24	NmkJ	5f Cls3 73-91 Hcap good.......................£16,200
82		5/24	Gdwd	5f Cls4 69-82 3yo Hcap soft...................£10,808
		4/24	Wolv	6f Cls3 3-5yo stand..................................£7,668
		3/24	Ling	6f Cls4 Mdn 3yo stand.............................£6,156

Remarkable success story last season, winning six times having been unraced until March; achieved her biggest win in a 5f Group 3 at Newbury and shaped better than bare form when fifth in the Prix de l'Abbaye (best of those drawn high); has also won a Listed race over 6f.

Noble Dynasty
7 b g Dubawi - Alina (Galileo)
Charlie Appleby   Godolphin
PLACINGS: 21/2157/1011/51185-3   RPR **118**

Starts	1st	2nd	3rd	4th	Win & Pl
16	7	2	1	-	£162,964

		6/24	NmkJ	7f Cls1 Gp3 gd-fm..................................£48,204
105		5/24	NmkR	7f Cls2 85-107 Hcap good.....................£25,770
		11/22	Ling	7f Cls3 stand..£7,560
102		9/22	NmkR	7f Cls2 84-103 Hcap good.....................£13,500
94		7/22	NmkJ	1m Cls3 76-96 Hcap gd-fm....................£16,200
93		9/21	Thsk	1m Cls3 84-93 3yo Hcap good...............£11,081
		10/20	Kemp	7f Cls5 2yo std-slw..................................£4,075

Returned from more than a year out in career-best form in the first half of last season; won over 7f at both Newmarket courses, adding a Group 3 to an easy handicap win at the Guineas meeting; well below par in stronger 7f races subsequently.

Nostrum
5 b g Kingman - Mirror Lake (Dubai Destination)
David O'Meara   Juddmonte
PLACINGS: 113/126/628-   RPR **116**

Starts	1st	2nd	3rd	4th	Win & Pl
9	3	2	1	-	£168,378

	7/23	NmkJ	1m Cls1 List 3yo gd-fm..........................£28,355
	9/22	NmkR	7f Cls1 Gp3 2yo good............................£34,026
	7/22	Sand	7f Cls4 Mdn 2yo gd-fm............................£5,346

Looked a future star when running away with a Listed race at Newmarket in 2023 but bitterly disappointing since; has failed to beat a single rival in three of his last four races, though close Group 3 second at Newmarket again confirmed ability; bought out of Sir Michael Stoute's yard last autumn.

Notable Speech
4 ch c Dubawi - Swift Rose (Invincible Spirit)
Charlie Appleby   Godolphin
PLACINGS: 11117153-   RPR **124+**

Starts	1st	2nd	3rd	4th	Win & Pl
8	5	-	1	-	£1,053,739

7/24	Gdwd	1m Cls1 Gp1 gd-fm	£567,100
5/24	NmkR	1m Cls1 Gp1 3yo good	£283,550
4/24	Kemp	1m Cls2 3yo std-slw	£15,462
2/24	Kemp	1m Cls3 3yo std-slw	£30,924
1/24	Kemp	1m Cls5 Mdn std-slw	£3,780

Remarkably won last season's 2,000 Guineas less than four months after making debut at Kempton; looked a top-class Guineas winner and backed up that impression in the Sussex Stakes, though also well beaten twice and came up short in third in the Breeders' Cup Mile.

Officer (Ire)
3 b c Dubawi - Hydrangea (Galileo)
Aidan O'Brien (Ire)   Magnier, Tabor & Smith
PLACINGS: 1-   RPR **91+**

Starts	1st	2nd	3rd	4th	Win & Pl
1	1	-	-	-	£10,260

8/24	Curr	7f Mdn 2yo good	£10,261

Beautifully bred colt who made a winning start on his sole run last season in a 7f Curragh maiden in August, showing a smart turn of foot; surely capable of better, most likely over middle distances, though wasn't the most imposing physical sort at that time.

Okeechobee
6 b g Time Test - Scuffle (Daylami)
Harry Charlton   Juddmonte
PLACINGS: 2111/21-   RPR **118+**

Starts	1st	2nd	3rd	4th	Win & Pl
6	4	2	-	-	£82,066

4/24	Sand	1m2f Cls1 Gp3 gd-sft	£48,204
92	9/22	Sals	1m2f Cls2 90-100 Hcap gd-sft	£11,597
8/22	Wolv	1m1½f Cls5 3-4yo stand	£4,320
8/22	Kemp	1m Cls4 std-slw	£5,346

Very lightly raced gelding who has run just twice since 2022 but showed huge potential in that time last season; finished second in a Listed race at Kempton after long layoff and then landed a Group 3 at Sandown in gritty fashion; had Group 1 aims when ruled out for the rest of the year.

Ombudsman (Ire)
4 b c Night Of Thunder - Syndicate (Dansili)
John & Thady Gosden   Godolphin
PLACINGS: 1111   RPR **114+**

Starts	1st	2nd	3rd	4th	Win & Pl
4	4	-	-	-	£68,036

9/24	Lonc	1m2f Gp3 3yo soft	£34,783
8/24	Deau	1m2f List 3yo good	£23,913
7/24	Leic	1m2f Cls5 gd-sft	£4,187
6/24	NmkJ	1m Cls4 3yo gd-fm	£5,154

Exciting unbeaten colt who won four times last season while being patiently handled with a view to 2025; won novice races at Newmarket and Leicester before adding Group 3 and Listed races over 1m2f in France; sent off odds-on for last three wins and much tougher tests await.

Passenger (USA)
5 b h Ulysses - Dilmun (War Front)
George Scott   Flaxman Stables Ireland Ltd
PLACINGS: 1301/13-   RPR **121+**

Starts	1st	2nd	3rd	4th	Win & Pl
6	3	-	2	-	£147,673

5/24	Ches	1m2½f Cls1 Gp2 gd-fm	£72,826
8/23	Wind	1m2f Cls1 Gp3 gd-fm	£34,026
4/23	NmkR	1m2f Cls3 Mdn 3yo good	£10,800

Long held in high regard (sent off just 8-1 when 12th in the 2023 Derby) and justified the faith when an impressive winner of the Huxley Stakes last season; had injuries subsequently, missing Royal Ascot and going lame at York; has switched from Sir Michael Stoute.

Peace Man
6 b g Kingman - Peacehaven (Rip Van Winkle)
John & Thady Gosden   John E Rose
PLACINGS: 44111/325-   RPR **113**

Starts	1st	2nd	3rd	4th	Win & Pl
8	3	1	1	2	£46,883

93	6/23	NmkL	1m2f Cls3 82-93 Hcap good	£10,800
86	5/23	Wind	1m2f Cls3 80-90 Hcap gd-fm	£9,936
	5/23	Wind	1m Cls5 Mdn soft	£4,320

Very lightly raced gelding who missed more than a year after winning his last three races in 2023 and couldn't quite deliver in a higher grade when returning in the autumn; still ran a career-best when beaten a nose in a 1m2f Listed race at Newmarket.

Persica (Ire)
4 ch c New Bay - Rubira (Lope De Vega)
Richard Hannon   Martin Hughes & Michael Kerr-Dineen
PLACINGS: 7101/34101318-   RPR **115**

Starts	1st	2nd	3rd	4th	Win & Pl
12	5	-	2	1	£134,515

	9/24	Ayr	1m2f Cls1 List gd-fm	£34,026
100	7/24	Sand	1m2f Cls2 87-102 Hcap gd-fm	£25,575
92	6/24	Epsm	1m2f Cls2 74-92 3yo Hcap gd-sft	£38,655
86	9/23	Kemp	1m Cls4 71-86 2yo Hcap std-slw	£6,281
	8/23	Sals	6f Cls4 2yo good	£5,400

Progressive middle-distance performer last season; won good 1m2f handicaps at Epsom and Sandown; forced into stronger company by 10lb rise for latter win and no better than fifth in two runs at Group level but split those efforts with another good win in a Listed race at Ayr.

169

RACING POST

Porta Fortuna (right): top-class filly who has won four times in Group 1 company

Poet Master (Ire)
5 b g Lope De Vega - Madeline (Kodiac)
Karl Burke   Sheikh Mohammed Obaid Al Maktoum

PLACINGS: 1181/15155-   RPR **120+**

Starts	1st	2nd	3rd	4th	Win & Pl
9	5	-	-	-	£135,020

	7/24	Curr	7f Gp2 good	£61,565
100	4/24	NmkR	7f Cls2 88-104 Hcap good	£25,770
92	9/23	Donc	7f Cls2 83-94 3yo Hcap gd-sft	£25,770
	7/23	Hayd	7f Cls5 good	£4,320
	6/23	Muss	7f Cls5 Mdn good	£3,780

Smart 7f performer on his day but has an increasingly patchy record; ran away with a Group 2 at the Curragh last season, building on impressive handicap wins at Doncaster and Newmarket; below that level when fifth in the Park Stakes and Prix de la Foret, albeit in hotter company.

Point Lynas (Ire)
6 b g Iffraaj - Initially (Dansili)
Edward Bethell   Julie & David R Martin & Dan Hall

PLACINGS: 0311d0/1622024/1401-2   RPR **115**

Starts	1st	2nd	3rd	4th	Win & Pl
26	5	8	2	2	£282,918

	7/24	Pont	1m Cls1 List gd-fm	£28,010
100	5/24	York	1m Cls2 85-106 Hcap good	£38,655
90	3/23	Newc	1m Cls3 79-91 Hcap stand	£8,640
84	7/22	Rdcr	1m Cls3 72-87 3yo Hcap gd-fm	£8,100
78	10/21	NmkR	7f Cls2 76-93 2yo Hcap good	£10,800

Front-running miler who developed into a very useful horse last season, winning twice in a light campaign; returned with a handicap win at York and finished with a runaway Listed victory at Pontefract, making all both times; best on quick ground.

170

GUIDE TO THE FLAT **2025**

Porta Fortuna (Ire)
4 b f *Caravaggio - Too Precious (Holy Roman Emperor)*
Donnacha O'Brien (Ire)   Medallion, S Weston, B Fowler & Reeves T'Bs

PLACINGS: 1112312/21118-   RPR **118**

Starts	1st	2nd	3rd	4th	Win & Pl
12	7	3	1	-	£1,331,344

9/24	Leop	1m Gp1 good	£205,217
7/24	NmkJ	1m Cls1 Gp1 good	£155,953
6/24	Asct	1m Cls1 Gp1 3yo gd-fm	£368,615
9/23	NmkR	6f Cls1 Gp1 2yo gd-fm	£155,953
6/23	Asct	6f Cls1 Gp3 2yo gd-fm	£56,710
5/23	Naas	6f Gp3 2yo good	£36,549
4/23	Curr	5f Mdn 2yo heavy	£8,876

Top-class filly who has won four Group 1 races and been placed in four more; followed near miss in last season's 1,000 Guineas by winning three times over a mile, most notably a runaway victory in the Falmouth Stakes; easily forgiven rare blip in the Breeders' Cup Mile (impeded).

Powerful Glory (Ire)
3 b c *Cotai Glory - Wouldntitbelovely (Kodiac)*
Richard Fahey   Sheikh Rashid Dalmook Al Maktoum

PLACINGS: 11-   RPR **106+**

Starts	1st	2nd	3rd	4th	Win & Pl
2	2	-	-	-	£73,240

9/24	Newb	6f Cls1 Gp2 2yo heavy	£61,360
8/24	Pont	6f Cls3 Mdn 2yo gd-fm	£11,880

Won both races as a two-year-old last season, maintaining unbeaten record with a gutsy win in the Mill Reef Stakes at Newbury; coped well with heavy ground that day having hacked up first time out on good to firm; looks a sprinter but could try further this year.

RACING POST

Prague (Ire)
5 b h Galileo - Princess Noor (Holy Roman Emperor)
Dylan Cunha   Amedeo Dal Pos

PLACINGS: 145210-   RPR **118**

Starts	1st	2nd	3rd	4th	Win & Pl
6	2	1	-	1	£114,455

9/24 NmkR 1m Cls1 Gp2 soft £70,888
6/24 Sand 1m2f Cls2 Mdn gd-sft £20,616

Ballydoyle cast-off who didn't race until last season but soon made up for lost time, ending the year a Group 2 winner; won at 40-1 on debut at Sandown and improved in defeat before striking again in the Joel Stakes at Newmarket; below par on final run in the Queen Elizabeth II Stakes.

Puppet Master (Ire)
3 gr c Camelot - Realtra (Dark Angel)
Aidan O'Brien (Ire)   Smith, Magnier & Tabor

PLACINGS: 214-   RPR **102**

Starts	1st	2nd	3rd	4th	Win & Pl
3	1	1	-	1	£19,165

8/24 Gway 1m½f Mdn 2yo soft £9,491

Useful middle-distance prospect who impressed when winning a Galway maiden by four lengths on soft ground last year; sent off joint-favourite for the Royal Lodge on only subsequent run but came up short in fourth; should improve over further.

Qirat
4 ch g Showcasing - Emulous (Dansili)
Ralph Beckett   Juddmonte

PLACINGS: 312/165122-   RPR **104+**

Starts	1st	2nd	3rd	4th	Win & Pl
9	3	3	1	-	£155,593

92 8/24 Gdwd 7f Cls2 82-105 Hcap gd-sft £38,655
88 5/24 Gdwd 7f Cls2 80-98 3yo Hcap good £51,540
   8/23 Kemp 7f Cls4 2yo std-slw £5,346

Half-brother to Bluestocking who was progressive in good 7f handicaps last season; won twice at Goodwood before finishing best of the rest behind runaway winner Volterra in the Challenge Cup at Ascot; second again in a Listed race on final run; needs cut in the ground.

Quddwah
5 b h Kingman - Sajjhaa (King's Best)
Simon & Ed Crisford   Sheikh Ahmed Al Maktoum

PLACINGS: 11/1145-   RPR **118+**

Starts	1st	2nd	3rd	4th	Win & Pl
6	4	-	-	1	£204,165

7/24 Asct 1m Cls1 Gp2 good £79,394
5/24 Asct 1m Cls1 List gd-sft £34,026
5/23 NmkR 1m Cls4 3yo good £5,400
5/23 Sals 7f Cls5 3yo gd-sft £4,590

Very smart miler who won his first four races, with both subsequent defeats coming in Group 1 company; returned from a long layoff to score twice at Ascot, most notably in the Summer Mile; fair fourth in the Prix Jacques le Marois but

172

GUIDE TO THE FLAT 2025

below par on soft ground in the Queen Elizabeth II Stakes.

Quickthorn
8 b g Nathaniel - Daffydowndilly (Oasis Dream)
H Morrison   Lady Blyth
PLACINGS: /2211165/64116/5461-   RPR **111+**

Starts	1st	2nd	3rd	4th	Win & Pl
27	10	3	1	3	£813,137

	9/24	Sals	1m6f Cls2 gd-sft	£10,308
	8/23	Gdwd	2m Cls1 Gp1 gd-sft	£283,550
	6/23	York	1m6f Cls1 List gd-fm	£39,697
	8/22	York	2m½f Cls1 Gp2 good	£141,775
	7/22	Lonc	1m6f Gp2 gd-sft	£62,269
	5/22	Sand	2m Cls1 Gp3 good	£45,368
	9/21	Sals	1m6f Cls2 good	£10,308
97	6/21	Asct	1m4f Cls2 94-104 Hcap heavy	£35,100
84	5/21	Hayd	1m4f Cls3 80-92 Hcap gd-sft	£5,927
	6/20	Kemp	1m3f Cls5 Auct Mdn 3-5yo std-slw	£3,493

Veteran stayer who ran away with the Goodwood Cup in 2023, landing a fourth Group victory; not at the same level last season, winning only an ordinary conditions race at Salisbury at 2-9 and no better than fourth in three other runs.

Quinault (Ger)
5 b g Oasis Dream - Queimada (Dansili)
Stuart Williams   TJE Racing
PLACINGS: 11111310/860911133-3   RPR **116**

Starts	1st	2nd	3rd	4th	Win & Pl
22	10	5	-	-	£344,701

	9/24	York	6f Cls1 List gd-sft	£39,697
	8/24	NmkJ	6f Cls1 List soft	£25,520
	8/24	Ches	6f Cls1 List gd-sft	£28,010
97	9/23	Asct	7f Cls2 81-101 Hcap gd-fm	£41,232
90	7/23	NmkJ	6f Cls2 84-105 3yo Hcap gd-fm	£51,540
85	6/23	York	6f Cls2 79-98 3yo Hcap gd-fm	£51,540
80	5/23	NmkR	6f Cls2 77-97 3yo Hcap good	£25,770
74	5/23	NmkR	6f Cls5 57-77 3yo Hcap good	£5,234
65	5/23	Brig	7f Cls5 59-71 3yo Hcap gd-fm	£4,606
59	4/23	Chmf	6f Cls6 46-62 3yo Hcap stand	£4,004

Prolific gelding who won six times during 2023 as he rose through the ranks and added a quickfire hat-trick of Listed wins last year, doing particularly well under a penalty at York; hasn't won in five runs at a higher level, though far from disgraced in third on final two runs.

Rashabar (Ire)
3 b c Holy Roman Emperor - Arnazonka (Camelot)
Brian Meehan   Manton Thoroughbreds Ix
PLACINGS: 32122-   RPR **112**

Starts	1st	2nd	3rd	4th	Win & Pl
5	1	3	1	-	£259,407

	6/24	Asct	6f Cls1 Gp2 2yo gd-fm	£99,243

Shock 80-1 winner of last season's Coventry Stakes at Royal Ascot, getting off the mark by a nose at the third attempt; built on that form

Rashabar (left): Royal Ascot winner who was placed on all five starts last season at two

despite failing to win again, finishing second in the Prix Morny and Prix Jean-Luc Lagardere; should stay a mile.

Rebel's Romance (Ire)
7 br g Dubawi - Minidress (Street Cry)
Charlie Appleby   Godolphin

PLACINGS: 011111/7U41/111311-1   RPR **123+**

Starts	1st	2nd	3rd	4th	Win & Pl
23	16	-	1	2	£10,314,327

2/25	Aluq	1m3½f Gp3 good	£1,140,000
11/24	Delm	1m4f Gd1 firm	£2,047,244
9/24	Colo	1m4f Gp1 gd-sft	£86,957
5/24	ShaT	1m4f Gp1 gd	£732,394
3/24	Meyd	1m4f Gp1 gd	£2,740,157
2/24	Doha	1m4f Gp3 gd	£1,122,047
12/23	Kemp	1m4f Listed std-slw	£28,355
11/22	Keen	1m4f Gd1 firm	£1,540,741
9/22	Colo	1m4f Gp1 gd-sft	£84,034
8/22	Hopp	1m4f Gp1 good	£84,034
7/22	Gdwd	1m4f Cls1 Gp3 gd-fm	£56,710
6/22	NmkJ	1m4f Cls1 List good	£29,489
3/21	Meyd	1m1½f Gp2 3yo fast	£328,467
1/21	Meyd	1m 3yo fast	£21,950
11/20	Kemp	1m Cls5 2yo std-slw	£4,075
10/20	Newc	1m Cls5 2yo std-slw	£3,429

Globetrotting superstar who has won seven Group 1 races, including four last year to put a below-par 2023 behind him; regained his Breeders' Cup Turf crown after top-level wins in Dubai, Hong Kong and Germany; third in the King George on second run in Britain since 2022.

Rebel's Romance and William Buick after landing the Amir Trophy in Qatar

Red Letter
3 gr f Frankel - Red Impression (Dark Angel)
Ger Lyons (Ire)   Juddmonte

PLACINGS: 214-   RPR **105**

Starts	1st	2nd	3rd	4th	Win & Pl
3	1	1	-	1	£27,478

7/24	Curr	7f Mdn 2yo good	£10,261

Promising filly who shone in two Curragh maidens last season (ran Lake Victoria to a head before winning easily) and was then a close fourth in the Moyglare Stakes; slightly unlucky that day having been short of room and could well make her mark at the top level this year.

Regional
7 b g Territories - Favulusa (Dansili)
Edward Bethell   Future Champions Racing Regional

PLACINGS: 32/4262305/1151/224-   RPR **119**

Starts	1st	2nd	3rd	4th	Win & Pl
20	5	5	2	3	£583,211

9/23	Hayd	6f Cls1 Gp1 good	£242,106
6/23	Hayd	5f Cls1 List gd-fm	£28,355
100 5/23	York	5f Cls2 88-104 Hcap good	£18,039
94 9/21	Hayd	6f Cls2 84-100 Hcap gd-fm	£13,500
7/20	Pont	5f Cls5 Mdn 2yo gd-fm	£4,140

High-class sprinter who made rapid progress in 2023 and won the Sprint Cup at Haydock; ran another huge race when best of the Europeans in the King Charles III Stakes at Royal Ascot last season, finishing second behind Asfoora, but not quite at that level in just two other runs.

TOTAL EQUESTRIAN CONSTRUCTION

Complete Projects | Indoor Arenas
Outdoor Arenas | Stables & Shelters
Gallops & Fencing | Horse Walkers
Concrete Bases & Groundworks

Design & Layout | 30 years' Experience
Planning Application Management
Free Consultation

A TOTAL design and build solution for all your equestrian projects

01380 818216 • info@teconstruction
www.teconstruction.co.uk

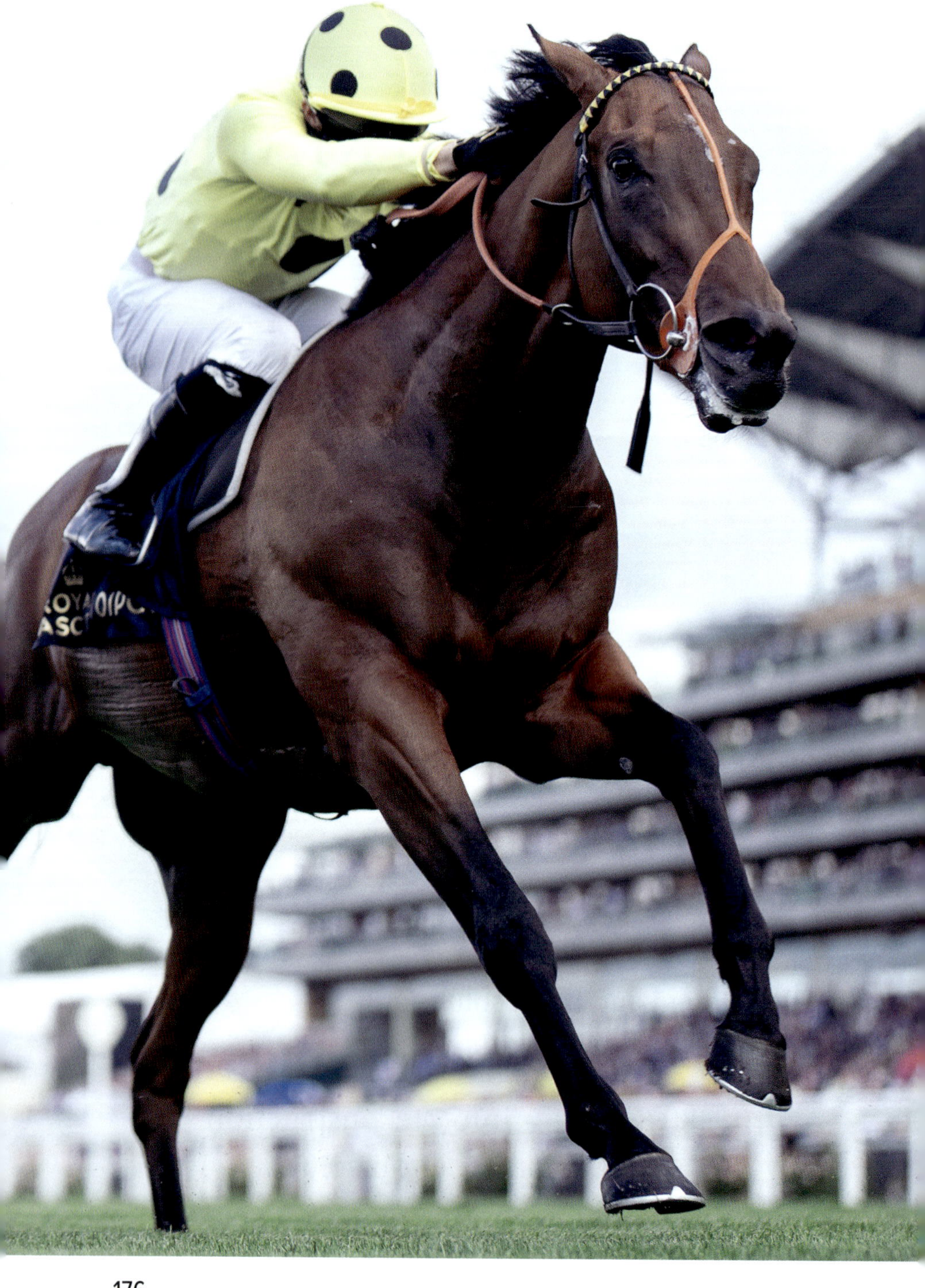

GUIDE TO THE FLAT 2025

Rhapsody (Ire)
3 ch f Ghaiyyath - Soul Searcher (Motivator)
William Haggas   Highclere Thoroughbred Racing
PLACINGS: 1-   RPR 80+

Starts	1st	2nd	3rd	4th	Win & Pl
1	1	-	-	-	£3,672
	10/24	Yarm	1m Cls5 2yo gd-sft		£3,672

Once-raced filly who caught the eye when making a winning start in a mile novice at Yarmouth last autumn; bred to come into her own over further and backed up that assessment by storming home powerfully late on; looks a smart prospect for middle distances.

Roi De France (Ire)
4 br c Sea The Stars - Danilovna (Dansili)
John & Thady Gosden   B E Nielsen
PLACINGS: 2/212012-   RPR 112+aw

Starts	1st	2nd	3rd	4th	Win & Pl
7	2	4	-	-	£35,296
	11/24	Kemp	1m Cls2 87-104 Hcap std-slw		£12,885
	7/24	Wind	1m Cls5 gd-fm		£4,320

Flopped when well fancied for the Cambridgeshire last season but otherwise progressed all year; had done well on much quicker ground and then resumed upward curve on the all-weather, overcoming adversity in a good handicap and finishing second in a Listed race.

Room Service (Ire)
4 b c Kodi Bear - Tamara Love (Tamayuz)
Kevin Ryan   Roddy O Byrne & Robert O Byrne
PLACINGS: 1331/761021-   RPR 115

Starts	1st	2nd	3rd	4th	Win & Pl
10	4	1	2	-	£242,315
	11/24	Donc	6f Cls1 List soft		£34,026
100	7/24	Pont	6f Cls2 84-102 Hcap soft		£13,916
	9/23	Donc	6½f Cls2 good		£147,540
	5/23	Weth	5½f Cls4 Mdn 2yo good		£4,860

Progressive colt who finished last season on a high with a Listed win at Doncaster over 6f, building on a fine weight-carrying performance when second in a valuable handicap at York; trainer expects him to appreciate return to 7f (had begun last season in the Greenham).

Rosallion (Ire)
4 b c Blue Point - Rosaline (New Approach)
Richard Hannon   Sheikh Mohammed Obaid Al Maktoum
PLACINGS: 1131/211-   RPR 124+

Starts	1st	2nd	3rd	4th	Win & Pl
7	5	1	1	-	£994,868
	6/24	Asct	1m Cls1 Gp1 3yo gd-fm		£390,094
	5/24	Curr	1m Gp1 3yo good		£247,826
	10/23	Lonc	7f Gp1 2yo gd-sft		£202,265
	7/23	Asct	7f Cls1 List 2yo good		£28,355
	6/23	Newb	6½f Cls4 Mdn 2yo gd-fm		£5,400

Top-class miler who has won three times at Group 1 level; no match for Notable Speech when second in last season's 2,000 Guineas but had that rival well beaten when landing the St James's Palace Stakes, building on Irish 2,000 Guineas win; missed the rest of the season.

Royal Dress (Ire)
5 b m Night Of Thunder - Wadaa (Dynaformer)
James Tate   Saeed Manana
PLACINGS: 642/13721407/13813-   RPR 112+

Starts	1st	2nd	3rd	4th	Win & Pl
16	4	2	3	2	£112,287
	7/24	Curr	1m1f Gp3 good		£28,217
	5/24	Gdwd	1m Cls1 List soft		£34,026
80	7/23	Hayd	7f Cls4 77-85 3yo Hcap heavy		£6,543
	4/23	Donc	6f Cls5 soft		£4,320

Massive improver last season, starting the year rated 87 and ending as a Pattern winner; sprang a 33-1 surprise in a Listed race at Goodwood first time out and was again underrated when scoring at 16-1 in a Group 3 at the Curragh; should stay 1m2f.

Royal Playwright
3 b c Lope De Vega - Arabian Queen (Dubawi)
Andrew Balding   J C Smith
PLACINGS: 1328-   RPR 106

Starts	1st	2nd	3rd	4th	Win & Pl
4	1	1	1	-	£39,269
	7/24	Sals	7f Cls4 2yo good		£5,400

Scopey colt who shaped with promise in some good races last season, notably when second in the Royal Lodge Stakes; well below that form in the Futurity Trophy but looks the type to do much better as a three-year-old.

Royal Rhyme (Ire)
5 b h Lope De Vega - Dubai Queen (Kingmambo)
Karl Burke   Sheikh Mohammed Obaid Al Maktoum
PLACINGS: 1/4310115/154673-   RPR 119

Starts	1st	2nd	3rd	4th	Win & Pl
14	5	-	2	2	£384,889
	5/24	Sand	1m2f Cls1 Gp3 soft		£45,368
	9/23	Ayr	1m2f Cls1 List gd-sft		£34,026
95	6/23	Gdwd	1m2f Cls2 83-104 3yo Hcap soft		£51,540
85	5/23	NmkR	1m2f Cls3 82-87 3yo Hcap soft		£15,462
	9/22	Thsk	7f Cls4 2yo soft		£8,100

Smart middle-distance performer who gained

Rosallion: Group 1 winner who returns this season after a curtailed campaign in 2024

RACING POST

his biggest win in a Group 3 at Sandown first time out last season; very highly tried since then and landed his first Group 1 place at the fifth attempt when third in the Champion Stakes at Ascot.

Royal Scotsman (Ire)
5 b h Gleneagles - Enrol (Pivotal)
Paul & Oliver Cole   Mrs Fitri Hay
PLACINGS: 413152/398/912-   RPR **117+**

Starts	1st	2nd	3rd	4th	Win & Pl
12	3	2	2	1	£366,586

6/24 Epsm 1m½f Cls1 Gp3 gd-sft..................£56,710
7/22 Gdwd 6f Cls1 Gp2 2yo gd-fm.................£85,065
5/22 Gdwd 6f Cls4 2yo gd-sft........................£5,994

Generally disappointing since finishing third in the 2,000 Guineas in 2023 but has been very lightly raced in that time and showed signs of a revival last season; won the Diomed Stakes at Epsom and outpaced on drop to 7f when a fair second in the Challenge Stakes.

Ruling Court (USA)
3 b c Justify - Inchargeofme (High Chaparral)
Charlie Appleby   Godolphin
PLACINGS: 13-   RPR **106**

Starts	1st	2nd	3rd	4th	Win & Pl
2	1	-	1	-	£23,154

7/24 Sand 7f Cls4 Mdn 2yo good...................£5,400

One-time Derby favourite who remains a fascinating prospect despite not adding to hugely impressive debut victory at Sandown; ran just once more subsequently, finishing third behind The Lion In Winter when evens favourite for a red-hot Acomb Stakes at York.

Running Lion: came good in last season's Duke of Cambridge at Royal Ascot

Running Lion
5 gr m Roaring Lion - Bella Nouf (Dansili)
John & Thady Gosden   D P Howden
PLACINGS: 411/110238/28172-   RPR **117**

Starts	1st	2nd	3rd	4th	Win & Pl
14	5	3	1	1	£328,679

6/24	Asct	1m Cls1 Gp2 gd-fm	£133,467
5/23	NmkR	1m2f Cls1 List 3yo soft	£28,355
4/23	Kemp	1m Cls2 3yo std-slw	£12,885
10/22	Chmf	1m Cls5 2yo stand	£3,725
8/22	Ling	1m Cls5 2yo stand	£3,672

Took a long time to fulfil potential but showed her class last season, notably when winning the Duke of Cambridge Stakes at Royal Ascot; benefited from drop in trip having finished 2023 racing over 1m4f but also did well over 1m2f when second in the Prix de l'Opera on final run.

Sallaal (Ire)
3 ch c Frankel - Nahrain (Selkirk)
Roger Varian   Sheikh Ahmed Al Maktoum
PLACINGS: 1-   RPR **89+**

Starts	1st	2nd	3rd	4th	Win & Pl
1	1	-	-	-	£5,372

10/24	Yarm	7f Cls4 2yo soft	£5,373

Beautifully bred (Frankel half-brother to Group 1 winners Benbatl and Elmalka) and did well to win on his sole start last season, finishing strongly to land what looked a good 7f novice; should have more to offer.

Saracen (Fr)
3 b c Siyouni - Soteria (Acclamation)
Joseph O'Brien (Ire)   Al Shaqab Racing
PLACINGS: 1-   RPR **94+**

Starts	1st	2nd	3rd	4th	Win & Pl
1	1	-	-	-	£10,260

10/24	Curr	6f Mdn 2yo soft	£10,261

€500,000 yearling who made an eyecatching start on his sole run last season, easily winning a 6f Curragh maiden by four lengths on soft ground; good mover who should appreciate better ground and seems sure to stay at least a mile.

Scorthy Champ (Ire)
3 ch c Mehmas - Fidaaha (New Approach)
Joseph O'Brien (Ire) Rectory Road Holdings, B Fowler & Mrs AM O'Brien
PLACINGS: 131-   RPR **112+**

Starts	1st	2nd	3rd	4th	Win & Pl
3	2	-	1	-	£223,843

9/24	Curr	7f Gp1 2yo good	£205,217
5/24	Leop	7f Mdn 2yo good	£9,235

Very smart two-year-old last season, winning two out of three races including the National Stakes; had finished only third in a red-hot Futurity Stakes but looked more professional when reversing that form with Henri Matisse, albeit helped by the runner-up looking awkward.

GUIDE TO THE FLAT 2025

Seagulls Eleven (Ire)
3 ch c Galileo Gold - Thrilled (Kodiac)
Hugo Palmer   Two Plus Three Two Plus Four
PLACINGS: 212340-   RPR **108**

Starts	1st	2nd	3rd	4th	Win & Pl
6	1	2	1	1	£96,954

6/24	Hayd	7f Cls4 2yo gd-fm	£5,400

Very useful two-year-old last season despite winning only a novice race at Haydock; chased home Shadow Of Light in the Superlative Stakes before a good third in the National; regressed subsequently when a well-beaten fourth in the Dewhurst and tenth at the Breeders' Cup.

See The Fire
4 ch f Sea The Stars - Arabian Queen (Dubawi)
Andrew Balding   J C Smith
PLACINGS: 123/0542135-   RPR **116**

Starts	1st	2nd	3rd	4th	Win & Pl
10	2	2	2	1	£456,689

8/24	York	1m1f Cls1 Gp3 gd-fm	£96,407
8/23	NmkJ	7f Cls2 Mdn 2yo good	£15,462

Very highly tried during her career and made the most of a rare window of opportunity to win a Group 3 at York last season; otherwise kept exclusively to Group 1 company, coming closest when second in the Nassau Stakes; seems best over that 1m2f trip.

Sevenna's Knight (Ire)
5 b h Camelot - Sevenna (Galileo)
Andre Fabre (Fr)   Oti Management Pty Ltd
PLACINGS: 0/4211443/46116152-   RPR **117**

Starts	1st	2nd	3rd	4th	Win & Pl
16	5	2	1	4	£417,637

9/24	Lonc	1m7½f Gp3 gd-fm	£34,783
5/24	Lonc	1m7½f Gp2 soft	£64,435
4/24	Lonc	1m7f Gp3 v soft	£34,783
8/23	Deau	1m6f List 3yo v soft	£24,336
6/23	Comp	1m6f 3yo gd-sft	£12,389

Smart and progressive French stayer; won three Group races last season and not far off a top-level success when second in the Prix Royal-Oak (sent off favourite); showed versatility when dropping back to 1m4f to finish a fine fifth in the Arc.

Shadow Of Light
3 ch c Lope De Vega - Winters Moon (New Approach)
Charlie Appleby   Godolphin
PLACINGS: 11211-   RPR **117+**

Starts	1st	2nd	3rd	4th	Win & Pl
5	4	1	-	-	£529,486

10/24	NmkR	7f Cls1 Gp1 2yo soft	£299,854
9/24	NmkR	6f Cls1 Gp1 2yo soft	£165,355
8/24	NmkJ	6f Cls4 2yo soft	£5,154
7/24	Yarm	6f Cls4 Mdn 2yo good	£5,373

Champion juvenile last season after winning four out of five races, including the Middle Park/Dewhurst double; relished soft ground both

179

times after a close second in the Gimcrack on good and not certain to prove as effective on a quicker surface; should stay a mile.

Shareholder (USA)
3 b c Not This Time - Cloudy Dancer (Invincible Spirit)
Karl Burke　　　　　　　　　　　　Wathnan Racing
PLACINGS: 1190-　　　　　　　　　　　RPR **104+**

Starts	1st	2nd	3rd	4th	Win & Pl
4	2	-	-	-	£110,835
	6/24	Asct	5f Cls1 Gp2 2yo gd-fm		£85,065
	6/24	Bevl	5f Cls2 2yo gd-fm		£25,770

Decisive winner of last season's Norfolk Stakes at Royal Ascot, making rapid strides having been bought at the breeze-ups less than six weeks earlier; didn't go on from there, failing to beat a single rival in the Prix Morny or at the Breeders' Cup, but retains raw ability.

Shuwari (Ire)
4 ch f New Bay - Lady Pimpernel (Sir Percy)
Ollie Sangster　　　Mrs Bv Sangster & Ballylinch Partnership
PLACINGS: 1122/

Starts	1st	2nd	3rd	4th	Win & Pl
4	2	2	-	-	£158,589
	7/23	Sand	7f Cls1 List 2yo soft		£22,684
	6/23	Newb	7f Cls4 2yo gd-fm		£5,400

Missed all of last season through injury but had looked a potentially very smart filly as a two-year-old in 2023; won first two races and sent off favourite when second in the May Hill Stakes (given too much to do) and Fillies' Mile (beaten just half a length).

Simmering
3 b f Too Darn Hot - Cashla Bay (Fastnet Rock)
Ollie Sangster　　　　　　　　　　　Al Shaqab Racing
PLACINGS: 321124-　　　　　　　　　　RPR **106**

Starts	1st	2nd	3rd	4th	Win & Pl
6	2	2	-	1	£216,655
	8/24	Deau	7f Gp2 2yo soft		£64,435
	7/24	Asct	6f Cls1 Gp3 2yo gd-fm		£36,862

Dual Group winner last season, adding a Group 2 at Deauville to the Princess Margaret Stakes at Ascot; excellent second behind Lake Victoria in the Moyglare before plugging on for fourth in the Prix Marcel Boussac, proving stamina for a mile.

Skellet (Ire)
4 b f Kingman - Dane Street (Street Cry)
Ralph Beckett　　　　　　　　　　　　　Juddmonte
PLACINGS: 412/8721-　　　　　　　　　RPR **107**

Starts	1st	2nd	3rd	4th	Win & Pl
7	2	2	-	1	£68,745
	9/24	Sand	1m Cls1 List good		£25,520
	9/23	Sals	7f Cls2 Mdn 2yo gd-fm		£15,462

Lightly raced filly who came up short in top company last season but bounced back at a more realistic level; finished no better than seventh in the Irish 1,000 Guineas and Coronation Stakes but was a head second in a Group 3 at Chantilly before winning a Listed race at Sandown.

Sky Majesty (Ire)
3 b f Blue Point - Majestic Alexander (Bushranger)
William Haggas　　　　　　Tony Bloom & Ian McAleavy
PLACINGS: 111-　　　　　　　　　　　RPR **108+**

Starts	1st	2nd	3rd	4th	Win & Pl
3	3	-	-	-	£137,316
	10/24	Chan	6f Gp2 2yo heavy		£94,174
	9/24	Ayr	6f Cls1 Gp3 2yo gd-fm		£36,862
	8/24	Newb	6f Cls4 Mdn 2yo gd-fm		£6,281

Exciting sprint prospect who won all three races as a two-year-old over 6f last season; followed

GUIDE TO THE FLAT 2025

Sky Majesty scores at Ayr, the second of three wins in an unbeaten juvenile campaign

up maiden win with a Group 3 victory at Ayr and then beat Cheveley Park runner-up Daylight (possibly below par) in a Group 2 at Chantilly; has won on good to firm and heavy ground.

Smoken
3 b f Too Darn Hot - Miss Marjurie (Marju)
Ralph Beckett   Andrew Rosen, Marc Chan & Mrs S Rogers
PLACINGS: 11-   RPR **94+**

Starts	1st	2nd	3rd	4th	Win & Pl
2	2	-	-	-	£23,857
11/24	NmkR	1m Cls1 List 2yo soft...			£20,132
10/24	Nott	1m¹/₂f Cls5 Mdn 2yo heavy.................................			£3,725

Fine middle-distance prospect who won both starts as a two-year-old last season; won a fair Nottingham maiden first time out and justified odds-on favouritism when following up in a Listed race at Newmarket, both over a mile; sure to stay further, though unproven on good ground.

Sosie (Ire)
4 b c Sea The Stars - Sosia (Shamardal)
Andre Fabre (Fr)   Wertheimer & Frere
PLACINGS: 12/13114-   RPR **120+**

Starts	1st	2nd	3rd	4th	Win & Pl
7	4	1	1	1	£807,865
9/24	Lonc	1m4f Gp2 3yo soft..			£64,435
7/24	Lonc	1m4f Gp1 3yo soft..			£298,122
4/24	Lonc	1m3f 3yo soft..			£15,217
9/23	Chan	1m 2yo gd-sft...			£22,124

High-class French colt who enjoyed his finest hour last season when comfortably beating

181

RACING POST

Illinois in the Grand Prix de Paris, relishing the step up in trip after coming third in the Prix du Jockey Club; returned from a break to land the Prix Niel before a creditable fourth in the Arc.

Space Legend (Ire)
4 b g Sea The Stars - Newton's Angel (Dark Angel)
William Haggas   Wathnan Racing
PLACINGS: 2/12244-   RPR **112**

Starts	1st	2nd	3rd	4th	Win & Pl
6	1	3	-	2	£106,654
	4/24	Leic	1m2f Cls5 Mdn soft.................................£3,664

Lightly raced middle-distance performer who has won only a maiden but ran well in defeat several times last season; unlucky to bump into Calandagan when second in the King Edward VII Stakes and not beaten far when fourth in the Great Voltigeur; has since been gelded.

Sparks Fly
5 b m Muhaarar - Stepping Out (Tagula)
David Loughnane   David Lowe
PLACINGS: 531111119116/557111-   RPR **116**

Starts	1st	2nd	3rd	4th	Win & Pl
21	11	-	1	-	£162,041
	11/24	StCl	1m List heavy......................................£22,609
	10/24	Nott	1m1½f Cls1 List soft..............................£25,520
	10/24	StCl	1m List v soft......................................£22,609
	10/23	StCl	1m List heavy......................................£23,009
98	9/23	Hayd	1m Cls2 86-100 Hcap heavy..................£25,770
93	7/23	Ayr	1m Cls3 71-93 Hcap gd-sft....................£10,308
87	6/23	Ches	1m2½f Cls3 68-87 Hcap gd-sft..............£12,740
77	5/23	Wind	1m Cls5 59-77 3yo Hcap soft.................£4,397
74	5/23	Thsk	1m Cls5 61-74 3yo Hcap heavy..............£4,187
65	5/23	Wind	1m Cls6 52-65 3yo Hcap soft..................£3,768
59	4/23	Wind	1m Cls6 48-60 3yo Hcap heavy..............£3,402

Prolific mare who won eight times during a remarkable 2023 and flourished again last autumn when rattling off a quickfire hat-trick of Listed victories; had looked out of sorts during the summer and seems increasingly reliant on soft or heavy ground up in class.

Square D'Alboni (Fr)
3 b g Zarak - Polonia Lady (Australia)
Ralph Beckett   The Obank Partnership
PLACINGS: 9111-   RPR **105+**

Starts	1st	2nd	3rd	4th	Win & Pl
4	3	-	-	-	£46,508
	10/24	Chan	1m1f List 2yo heavy............................£26,087
	9/24	Sals	1m Cls4 2yo gd-sft..................................£4,860
	8/24	Epsm	7f Cls2 Mdn 2yo good..........................£15,462

Sharply progressive two-year-old last season, winning his last three races in impressive fashion; signed off by landing a Listed race at Chantilly by four lengths, making all over 1m1f, having won a novice at Salisbury under similar tactics by even further.

Stanhope Gardens (Ire)
3 ch c Ghaiyyath - Pure Art (Dutch Art)
Ralph Beckett   Marc Chan & Chelsea Thoroughbreds
PLACINGS: 312-   RPR **105**

Starts	1st	2nd	3rd	4th	Win & Pl
3	1	1	1	-	£19,953
	8/24	Bevl	7½f Cls4 Mdn 2yo gd-fm........................£4,711

Ran a big race on only run outside maiden company when a neck second behind subsequent Futurity Trophy runner-up Delacroix in the Autumn Stakes at Newmarket (pair clear); had won well at Beverley and should continue to progress.

Starlust
4 b c Zoustar - Beyond Desire (Invincible Spirit)
Ralph Beckett   Mrs Fitri Hay
PLACINGS: 1122153/23618163910-   RPR **121**

Starts	1st	2nd	3rd	4th	Win & Pl
19	6	3	3	-	£724,712
	11/24	Delm	5f Gd1 firm..£409,449
	7/24	York	5f Cls1 List gd-sft...............................£39,697
105	5/24	York	5f Cls2 81-107 Hcap gd-sft...................£25,770
	9/23	Kemp	6f Cls1 Gp3 2yo std-slw......................£39,697
	7/23	Newb	6f Cls4 2yo good..................................£5,400
	6/23	Chmf	6f Cls5 Mdn 2yo stand..........................£3,725

Tough and durable sprinter who raced 11 times last year and gained his biggest success on his penultimate start when winning the Breeders' Cup Turf Sprint; produced his best run at home when third in the Nunthorpe, having also won twice at York; has won over 6f but seems better over 5f.

Starzintheireyes
3 ch c Starspangledbanner - Crystal Hope (Nathaniel)
Ralph Beckett   Marcstown Ltd
PLACINGS: 211-   RPR **107+**

Starts	1st	2nd	3rd	4th	Win & Pl
3	2	1	-	-	£46,797
	10/24	NmkR	1m2f Cls1 Gp3 2yo gd-sft.....................£36,862
	9/24	Leic	7f Cls4 2yo soft....................................£4,860

Fine staying type who won two out of three races as a two-year-old last season; showed useful form over 7f in maidens before taking a big leap forward when stepped up to 1m2f for the Zetland Stakes at Newmarket, coming from last to first; should progress as a three-year-old.

Subsequent (Ire)
4 ch g Galileo - After (Danehill Dancer)
Andrew Balding   Mrs Fitri Hay
PLACINGS: 92115121-   RPR **107+**

Starts	1st	2nd	3rd	4th	Win & Pl
8	4	2	-	-	£105,480
	10/24	Asct	1m6f Cls1 List 3yo soft.........................£56,710
91	8/24	NmkJ	1m6f Cls3 80-94 Hcap soft....................£9,020
84	6/24	Sals	1m4f Cls3 80-89 3yo Hcap gd-fm.........£12,885
	6/24	Hayd	1m3½f Cls4 4yo gd-fm..........................£5,405

Hugely promising stayer who went from strength

GUIDE TO THE FLAT 2025

to strength last season, winning four of his last six races; was also a short-head away from winning the Mallard Stakes at Doncaster before stepping up again to easily land a 1m6f Listed race at Ascot on final run.

Sun God
4 b g Fastnet Rock - Seaduced (Lope De Vega)
Hughie Morrison   Ben & Sir Martyn Arbib
PLACINGS: 05541/24551-   RPR **98**

Starts	1st	2nd	3rd	4th	Win & Pl
10	1	-	-	-	£75,671
82	10/24	NmkR	1m4f Cls2 78-98 3yo Hcap gd-sft		£51,540
68	12/23	Ling	1m2f Cls5 62-76 2yo Hcap stand		£3,873

Remarkable winner of the Old Rowley Cup at Newmarket on final run last season, tearing apart a field of promising three-year-olds; had run well in other good handicaps, including when fifth in the Melrose, but left that form well behind and could have more to offer.

Sunway (Fr)
4 b c Galiway - Kensea (Kendargent)
David Menuisier   Guy Pariente Holding & Qatar Racing Ltd
PLACINGS: 1621/5272430-   RPR **118+**

Starts	1st	2nd	3rd	4th	Win & Pl
11	2	3	1	1	£530,218
	10/23	StCl	1m Gp1 2yo v soft		£126,416
	6/23	Sand	7f Cls4 Mdn 2yo good		£5,400

Failed to win last season but ran well in the face of some stiff tasks; Group 1 winner as a two-year-old in 2023 and had last five runs at the top level again after two odds-on defeats early in the year, finishing second in the Irish Derby and third in the St Leger.

Sweet William (Ire)
6 b g Sea The Stars - Gale Force (Shirocco)
John & Thady Gosden   Normandie Stud Ltd
PLACINGS: 22/2111223/313212-   RPR **118**

Starts	1st	2nd	3rd	4th	Win & Pl
15	5	7	3	-	£700,662
	9/24	Donc	2m2f Cls1 Gp2 gd-sft		£79,394
	5/24	Sand	2m Cls1 Gp3 soft		£45,368
95	8/23	Gdwd	1m6f Cls2 87-100 Hcap heavy		£51,540
88	7/23	Newb	2m½f Cls2 86-101 Hcap good		£38,655
	7/23	Donc	1m4f Cls2 gd-fm		£21,040

Smart stayer who progressed throughout a remarkably consistent campaign last season; gained his biggest win in the Doncaster Cup to add to Group 3 strike at Sandown earlier in the year; got steadily closer in three runs behind Kyprios, finishing with a second in the Long Distance Cup.

Swelter
3 b f Kingman - Hot Snap (Pivotal)
Dermot Weld (Ire)   Juddmonte
PLACINGS: 1-   RPR **89+**

Starts	1st	2nd	3rd	4th	Win & Pl
1	1	-	-	-	£9,234
	7/24	Leop	1m Mdn 2yo good		£9,235

From a top-class Juddmonte family (out of a Group 3-winning half-sister to the great Midday) and impressed when making a winning start in a mile maiden at Leopardstown last July; didn't run again but could well develop into a smart filly.

Swingalong (Ire)
5 ch m Showcasing - Pilates (Shamardal)
Karl Burke   Sheikh Juma Dalmook Al Maktoum
PLACINGS: 24114/303144/82272-   RPR **117**

Starts	1st	2nd	3rd	4th	Win & Pl
16	3	4	2	4	£796,074
	7/23	York	6f Cls1 Gp3 good		£48,204
	8/22	York	6f Cls1 Gp2 2yo good		£151,699
	8/22	Ripn	6f Cls4 2yo gd-sft		£4,860

High-class mare who has been desperately unlucky not to win a Group 1; beaten a head in last season's Champions Sprint having also finished within half a length in the Jubilee Stakes and July Cup; hasn't won since a Group 3 in July 2023 but has run just once below Group 1 level.

Tabiti
3 b f Kingman - Lilyfire (First Defence)
Ralph Beckett   Juddmonte
PLACINGS: 115-   RPR **101**

Starts	1st	2nd	3rd	4th	Win & Pl
3	2	-	-	-	£59,585
	9/24	Sals	6f Cls1 Gp3 2yo gd-sft		£25,520
	8/24	NmkJ	7f Cls2 Mdn 2yo gd-fm		£20,616

Who won first two races, making a big impression on her debut at Newmarket and following up narrowly in a 6f Group 3 at Salisbury; couldn't land a blow when only fifth in the Fillies' Mile on final run but should be suited by that trip in time.

Tabletalk (Ire)
4 b c Camelot - Dillydallydo (Holy Roman Emperor)
Tom Clover   Abdulla Al Mansoori
PLACINGS: 3/10315-   RPR **105**

Starts	1st	2nd	3rd	4th	Win & Pl
6	2	-	2	-	£100,930
95	8/24	York	1m6f Cls2 80-101 3yo Hcap gd-fm		£87,618
	5/24	Chmf	1m2f Cls2 Mdn 3-5yo stand		£4,320

Below par on final run last season at Ascot but had been sharply progressive until then, winning the valuable Melrose Stakes at York on his previous start; relished step up to 1m6f having come tenth when given an ambitious tilt at the Derby and third in a good handicap at Ascot.

183

RACING POST

Tamfana (Ger)
4 b f Soldier Hollow - Tres Magnifique (Zoffany)
David Menuisier   Quantum Leap Racing & Friends
PLACINGS: 311/3434113-   RPR **120**

Starts	1st	2nd	3rd	4th	Win & Pl
10	4	-	4	2	£536,166

10/24	NmkR	1m Cls1 Gp1 gd-sft	£155,953
8/24	Sand	1m Cls1 Gp3 good	£48,204
10/23	Chan	7f Gp3 2yo heavy	£35,398
10/23	Kemp	1m Cls5 Mdn 2yo std-slw	£3,672

Last season's highest-rated three-year-old filly who landed a long-overdue Group 1 win in the Sun Chariot Stakes, ruining Inspiral's swansong; had been a luckless fourth in the 1,000 Guineas over course and distance; stays further and will have lots of Group 1 options.

Tennessee Stud (Ire)
3 b c Wootton Bassett - In My Dreams (Sadler's Wells)
Joseph O'Brien (Ire)   Westerberg, Tabor, Magnier & Smith
PLACINGS: 3121-   RPR **110+**

Starts	1st	2nd	3rd	4th	Win & Pl
4	2	1	1	-	£154,726

| 10/24 | StCl | 1m2f Gp1 2yo heavy | £124,217 |
| 9/24 | Tipp | 1m1f Mdn 2yo good | £9,235 |

Fine middle-distance prospect who found a soft Group 1 opening last season, winning a three-runner Criterium de Saint-Cloud at 3-5; had been a solid second behind subsequent Group 1 winner Hotazhell and improved for step up to 1m2f on heavy ground.

Term Of Endearment
6 b m Sea The Moon - Miss You Too (Montjeu)
William Haggas   C Acheson
PLACINGS: 6/1432/5210/117-   RPR **109**

Starts	1st	2nd	3rd	4th	Win & Pl
12	4	2	1	1	£289,288

8/24	Gdwd	1m6f Cls1 Gp2 gd-fm	£170,130
5/24	York	1m6f Cls1 Gp3 gd-sft	£56,710
8/23	Cork	1m4f Gp3 sft-hvy	£33,938
6/22	Gowr	1m1½f Mdn 3yo yield	£6,445

Progressive and lightly raced mare; won two out of three races for Henry de Bromhead when

Topgear: ended last season with back-to-back wins at Longchamp and Newmarket

stepped up in trip last season, most notably the Lillie Langtry Stakes at Glorious Goodwood; below-par seventh in the Prix de Royallieu on final run; switched to William Haggas.

That's Amore (Ire)
3 ch f New Bay - Rubira (Lope De Vega)
Ralph Beckett   Lady Bamford
PLACINGS: 1-   RPR 90+

Starts	1st	2nd	3rd	4th	Win & Pl
1	1	-	-	-	£6,480
10/24	Newb	1m Cls4 2yo heavy £6,480

Once-raced filly who made a big impression on sole start at Newbury last season when making all to win a mile novice by six lengths on heavy ground; full sister to 1m2f Listed winner Persica and should flourish over middle distances.

The Lion In Winter (Ire)
3 b c Sea The Stars - What A Home (Lope De Vega)
Aidan O'Brien (Ire)   Tabor, Smith & Magnier
PLACINGS: 11-   RPR 116+

Starts	1st	2nd	3rd	4th	Win & Pl
2	2	-	-	-	£103,832
8/24	York	7f Cls1 Gp3 2yo gd-fm £93,572
7/24	Curr	7f Mdn 2yo good £10,261

Winter favourite for the 2,000 Guineas and Derby after a highly promising but abbreviated two-year-old campaign last season; ran just twice and looked a future star when winning what proved a red-hot Acomb Stakes at York.

The Reverend
4 b g Lope De Vega - Burning Rules (Aussie Rules)
William Haggas   Tony Bloom & Ian McAleavy
PLACINGS: 1/22149-   RPR 102+

Starts	1st	2nd	3rd	4th	Win & Pl
6	2	2	-	1	£73,596
86	9/24	Asct	1m4f Cls5 79-97 3yo Hcap soft £51,540
	11/23	NmkR	7f Cls4 2yo heavy £4,320

Impressive winner of a valuable handicap at Ascot last autumn on first run over 1m4f following a second after being gelded; beaten favourite twice subsequently but didn't quite stay 1m6f and looked outpaced back at 1m2f; retains potential over his preferred trip.

Thunder Run (Ire)
4 ch g Night Of Thunder - Astonished (Sea The Stars)
Karl Burke   Clipper Logistics
PLACINGS: 211314-   RPR 104+

Starts	1st	2nd	3rd	4th	Win & Pl
6	3	1	1	1	£103,469
96	8/24	York	1m Cls2 85-107 Hcap gd-fm £77,310
	7/24	Haml	1m¹/₂f Cls5 good £4,050
	7/24	Thsk	1m Cls5 gd-sft £4,420

Progressive gelding who won three times last

GUIDE TO THE FLAT 2025

season, most notably at York's Ebor meeting; fair fourth when favourite for the Balmoral on Champions Day on final run, though not quite as effective on softer ground; likely type for more top handicaps.

Tiber Flow (Ire)
6 b g Caravaggio - Malabar (Raven's Pass)
William Haggas   Jon & Julia Aisbitt
PLACINGS: 1121865/4213/5F1610-   RPR 116+

Starts	1st	2nd	3rd	4th	Win & Pl
18	7	2	1	1	£261,921
8/24	Newb	7f Cls1 Gp2 gd-fm £70,888
6/24	Hayd	7f Cls1 Gp3 good £48,204
7/23	Newc	6f Cls1 Gp3 std-slw £39,697
5/22	Newb	6f Cls1 List 3yo good £25,520
89 3/22	Sthl	7f Cls3 80-91 3yo Hcap std-slw £6,480
1/22	Newc	7f Cls5 3yo std-slw £3,942
12/21	Newc	6f Cls5 2yo stand £3,780

Smart gelding who won two 7f Group races last season, most notably the Hungerford Stakes by a nose; had also won a 6f Group 3 in 2023 but seemed to appreciate stepping up to 7f, winning at Haydock on first run at the trip since 2022 before narrow victory at Newbury.

Tiffany (Ire)
5 b m Farhh - Affinity (Sadler's Wells)
Sir Mark Prescott   Elite Racing Club
PLACINGS: 8/71V1121/112132-   RPR 112

Starts	1st	2nd	3rd	4th	Win & Pl
14	7	3	1	-	£243,393
8/24	Badn	1m4f Gp2 gd-sft £34,783
6/24	Newc	1m2f Cls1 Gp3 std-slw £36,862
5/24	Newc	1m3f List good £13,043
9/23	Hanv	1m2f List good £13,274
76 7/23	Newc	1m2f Cls4 61-82 App Hcap stand £5,129
72 7/23	Wind	1m2f Cls5 58-76 3yo good £4,397
6/23	Wolv	7f Cls5 stand £4,104

Progressive mare over middle distances; was winning for the sixth time in her last eight races when landing a Group 2 in Germany last season; twice ran well at Group 1 level subsequently, finishing third on Champions Day at Ascot and a neck second back in Germany.

Topgear (Fr)
6 b h Wootton Bassett - Miss Lech (Giant's Causeway)
Christopher Head (Fr)   Hisaaki Saito
PLACINGS: 111/122260/23211-   RPR 120+

Starts	1st	2nd	3rd	4th	Win & Pl
14	6	5	1	-	£247,494
10/24	NmkR	7f Cls1 Gp2 gd-sft £70,888
9/24	Lonc	7f Gp3 soft £34,783
4/23	Chan	7f 4yo soft £7,965
9/21	Chan	6f Gp3 2yo soft £35,714
8/21	Deau	6½f 2yo good £15,179
8/21	Deau	6f 2yo good £12,054

Smart and progressive horse who ran away with the Challenge Stakes at Newmarket last season; has largely run over a mile since unbeaten two-year-old campaign (missed all of 2022 in between) but seemed well suited by drop to 7f when winning final two races.

185

RACING POST

Torito
5 b g Kingman - Montare (Montjeu)
John & Thady Gosden   Wathnan Racing
PLACINGS: 3/1214/33-   RPR **113**

Starts	1st	2nd	3rd	4th	Win & Pl
7	2	1	3	1	£88,896

95 6/23 Epsm 1m2f Cls2 76-97 3yo Hcap gd-fm £38,655
    4/23 Nott 1m¹/₂f Cls5 3yo soft.................................... £3,847

Continued to show promise in just three runs since winning a valuable handicap at Epsom in 2023; finished third in the Wolferton Stakes at Royal Ascot on his final run last year, improving on his fourth in the Hampton Court at the same meeting 12 months earlier.

Tower Of London (Ire)
5 b h Galileo - Dialafara (Anabaa)
Aidan O'Brien (Ire)   Smith, Magnier, Tabor & Westerberg
PLACINGS: 15/611249/1151-   RPR **119+**

Starts	1st	2nd	3rd	4th	Win & Pl
12	6	1	-	1	£1,886,837

        7/24 Curr 1m6f Gp2 good................................... £76,957
        3/24 Meyd 2m Gp2 good.................................... £456,693
0   2/24 Jana 1m7f Gd3 Hcap gd-fm....................... £1,181,102
99   6/23 DRoy 1m5f 80-99 3yo Hcap good.................... £52,212
        6/23 Leop 1m4f List 3yo good................................ £20,885
        7/22 Leop 1m Mdn 2yo good.................................. £8,181

Smart stayer who won three out of four races last season; landed valuable prizes in Saudi Arabia and Dubai before disappointing on return to Europe in the Yorkshire Cup; bounced back with an impressive win in the Curragh Cup.

Trawlerman (Ire)
7 b g Golden Horn - Tidespring (Monsun)
John & Thady Gosden   Godolphin
PLACINGS: 16/100113/80111/323-   RPR **120**

Starts	1st	2nd	3rd	4th	Win & Pl
18	7	1	5	-	£1,019,468

        10/23 Asct   1m7¹/₂f Cls1 Gp2 gd-sft..................... £283,550
        9/23   NmkR 2m Cls1 List gd-fm............................ £31,045
        9/23   Sals   1m6f Cls2 gd-fm................................ £10,308
101   8/22   York   1m6f Cls2 100-110 Hcap gd-fm......... £300,000
97   7/22   Gdwd 1m6f Cls2 85-102 Hcap gd-fm............. £51,540
93   4/22   Chmf   1m2f Cls2 84-95 Hcap stand............. £15,462
        4/21   Pont   1m4f Cls4 Mdn 3yo gd-fm..................... £5,130

High-class stayer who was the last horse to beat Kyprios in the 2023 Long Distance Cup on Champions Day; fine second behind that rival in last season's Gold Cup but not quite as effective on soft ground when a well-beaten third back on Champions Day.

Treble Tee (Ire)
3 b c Persian King - Sefroua (Kingmambo)
Simon & Ed Crisford   Michael Geoghegan Et Al
PLACINGS: 1-   RPR **88+**

Starts	1st	2nd	3rd	4th	Win & Pl
1	1	-	-	-	£4,380

        10/24 NmkR 7f Cls4 2yo soft..................................... £4,581

Once-raced colt who made a bright start when winning a 7f maiden at Newmarket last autumn, justifying market confidence; showed good speed and comfortably drew clear; looks a good physical specimen and likely to be best at a mile.

Trueshan (Fr)
9 b g Planteur - Shao Line (General Holme)
Alan King   Singula Partnership
PLACINGS: 1/26111/11321/24114-4314223-   RPR **116**

Starts	1st	2nd	3rd	4th	Win & Pl
33	16	6	3	5	£2,016,340

        7/24   Sand   2m Cls1 List good............................ £25,520
        9/23   Lonc   2m4f Gp1 gd-sft.............................. £151,699
        9/23   Donc   2m2f Gp2 soft................................. £73,723
        10/22 Asct   2m Cls1 Gp2 gd-sft......................... £283,550
120   6/22   Newc   2m¹/₂f Cls2 90-120 Hcap std-slw......... £81,000
        4/22   Nott   1m6f Cls1 List gd-sft........................ £31,191
        10/21 Asct   2m Cls1 Gp2 gd-sft......................... £283,550
        10/21 Lonc   2m4f Gp1 v soft............................ £153,054
        7/21   Gdwd   2m Cls1 Gp1 soft........................... £294,183
        10/20 Asct   2m Cls1 Gp2 soft........................... £170,130
        9/20   Sals   1m6f Cls2 good............................... £12,291
        7/20   Hayd   1m4f Cls1 List gd-sft......................... £14,461
        10/19 Newb   1m5¹/₂f Cls2 3yo heavy...................... £32,345
93   10/19 NmkR 1m4f Cls2 79-100 3yo gd-sft.............. £74,700
        8/19   Ffos   1m4f Cls5 good................................ £3,429
        8/19   Wolv   1m4f Cls5 stand............................... £3,429

Veteran stayer who has a wonderful CV, winning three Group 1 races and three runnings of the Long Distance Cup at Ascot; won only a Listed race at Sandown last season but remained a force in stronger races and was second when going for a second successive Prix du Cadran.

Truly Enchanting (Ire)
3 b f No Nay Never - Alluringly (Fastnet Rock)
Aidan O'Brien (Ire)   Magnier, Tabor & Smith
PLACINGS: 101-   RPR **97+**

Starts	1st	2nd	3rd	4th	Win & Pl
3	2	-	-	-	£67,721

        6/24 Curr 6f Gp2 2yo good................................. £61,565
        5/24 Tipp 5f Mdn 2yo soft.................................. £6,157

Missed the second half of last season but had made a good impression in winning two out of three races, most notably a 6f Group 2 at the Curragh; suffered sole defeat when well beaten in the Albany Stakes but looked more professional when soon back to winning ways.

Tuscan Hills (Fr)
3 b c Night Of Thunder - Taqleed (Sea The Stars)
Raphael Freire   Amo Racing Limited
PLACINGS: 11-   RPR **100+**

Starts	1st	2nd	3rd	4th	Win & Pl
2	2	-	-	-	£27,004

        10/24 Pont 1m Cls1 List 2yo soft......................... £22,684
        8/24   Thsk 1m Cls5 2yo good.............................. £4,320

Exciting colt who won both races last season as a two-year-old by wide margins; didn't beat much on debut at Thirsk but followed up even more decisively in a Listed race at Pontefract, enjoying soft ground; should stay at least 1m2f.

Twain (Ire)

3 b c Wootton Bassett - Wading (Montjeu)
Aidan O'Brien (Ire) Tabor, Smith & Magnier

PLACINGS: 11- RPR **112+**

Starts	1st	2nd	3rd	4th	Win & Pl
2	2	-	-	-	£133,452
	10/24 StCl	1m Gp1 2yo heavy			£124,217
	10/24 Leop	7f Mdn 2yo soft			£9,235

Exciting colt who won the Group 1 Criterium International at Saint-Cloud last season just eight days after a successful debut at Leopardstown; coped with heavy ground that day but expected to prove better on a quicker surface; seen as a 2,000 Guineas horse by his trainer.

Unequal Love

5 ch m Dutch Art - Heavenly Dawn (Pivotal)
William Haggas Cheveley Park Stud

PLACINGS: 4111014/151330- RPR **114+**

Starts	1st	2nd	3rd	4th	Win & Pl
13	6	-	2	2	£214,858
102	6/24 Asct	6f Cls2 95-107 Hcap gd-fm			£90,195
	5/24 NmkR	6f Cls1 List good			£34,026
90	9/23 Pont	6f Cls2 78-91 Hcap gd-sft			£15,462
85	8/23 Hayd	7f Cls4 78-87 Hcap good			£6,543
	7/23 Ripn	6f Cls5 3-5yo soft			£5,400
	7/23 Leic	6f Cls5 Mdn 3-5yo good			£4,320

Progressive mare who won last season's Wokingham and went on to prove herself at Group 1 level with a length third in the Sprint Cup at Haydock; had won a Listed race first time out and also went close in a Group 3; has won over 7f but kept to 6f since mid-2023.

Unquestionable (Fr)

4 b c Wootton Bassett - Strawberry Lace (Sea The Stars)
Richard Hannon Al Shaqab Racing

PLACINGS: 312421/44- RPR **113**

Starts	1st	2nd	3rd	4th	Win & Pl
8	2	2	1	3	£612,939
	11/23 SnAt	1m Gd1 2yo firm			£433,333
	5/23 Curr	6f Mdn 2yo good			£10,442

Won the Breeders' Cup Juvenile Turf in 2023 but came up short at the top level last season, albeit in just two runs; well-beaten fourth in the Irish 2,000 Guineas but got a little closer when filling the same spot in the St James's Palace Stakes; has since left Aidan O'Brien.

Uxmal (Ire)

6 b g Galileo - Only Mine (Pour Moi)
Joseph O'Brien (Ire) Flaxman Stables Ireland Ltd

PLACINGS: 4/2/4212/11- RPR **112**

Starts	1st	2nd	3rd	4th	Win & Pl
8	3	3	-	2	£87,326
	6/24 Asct	2m5½f Cls2 gd-fm			£59,400
	5/24 Klny	1m6f soft			£7,696
	9/23 Tram	2m Mdn good			£6,265

Has gone from strength to strength since needing five runs to break his maiden and was a runaway winner of the Queen Alexandra at Royal Ascot last season; likely type for Group races over long trips on that evidence.

Verse Of Love

3 b f Siyouni - Vercelli (Shamardal)
Charlie Appleby Godolphin

PLACINGS: 1- RPR **94**

Starts	1st	2nd	3rd	4th	Win & Pl
1	1	-	-	-	£10,308
	10/24 NmkR	7f Cls2 Mdn 2yo gd-sft			£10,308

Once-raced filly who looked a potential Guineas horse when running away from a 7f maiden at Newmarket on debut last autumn; drew clear by five lengths despite running green; looks a miler on pedigree.

Vertical Blue (Ire)

3 b f Mehmas - Krunch (Sea The Stars)
Francis Graffard (Fr) Gemini Stud & Argella Racing

PLACINGS: 22121- RPR **110**

Starts	1st	2nd	3rd	4th	Win & Pl
5	2	3	-	-	£232,660
	10/24 Lonc	1m Gp1 2yo soft			£198,748
	7/24 Claf	1m 2yo gd-sft			£13,043

Left behind previous form when a 33-1 winner of last season's Prix Marcel Boussac, edging out better-fancied stablemate Zarigana; had been a beaten favourite in a Listed race at Lyon the time before but had the benefit of experience and proven stamina; might struggle to go on.

Volterra (Ire)

4 b c Farhh - Lajatico (Equiano)
Kevin Ryan Sheikh Mohammed Obaid Al Maktoum

PLACINGS: 431/10021- RPR **111+**

Starts	1st	2nd	3rd	4th	Win & Pl
8	3	1	1	1	£144,604
94	10/24 Asct	7f Cls2 90-104 Hcap soft			£92,772
82	5/24 Curr	1m Cls3 75-89 3yo Hcap good			£15,462
	10/23 Rdcr	7f Cls2 2yo good			£4,320

Stunning winner of the Challenge Cup at Ascot on final run last season, making all the running to turn a valuable handicap into a procession; benefited from drop to 7f having not quite lived up to expectations since reappearance win at Newmarket; still feasibly handicapped after 9lb rise.

Washington Heights

5 b g Washington Dc - Epping Rose (Kodiac)
Kevin Ryan Hambleton Racing Ltd

PLACINGS: 223/9222441/140657-2 RPR **117**

Starts	1st	2nd	3rd	4th	Win & Pl
19	3	6	1	4	£305,524
	4/24 NmkR	6f Cls1 Gp3 good			£48,204
	9/23 BroP	6f List good			£31,847
	6/22 Carl	5f Cls5 Mdn 2yo good			£5,400

Hugely consistent in good sprint handicaps in

187

RACING POST

2023 but left those days behind when winning the Abernant Stakes at Newmarket first time out last year; far from disgraced in a higher grade subsequently, though no better than fifth in four runs at Group 1 level.

Whirl (Ire)
3 b f Wootton Bassett - Salsa (Galileo)
Aidan O'Brien (Ire) — Tabor, Smith & Magnier
PLACINGS: 4511-   RPR **93**

Starts	1st	2nd	3rd	4th	Win & Pl
4	2	-	-	1	£47,395

| 10/24 | Curr | 1m Gp3 2yo soft | £28,217 |
| 9/24 | Donc | 7f Cls2 Mdn 2yo good | £15,462 |

Progressive as a two-year-old last season, winning her last two races; got off the mark at the third attempt in a Doncaster maiden before taking a big step forward to land a mile Group 3 at the Curragh; big filly who should progress as a three-year-old, most likely over middle distances.

Whistlejacket (Ire)
3 ch c No Nay Never - Adventure Seeker (Bering)
Aidan O'Brien (Ire) — Brant, Magnier, Tabor & Smit
PLACINGS: 21412125-   RPR **111+**

Starts	1st	2nd	3rd	4th	Win & Pl
8	3	3	3	1	£406,618

8/24	Deau	6f Gp1 2yo gd-sft	£173,904
7/24	NmkJ	6f Cls1 Gp2 2yo gd-sft	£56,710
5/24	Curr	5f List 2yo soft	£20,522

Standing dish in top two-year-old sprints last season and won three times, including the Prix Morny; had limitations exposed in stronger Group 1 races, notably when a four-length second behind Shadow Of Light in the Middle Park; found 5f too sharp at the Breeders' Cup.

White Birch
5 gr h Ulysses - Diagnostic (Dutch Art)
John Joseph Murphy (Ire) — Mrs C C Regalado-Gonzalez
PLACINGS: 51/12384/111-   RPR **125+**

Starts	1st	2nd	3rd	4th	Win & Pl
10	5	1	1	1	£593,055

5/24	Curr	1m2½f Gp1 gd-yld	£256,522
5/24	Curr	1m2f Gp1 2yo soft	£61,565
4/24	Curr	1m2f Gp3 heavy	£28,217
4/23	Leop	1m2f Gp3 3yo heavy	£26,106
11/22	Dund	7f Mdn 2yo stand	£7,437

Good third in the 2023 Derby but looked a much better four-year-old early last season when winning all three races; completed the hat-trick with first Group 1 triumph in the Tattersalls Gold Cup, easily beating Auguste Rodin; missed the rest of the season through injury.

Wimbledon Hawkeye
3 b c Kameko - Eva Maria (Sea The Stars)
James Owen — The Gredley Family
PLACINGS: 13213-   RPR **110+**

Starts	1st	2nd	3rd	4th	Win & Pl
5	2	1	2	-	£146,582

| 9/24 | NmkR | 1m Cls1 Gp2 2yo soft | £70,888 |
| 5/24 | Kemp | 7f Cls4 2yo std-slw | £5,346 |

Smart and consistent two-year-old last season; won the Royal Lodge Stakes at Newmarket and placed in three other Group races, notably when second behind The Lion In Winter in the Acomb and third behind Hotazhell in the Futurity Trophy.

Yaroogh (Ire)
3 b c Dubawi - Lawahed (Invincible Spirit)
William Haggas — Sheikh Ahmed Al Maktoum
PLACINGS: 7119112-4   RPR **103**

Starts	1st	2nd	3rd	4th	Win & Pl
8	4	1	-	1	£85,896

10/24	Chan	7f List 2yo heavy	£26,087
9/24	Donc	7f Cls3 72-90 2yo Hcap good	£18,039
8/24	Kemp	7f Cls4 2yo std-slw	£5,346
5/24	Hayd	7f Cls3 2yo soft	£5,400

Prolific and progressive two-year-old last season, winning four of his last six races; won two novices before adding a nursery at Doncaster and a Listed race at Chantilly; coped well with heavy ground that day and finished a nose second in the Horris Hill in similar conditions.

You Got To Me
4 b f Nathaniel - Brushing (Medicean)
Ralph Beckett — Valmont & Newsells Park Stud Bldstk
PLACINGS: 15/144127-   RPR **116**

Starts	1st	2nd	3rd	4th	Win & Pl
8	3	1	-	2	£445,931

7/24	Curr	1m4f Gp1 3yo good	£247,826
5/24	Ling	1m3½f Cls1 List 3yo good	£34,488
9/23	Kemp	1m Cls5 Mdn 2yo std-slw	£3,672

Standing dish in top middle-distance fillies' races last season and enjoyed her finest hour when winning the Irish Oaks; stepped up on previous fourths in the Oaks and Ribblesdale Stakes but couldn't quite confirm that form with Content when a good second in the Yorkshire Oaks.

Zarigana
3 b f Siyouni - Zarkamiya (Frankel)
Francis Graffard (Fr) — Aga Khan
PLACINGS: 112-   RPR **110**

Starts	1st	2nd	3rd	4th	Win & Pl
3	2	1	-	-	£127,339

| 9/24 | Lonc | 1m Gp3 2yo soft | £34,783 |
| 7/24 | Chan | 7f 2yo gd-sft | £13,043 |

Top filly who won her first two races by wide margins last season before a narrow defeat when 1-2 for the Prix Marcel Boussac; given plenty to do that day but remains hugely exciting.

KEY HORSES LISTED BY TRAINER

Charlie Appleby
Ancient Truth
Ancient Wisdom
Aomori City
Arabian Crown
Dance Sequence
Desert Flower
Masai Moon
Noble Dynasty
Notable Speech
Rebel's Romance
Ruling Court
Shadow Of Light
Verse Of Love

Michael Appleby
Big Mojo

Andrew Balding
Alsakib
Bellum Justum
Coltrane
Cool Hoof Luke
Flora Of Bermuda
Kalpana
Mount Atlas
New Century
Royal Playwright
See The Fire
Subsequent

Mario Baratti
Misunderstood

Y Barberot
Beauvatier

Ralph Beckett
Bright Times Ahead
Cathedral
Centigrade
Grey's Monument
King's Gamble
Kinross
Qirat
Skellet
Smoken
Square D'Alboni
Stanhope Gardens
Starlust
Starzintheireyes
Tabiti
That's Amore
You Got To Me

Michael Bell
Carrytheone

Ed Bethell
Point Lynas
Regional

Marco Botti
Giavellotto

George Boughey
Believing
Botanical
Hopewell Rock

Karl Burke
Al Qareem
Arabie
Beautiful Diamond
Bolster

Elite Status
Fallen Angel
Ice Max
Lethal Levi
Liberty Lane
Marshman
Night Raider
Poet Master
Royal Rhyme
Shareholder
Swingalong
Thunder Run

Owen Burrows
Alflaila
Alyanaabi
Anmaat
Deira Mile
Falakeyah
Jarraaf
Nakheel

Jack Channon
Certain Lad

P Charalambous & J Clutterbuck
Apollo One

Harry Charlton
Cosmic Year
Hand Of God
Kikkuli
King's Gambit
Okeechobee

Tom Clover
Al Nayyir
Tabletalk

Paul & Oliver Cole
Royal Scotsman

Patrice Cottier
Daylight
Horizon Dore

Clive Cox
Ghostwriter
James's Delight
Jasour
Kerdos

Simon & Ed Crisford
Arabian Dusk
Coto De Caza
Quddwah
Treble Tee

Dylan Cunha
Prague

Henry de Bromhead
Higher Leaves
Magical Zoe
Term Of Endearment

Tim Easterby
Art Power

Harry Eustace
Docklands

Andre Fabre
Alcantor
Sevenna's Knight
Sosie

Richard Fahey
Powerful Glory

James Fanshawe
Ambiente Friendly
Kind Of Blue

Christophe Ferland
Aventure
Double Major

Raphael E Freire
Tuscan Hills

John & Thady Gosden
Audience
Chancellor
Courage Mon Ami
Damysus
Danielle
Detain
Field Of Gold
Friendly Soul
Gregory
Lead Artist
Military Academy
Ombudsman
Peace Man
Roi De France
Running Lion
Sweet William
Torito
Trawlerman

Francis-Henri Graffard
Calandagan
Goliath
Vertical Blue
Zarigana

William Haggas
Al Aasy
Alobayyah
Desert Hero
Dubai Honour
Economics
Elmonjed
Lake Forest
Maljoom
Montassib
Rhapsody
Sky Majesty
Space Legend
The Reverend
Tiber Flow
Unequal Love
Yaroogh

Richard Hannon
Haatem
Persica
Rosallion
Unquestionable

Jessica Harrington
Green Impact
Hotazhell

Christopher Head
Maranoa Charlie
Topgear

Waldemar Hickst
Lazio

Charlie Hills
Cicero's Gift
Iberian
Khaadem
Mitbaahy

Richard Hughes
No Half Measures

Gerard Keane
Crystal Black

Alan King
Trueshan

David Loughnane
Sparks Fly

Ger Lyons
Babouche
Chantez
Magnum Force
Mutasarref
My Mate Alfie
Red Letter

Willie McCreery
Jancis

Brian Meehan
Rashabar

David Menuisier
Caius Chorister
Sunway
Tamfana

Hughie Morrison
Quickthorn
Sun God

John Joseph Murphy
White Birch

Adrian Murray
Arizona Blaze

Fawzi Abdulla Nass
Calif

Aidan O'Brien
Acapulco Bay
Aftermath
Ballet Slippers
Bedtime Story
Bubbling
Camille Pissarro
Continuous
Delacroix
Diego Velazquez
Dreamy
Exactly
Expanded
Fairy Godmother
Giselle
Henri Matisse
Ides Of March
Illinois
Jan Brueghel
January
Kyprios
Lake Victoria
Los Angeles
Merrily
Mount Kilimanjaro
Officer
Puppet Master

The Lion In Winter
Tower Of London
Truly Enchanting
Twain
Whirl
Whistlejacket

Donnacha O'Brien
Falling Snow
Porta Fortuna

Joseph O'Brien
Al Riffa
Saracen
Scorthy Champ
Tennessee Stud
Uxmal

David O'Meara
Estrange

James Owen
Wimbledon Hawkeye

Hugo Palmer
Seagulls Eleven

Sir Mark Prescott
Tiffany

Jerome Reynier
Facteur Cheval
Lazzat

Kevin Ryan
Inisherin
Room Service
Volterra
Washington Heights

Ollie Sangster
Celestial Orbit
Shuwari
Simmering

George Scott
Bay City Roller
Isle Of Jura

Sir Michael Stoute
Formal
Nostrum
Passenger

James Tate
Royal Dress

Roger Teal
Dancing Gemini

Roger Varian
Elmalka
Enfjaar
Jabaara
Sallaal

Ed Walker
Almaqam
Celandine
English Oak
Harper's Ferry

Archie Watson
Aesterius

Dermot Weld
Hazdann
Swelter

Stuart Williams
Quinault

189

INDEX OF HORSES

Acapulco Bay 100, 117
Aesterius 117, 127
Aftermath 117
Against The Wind 66
Ain't Nobody 62
Al Aasy 117
Al Nayyir 117
Al Qareem 18-19, 117
Al Riffa 117
Alcantor 111, 118
Alfareqa 30
Alflaila 26-27, 118-119
Allezdancer 64
Almaqam 119
Almeraq 100
Alobayyah 119
Alsakib 120
Alyanaabi 28-29, 120-121
Ambiente Amigo 44
Ambiente Friendly 121
American Affair 96
Ammes 44
Ancient Truth 102, 121
Ancient Wisdom 121
Andesite 19-20
Anmaat 26, 27, 121
Aomori City 121
Apiarist 64
Apollo One 96, 121-122
Arabian Crown 122
Arabian Dusk 122
Arabie 122
Arizona Blaze 122
Art Power 122, 123
Asuka 100-101
Audience 122
Audubon Park 112
Aventure 112, 122
Azimpour 108, 110
Azure Angel 12-13
Babouche 93, 123
Baileys Khelstar 96-97
Ballet Slippers 106, 123, 143
Bay City Roller 68-70, 114, 124
Beautiful Diamond 124
Beauvatier 126
Bedtime Story 126, 142
Believing 127
Bellum Justum 127
Bethnal Green 44-47
Big Mojo 117, 127

Bolster 127
Bonnet 111
Botanical 128
Bragbor 74
Bright Times Ahead 128
Bryant 74
Bubbling 128-129
Burdett Road 40-42, 164
Caballo De Mar 75
Caius Chorister 128-130
Calandagan 112, 121, 130, 182
Calif 130-131
Callisto Dream 9
Camille Pissarro 94, 131
Cankoura 110
Carlton 44
Carrytheone 131
Cathedral 101-102, 132
Celandine 38, 132
Celestial Orbit 132
Centigrade 132-133
Certain Lad 33-34, 133
Chancellor 133
Chantez 93, 132, 133-134
Charging Thunder 47
Cicero's Gift 134
City House 70-73
City Of God 21-22
Clarendon House 16
Codiak 13
Coltrane 134
Content 188
Continuous 134
Cool Hoof Luke 13, 134
Cosmic Year 114, 134
Coto De Caza 134
Counting Cards 13
Courage Mon Ami 134-136
Crestofdistinction 37
Crystal Black 136, 137
Damysus 136
Dance Sequence 136
Dancing Gemini 136
Danger Bay 9-10
Danielle 137, 142
Dark Moon Rising 65-66
Daylight 111-112, 137, 181
Deira Mile 27, 138
Deira Storm 30
Delacroix 93, 100, 139, 149, 182
Desert Flower 95, 138,

139, 158
Desert Hero 105, 139
Destinado 44
Detain 139
Diego Velazquez 139
Docklands 139
Dopamine 75
Double Major 112, 139
Dreamy 95, 140
Dubai Honour 140
East India Dock 43
Economics 121, 140, 141
Ectocross 97
El Megeeth 30
Elim 6-7
Elite Status 16, 104, 140
Elmalka 141
Elmonjed 141
Elsie's Ruan 114
Enfjaar 141
English Oak 141
Eponine 112
Estrange 142
Exactly 142
Expanded 92, 102-103, 142
Facteur Cheval 111, 142
Fair Wind 27
Fairy Godmother 93, 143
Falakeyah 29-30, 143
Fallen Angel 143
Falling Snow 143
Fast Tracker 112
Ferrous 36
Field Of Gold 94, 144
First Look 112
Flight Plan 20
Flora Of Bermuda 144
Fluorescence 10
Force And Valour 75
Formal 146
Forza Orta 66, 67
Friendly Soul 146-147
Galene 111
Gallant 103-104
Galyx 36
Gethin 29
Ghostwriter 146
Giavellotto 146
Giselle 94-95, 146
Glittering Surf 30
Goliath 70, 112, 146-149
Green Impact 148-149
Gregory 149

Grey Cuban 52-53
Greydreambeliever 22, 23
Grey's Monument 149
Gun Of Brixton 110-111
Haatem 150, 159
Hand Of God 150
Harper's Ferry 150
Hawksbill 52
Hazdann 150
He's A Gentleman 53, 54
Henri Matisse 121, 150, 151, 179
Hey Boo 38
Higher Leaves 151
HK Fourteen 97
Holloway Boy 19
Hope Horizon 38
Hopewell Rock 151
Horizon Dore 151-152
Hot Cash 36
Hotazhell 93, 95, 152, 184, 188
Iberian 152
Ice Max 152
Ides Of March 91, 154
Illinois 154, 182
Inisherin 58, 59-60, 154
Intrusively 12
Isle Of Jura 70, 75, 154-156
Isneauville 112
Jabaara 156
James McHenry 7
James's Delight 156
Jan Brueghel 156, 157
Jancis 158
Janey Mackers 95
January 158
Jarraaf 28, 31, 159
Jasour 159
Johan 34-35
Kalpana 158, 159
Kerdos 159
Khaadem 16, 159
Kikkuli 159-160
Kind Of Blue 16, 104, 160, 164
King Of Bears 74
King's Gambit 160
King's Gamble 160
Kings Merchant 10
Kinross 160
Kirkdale 13
Korker 16

190

GUIDE TO THE FLAT 2025

INDEX OF HORSES

Kyprios 40, 93, 115, 136, 149, 161, 183, 186
Lake Forest 105, 161
Lake Victoria 93, 94, 95, 105, 106, 114, 137, 161, 174, 180
Lavender Hill Mob 43-44
Lazio 161-162
Lazzat 111, 112, 162
Lead Artist 162
Lethal Levi 16-18, 162
Letsbefrank 97
Liam Swagger 43
Liberty Lane 21, 163
Los Angeles 163
Lothlorien 63-64
Magical Zoe 163
Magnum Force 163
Majestic 36
Maljoom 163
Map Of Stars 112
Maranoa Charlie 110, 163
Marshman 16, 163
Masai Moon 164
Merrily 102, 132, 164
Metal Merchant 34
Metallo 35
Mighty Quiet 97-98
Military Academy 164
Miss Lamai 20
Misty Sky 53-54
Misunderstood 110, 164
Mitbaahy 164
Modern Utopia 74
Montassib 104, 164
Mount Atlas 164
Mount Kilimanjaro 92, 94, 167
Mutasarref 166, 167
My Mate Alfie 168
Naepoint 7
Nakheel 28, 168
Nardra 104-105
Nariko 54
Native Warrior 21
Nebras 105
Nesthorn 110
New Century 94, 168
Night Raider 18, 168
Nitoi 111
No Half Measures 168
Noble Dynasty 168
Noisy Jazz 147

Nostrum 168
Notable Speech 169, 177
Officer 169
Okeechobee 139, 169
Old Cock 7-9
Ombudsman 169
One Eye Jack 56
Paborus 11-12
Passenger 169
Peace Man 169
Pellitory 47
Percival 111
Persica 169, 185
Phantom Flight 70
Pocklington 114
Poet Master 16, 170
Point Lynas 7, 170
Polly Darling 22
Porta Fortuna 156, 171
Powerful Glory 114, 171
Prague 114-115, 172
Prydwen 72, 73-74
Puppet Master 172
Qirat 172
Quddwah 172-173
Quickthorn 173
Quinault 173
Rashabar 173-174
Rathgar 36
Raveena 37-38
Rebel's Gamble 22
Rebel's Romance 174
Red Letter 93, 105-106, 174
Regional 4-6, 174
Reine De Medicis 111
Remmooz 30
Return Of The Gods 13
Rhapsody 177
Roaring Legend 49-51
Rogue Diplomat 44
Rogue Sensation 12
Roi De France 177
Room Service 62-63, 177
Rosallion 176, 177
Royal Dress 177
Royal Playwright 177
Royal Rhyme 177-178
Royal Scotsman 178
Ruling Court 91, 178
Running Lion 178, 179
Sacred Falls 98
Sallaal 179
Sarab Star 37

Saracen 179
Scorthy Champ 92-93, 179
Sea Poetry 30
Seagolazo 54-56
Seagulls Eleven 51-52, 179
See The Fire 179
Sergeant Wilko 63
Serving With Style 18
Sevenna's Knight 179
Shadow Of Light 91, 92, 94, 102, 134, 142, 179-180, 188
Shareholder 180
Shaw Park 98
Shuwari 180
Silky Wilkie 16
Simmering 180
Sir Edward Lear 47
Sisyphean 65
Skellet 180
Sky Majesty 180-181
Smoken 181
Sosie 111, 112, 181-182
Space Legend 182
Sparks Fly 115, 182
Square D'Alboni 182
Stanhope Gardens 182
Star Of Light 107
Starlust 182
Start Of Day 112
Starzintheireyes 94, 182
Stratusnine 54
Subsequent 182-183
Sukanya 38
Sun God 164, 183
Sunway 183
Sweet William 183
Swelter 183
Swingalong 16, 104, 183
Tabiti 183
Tabletalk 183
Tamfana 184
Tasalla 30
Tennessee Stud 184
Term of Endearment 184-185
That's Amore 185
The Cavern Club 46, 47
The Lion In Winter 91, 92, 94, 95, 102, 178, 185, 188
The Reverend 185
The Waco Kid 52
The Watcher 22

Thunder Run 21, 185
Tiber Flow 185
Tiffany 185
Tito Mo Cen 112
Topgear 112, 184, 185
Torito 186
Touch The Moon 75
Tower Of London 186
Trad Jazz 43
Trawlerman 186
Treasure Time 107
Treble Tee 186
Trueshan 186
Truly Enchanting 186
Tuscan Hills 186
Twain 92, 110, 167, 187
Tycoon 115
Uncle Dick 98
Unequal Love 187
Unquestionable 187
Uther 111
Uxmal 115, 187
Vantheman 66
Venture Capital 64-65
Verse Of Love 187
Vertical Blue 108, 109, 110, 112, 187
Volterra 63, 107, 115, 172, 187
Waardah 30
Waleefy 115
Washington Heights 60, 187-188
We Never Stop 64
West Acre 74, 103
Whirl 95, 188
Whistlejacket 123, 188
White Birch 188
William Walton 30
Wimbledon Hawkeye 42-43, 47, 95, 188
Wisper 98
Wolf Of Badenoch 52, 56
Yaroogh 188
Yorkshire 10-11
You Got To Me 188
Zarigani 108, 110, 111, 112, 187, 188
Zerket 111
Zeus Olympios 22
Zoffee 48, 49
Zubaru 75

191

GET
Global Equine Transport

> GET provided an excellent service with our first runner in the Breeders Cup. Stephan was reachable 24/7 for any questions and arranged everything to perfection during the whole trip. We will definitely use GET for all our horse shipments in Europe and around the Globe.
>
> **Holger Faust**
> Darius Racing Manager

Sales
Racing & Bloodstock

In attendance, at all the major sales across Europe
Your key point of call

Transport
Road, Air & Sea

Offering a wealth of experience in all areas of equine transportation.
Packages tailored to you

Charter
Exclusivity Guaranteed

Global access to the top locations and best handlers
The 5-star treatment

GET in touch
Office | +44 1638 410 012
UK Mobile | +44 7960 377 972
GER Mobile | +49 152 053 762 07

info@globalequinetransport.com
www.globalequinetransport.com
Address | Suite 16, 341 Exning Road, Newmarket, CB8 0AT, UK